JOHN M. MUNRO is Associate Professor
and Chairman of the Department of
English at the American University in
Beirut, Lebanon. He received a B.A.
(with honors) from Durham University,
in England, in 1955, and received a
Ph.D. from Washington University in
St. Louis, Missouri, in 1962. He is the
editor, with T. Y. Greet and Charles
Edge, of *The Worlds of Fiction*
(1965) and has written numerous
articles for journals and magazines.
Professor Munro, who is a citizen of the
U.K., is married and the father of four
children.

English Poetry in Transition
1880 – 1920

English Poetry

IN TRANSITION

1880 – 1920

Edited by

JOHN M. MUNRO

184

PEGASUS

A Division of Western Publishing Co., Inc.

New York · 1968

141914

Library of Congress Catalogue Card Number 67–25502

Acknowledgments

We are indebted to and hereby thank the more than thirty publishers and
agents who have granted us permission to reprint these poems:

By Lascelles Abercrombie, "Indignation: An Ode," "Ceremonial Ode Intended
for a University," "Mary and the Bramble," "Witchcraft: New Style," Oxford
University Press, London, publishers of *Collected Poems,* 1930, in the
Oxford Standard Authors series.

By Hilaire Belloc, "Sonnet XIX," "To Dives," "Drinking Dirge," "Ballade of
Genuine Concern," "Ballade of Gentlemanly Feeling and Railway Strikes,"
"On Mundane Acquaintances," and "On His Books," A. D. Peters & Co.,
London, agents for George Duckworth and Co., London, publishers of
Hilaire Belloc, *Sonnets and Verse,* 1954.

By Robert Bridges, "London Snow," "Nightingales," "Peace Ode," "There Is a
Hill Beside the Silver Thames," and "Christmas Eve, 1917," The Clarendon
Press, Oxford, publishers of Robert Bridges, *Poetical Works,* Oxford Standard
Authors series, 1953.

Acknowledgments

By G. K. Chesterton, "The Donkey," from *The Collected Poems of G. K. Chesterton,* A. P. Watt & Son, London, by permission of Miss D. E. Collins and J. M. Dent & Sons, Ltd., London; "The Rolling English Road," "Wine and Water," "Lepanto," and a two-page excerpt from "The Ballad of the White Horse," from *The Collected Poems of G. K. Chesterton,* by permission of Methuen & Co., Ltd., London. American rights are granted by Dodd, Mead & Company, Inc., New York, publishers of *The Collected Poems of G. K. Chesterton* in the United States.

By W. H. Davies, "School's Out," "The Sluggard," "Leisure," "The Hospital Waiting-Room," "The Inquest," "I Am the Poet Davies, William," "One Thing Wanting," and "All in June," Jonathan Cape Ltd., London, publishers of *The Complete Poems of W. H. Davies,* 1963, on behalf of Mrs. H. M. Davies; and Wesleyan University Press, Middletown, Connecticut.

By Walter de la Mare, "Evening," "Sea-Magic," "Drugged," "The Feckless Dinner-Party," "Silence," "The Dove," "Moonlight," "The Quarry," and "The Listeners," The Literary Trustees of Walter de la Mare and The Society of Authors, London, their representative.

By Austin Dobson, "Ars Victrix," "On a Fan That Belonged to the Marquise de Pompadour," "The Ballad of Imitation," "The Ballad of Prose and Rhyme," and "The Ballad of the Bore," Oxford University Press, London, publishers of *The Complete Poetical Works of Austin Dobson,* edited by Alban Dobson, 1924.

By James Elroy Flecker, "To a Poet a Thousand Years Hence," "Tenebris Interlucentem," "A Ship, an Isle, a Sickle Moon," "In Hospital," and "Brumana," The Richards Press, London, publishers of Flecker's *Selected Poems,* 1964.

By Edmund Gosse, "Lying in the Grass," "In the Grass," and "Revelation," William Heinemann, Ltd., London, publishers of Edmund Gosse, *Collected Poems,* 1911, and for "The Shepherdess" and "Renouncement," Misses Sylvia and Jennifer Gosse, Berkshire, England.

By Thomas Hardy, "Nature's Questioning," "Drummer Hodge," "At a Lunar Eclipse," "The Lacking Sense," "An August Midnight," "Reminiscences of a Dancing Man," "The Minute Before Meeting," "New Year's Eve," "The Blinded Bird," "The Ballet," "In Time of 'The Breaking of Nations,'" "Weathers," "Snow in the Suburbs," "God-Forgotten," "Channel Firing," "The Darkling Thrush," "Under the Waterfall," "Drinking Song," and "At Wynyard's Gap," Macmillan & Co., Ltd., London, publishers of Thomas Hardy, *Collected Poems,* 1930, 4th edition, and The Macmillan Company, New York, for "Snow in the Suburbs" and "At Wynyard's Gap" from *Collected Poems* by Thomas Hardy, copyright 1925 by The Macmillan Company, renewed 1953 by Lloyd's Bank, Ltd.; for "Drinking Song" from *Collected Poems* by Thomas Hardy, copyright 1928 by Florence E. Hardy and Sydney E. Cockerell, re-

vii

of D. H. Lawrence, Volume I, edited by Vivian de Sola Pinto and Warren Roberts, copyright 1923 and 1951 by Frieda Lawrence, for "How Beastly the Bourgeois Is," and "The Elephant Is Slow to Mate" from *The Complete Poems of D. H. Lawrence,* Volume I, edited by Vivian de Sola Pinto and Warren Roberts, copyright 1929 by Frieda Lawrence Roberts, all rights reserved, and for "Bavarian Gentians," from *The Complete Poems of D. H. Lawrence,* Volume II, edited by Vivian de Sola Pinto and Warren Roberts, copyright 1933 by Frieda Lawrence, and 1964 by Angelo Ravagli and C. M. Weekley, Executors of The Estate of Frieda Lawrence Ravagli, all rights reserved.

By John Masefield, "Cape Horn Gospel I," "Cape Horn Gospel II," "Sea-Fever," "A Wanderer's Song," "Cargoes," and 116 lines from "Reynard, the Fox," The Society of Authors, London, and The Macmillan Company, New York; for "Cape Horn Gospel" and "A Wanderer's Song" from *Poems* by John Masefield, copyright 1916 by John Masefield and renewed 1944 by John Masefield; for "Cargoes" and "Sea-Fever" from *Poems* by John Masefield, copyright 1912 by John Masefield and renewed 1940 by John Masefield; for 116 lines from "Reynard the Fox" from *Poems* by John Masefield, copyright 1919 by John Masefield, renewed 1947 by John Masefield.

By Alice Meynell, "The Visiting Sea," "The Young Neophyte," "To the Body," "Summer in England, 1914," and "The Threshing-Machine," Oxford University Press, London, publishers of the Oxford Standard Authors edition of Alice Meynell, *Poems,* edited by F. Page, 1940, and on behalf of Sir Francis Meynell.

By Harold Monro, "Week-End," "Milk for the Cat," and "Bitter Sanctuary," Gerald Duckworth & Co., Ltd., London, publishers of Harold Monro's *Collected Poems,* and on behalf of Alida Monro.

By Henry Newbolt, "Drake's Drum," "The Death of Admiral Blake," and "Clifton Chapel," A. P. Watt & Son, London, publishers of *Poems New and Old* by Sir Henry Newbolt, and on behalf of Mr. Peter Newbolt.

By Wilfred Owen, "Music," "Insensibility," "Strange Meeting," "Apologia Pro Poemate Meo," "Greater Love," "Anthem for Doomed Youth," "Dulce et Decorum Est," "Futility," and "The Dead-Beat," Chatto and Windus, Ltd., London, publishers of *The Collected Works of Wilfred Owen,* edited by C. Day Lewis, 1964, and on behalf of Mr. Harold Owen; and New Directions Publishing Corporation, New York, publishers of *The Collected Poems* of Wilfred Owen, copyright by Chatto and Windus, Ltd., 1963.

By Isaac Rosenberg, "Dawn," "God," "Break of Day in the Trenches," "Louse Hunting," "Returning, We Hear the Larks," and "Dead Man's Dump," Chatto and Windus, Ltd., London, publishers of *The Collected Poems of Isaac Rosenberg,* 1962, and on behalf of the Literary Estate of Isaac Rosenberg; Schocken Books, Inc., New York, publishers of *Collected Poems* by Isaac Rosenberg, copyright 1949 by Schocken Books, Inc.

Contents

Introduction   19

Abercrombie, Lascelles   37
    Indignation: An Ode   38
    Ceremonial Ode Intended for a University   42
    Mary and the Bramble   43
    Witchcraft: New Style   48

Belloc, Hilaire   53
    Sonnet XIX   54
    To Dives   54
    Drinking Dirge   55
    Ballade of Genuine Concern   56
    Ballade of Gentlemanly Feeling and Railway Strikes   57
    On Mundane Acquaintances   58
    On His Books   58

Bridges, Robert   59
    London Snow   60
    Nightingales   61
    Peace Ode   61
    There Is a Hill Beside the Silver Thames   63
    Christmas Eve, 1917   66

Brooke, Rupert   69
    A Channel Passage   70
    The Old Vicarage, Grantchester   70
    The Busy Heart   74
    Waikiki   74
    The Dead, III   75
    The Dead, IV   75
    The Soldier   76

Chesterton, G. K.   77
    The Donkey   78
    The Rolling English Road   78
    Wine and Water   79
    Lepanto   80
    From The Ballad of the White Horse   84

Davidson, John   89
    A Ballad of a Nun   90
    Thirty Bob a Week   95
    In Romney Marsh   98
    A Cinque Port   99
    War Song   99
    Insomnia   102
    From The Testament of a Prime Minister   102

Davies, W. H.   105
    School's Out   106
    The Sluggard   106
    Leisure   107
    The Hospital Waiting-Room   107
    The Inquest   108
    I Am the Poet Davies, William   109
    One Thing Wanting   110
    All in June   110

de la Mare, Walter   111
    Evening   112
    Sea-Magic   112
    Drugged   113
    The Feckless Dinner-Party   114
    Silence   116
    The Dove   117
    Moonlight   117
    The Quarry   117
    The Listeners   118

Dobson, Austin   121
    Ars Victrix   122
    The Ballad of Prose and Rhyme   123
    On a Fan That Belonged to
        the Marquise de Pompadour   124
    The Ballad of Imitation   125
    The Ballad of the Bore   126

Dowson, Ernest 129
  Nuns of the Perpetual Adoration 130
  To One in Bedlam 131
  Ad Manus Puellae 131
  Non Sum Qualis Eram Bonae Sub Regno Cynarae 132
  Beata Solitudo 133
  Terre Promise 134
  Carthusians 134

Flecker, James Elroy 137
  To a Poet a Thousand Years Hence 138
  Tenebris Interlucentem 138
  A Ship, an Isle, a Sickle Moon 139
  In Hospital 139
  Brumana 140

Flint, F. S. 143
  Poems in Unrhymed Cadence 144

Gosse, Edmund 147
  The Shepherdess 148
  In the Grass 148
  Lying in the Grass 149
  Impression 151
  Revelation 152
  Renouncement 153

Grenfell, Julian 155
  Into Battle 156

Hardy, Thomas 159
  Nature's Questioning 160
  Drummer Hodge 161
  At a Lunar Eclipse 161
  The Lacking Sense 162
  God-Forgotten 164
  An August Midnight 165
  The Darkling Thrush 166
  Reminiscences of a Dancing Man 167
  The Minute Before Meeting - 168
  New Year's Eve 168
  Channel Firing 169
  Under the Waterfall 171
  The Blinded Bird 172

The Ballet   173
In Time of "The Breaking of Nations"   173
Weathers   174
Snow in the Suburbs   175
At Wynyard's Gap   175
Drinking Song   181

Henley, W. E.   185
    From In Hospital   186
        I   Enter Patient   186
        IV   Before   186
        VI   After   187
        XXIV   Suicide   187
        XXVIII   Discharged   188
    Ballade of a Toyokuni Colour-Print   189
    Ballade of Dead Actors   190
    London Voluntaries   191
    To James McNeill Whistler   200
    What Have I Done for You, England, My England?   201
    Invictus   203

Housman, A. E.   205
    Leave your home behind, lad   206
    On moonlit heath and lonesome bank   207
    On your midnight pallet lying   208
    When I was one-and-twenty   208
    With rue my heart is laden   209
    "Terence, this is stupid stuff"   209
    Her strong enchantments failing   211
    The chestnut casts his flambeaux   211
    Parta Quies   212

Hulme, T. E.   215
    Autumn   216
    The Embankment   216

Johnson, Lionel   217
    By the Statue of King Charles at Charing Cross   218
    Mystic and Cavalier   219
    The Dark Angel   221
    To a Passionist   222
    The Church of a Dream   223
    The Destroyer of a Soul   224
    Our Lady of the Snows   224

Ninety-Eight 227
Nihilism 228

Kipling, Rudyard 229
M'Andrew's Hymn 230
A Song of the English 236
Our Lady of the Snows 237
The Ballad of East and West 238
The Islanders 242
The Old Men 245
The White Man's Burden 247
Hymn Before Action 248
Recessional 250
The Conundrum of the Workshops 251
"Mary, Pity Women!" 253
The Return 254
The Storm Cone 256

Lawrence, D. H. 259
Snake 260
How Beastly the Bourgeois Is 262
The Elephant Is Slow to Mate 263
Bavarian Gentians 264

Masefield, John 267
Cape Horn Gospel I 268
Cape Horn Gospel II 269
Sea-Fever 270
A Wanderer's Song 270
Cargoes 271
From Reynard the Fox 272

Meynell, Alice 277
The Visiting Sea 278
The Young Neophyte 278
To the Body 279
Summer in England, 1914 279
The Threshing-Machine 280

Monro, Harold 283
Week-End 284
Milk for the Cat 289
Bitter Sanctuary 290

Newbolt, Henry 293
    Drake's Drum 294
    The Death of Admiral Blake 294
    Clifton Chapel 296

Owen, Wilfred 299
    Music 300
    Insensibility 300
    Strange Meeting 302
    Apologia Pro Poemate Meo 304
    Greater Love 305
    Anthem for Doomed Youth 306
    Dulce et Decorum Est 306
    Futility 307
    The Dead-Beat 307

Rosenberg, Isaac 309
    Dawn 310
    God 310
    Break of Day in the Trenches 311
    Louse Hunting 312
    Returning, We Hear the Larks 313
    Dead Man's Dump 313

Sassoon, Siegfried 317
    The Death-Bed 318
    Counter-Attack 319
    Dreamers 320
    Attack 320
    Aftermath 321
    "They" 322
    Storm on Fifth Avenue 322
    Falling Asleep 323

Seaman, Owen 325
    A Ballad of a Bun 326
    The Rhyme of the Kipperling 329
    To a Boy-Poet of the Decadence 332
    Pro Patria 333
    Thomas of the Light Heart 334
    To the Enemy, on His Achievement 335

Sitwell, Edith 337
    Green Geese 338

Two Kitchen Songs 339
Solo for Ear-Trumpet 341
Eventail 341
Fox Trot 342

Sorley, Charles 345
To Poets 346
German Rain 346
All the Hills and Vales Along 347
To Germany 348

Squire, J. C. 349
To a Bull-Dog 350
The Discovery 352
Crepuscular 352
Ballade of the Poetic Life 353
The Lily of Malud 354
How They Do It 357

Stevenson, Robert Louis 359
The Land of Nod 360
My Kingdom 360
The Canoe Speaks 361
Et Tu in Arcadia Vixisti 362
To W. E. Henley 364
The Celestial Surgeon 365
Our Lady of the Snows 366
"My body which my dungeon is" 368
"I will make you brooches and toys" 369
To My Old Familiars 370
To S. C.

Symons, Arthur 373
The Opium-Smoker 374
Maquillage 374
At the Cavour 374
Javanese Dancers 375
Prologue: In the Stalls 376
To a Dancer 376
Air de Ballet 377
La Mélinite: Moulin-Rouge 378
Art Poétique 379
Cortège 380
Amends to Nature 381

Thomas, Edward   383
    Tears   384
    The Owl   384
    Swedes   385
    The Path   385
    Adlestrop   386
    Tall Nettles   386
    Rain   387
    Lights Out   387
    February Afternoon   388
    The New House   389
    Out in the Dark   389

Thompson, Francis   391
    Daisy   392
    The Hound of Heaven   394

Watson, William   399
    Wordsworth's Grave   400
    Shelley's Centenary   406
    After the Titans   409
    Ode on the Day of the Coronation
      of King Edward VII   410
    England   414

Wilde, Oscar   417
    Theoretikos   418
    Impression du Matin   418
    The Grave of Keats   419
    In the Gold Room   419
    Taedium Vitae   420
    The Harlot's House   420
    Symphony in Yellow   421

General Bibliography   423

Bibliographies of the Poets   427

Introduction

IN HIS essay on "The Metaphysical Poets" (1921), T. S. Eliot put forward his notion of the "dissociation of sensibility," a phenomenon which he maintained became apparent in the seventeenth century and persisted into the twentieth. Comparing passages from Chapman and Lord Herbert of Cherbury with extracts from Tennyson and Browning, he found that "something had happened to the mind of England" during the period in between, and that poetry had changed from being "intellectual" to "reflective":

> Tennyson and Browning are poets, and they think; but they do not feel their thought as immediately as the odour of a rose. A thought to Donne was an experience; it modified his sensibility. When a poet's mind is perfectly equipped for its work, it is constantly amalgamating disparate experience; the ordinary man's experience is chaotic, irregular, fragmentary. The latter falls in love, or reads Spinoza, and these two experiences have nothing to do with each other, or with the noise of the typewriter, or the smell of cooking; in the mind of the poet these experiences are always forming new wholes.

The difference between these two modes of perception Eliot accounted for by the fact that the poets of the seventeenth century "possessed a mechanism of sensibility which could devour any kind of experience," but afterward a "dissociation of sensibility set in from which we have never recovered." The poet's response to phenomena became increasingly restricted and predictable, and consequently the poetry of more recent times failed to communicate the rich totality of human

19

experience. Therefore, Eliot concluded, it was the modern poet's task to effect a return to the early seventeenth-century tradition. "It appears likely," he wrote, "that poets in our civilisation as it exists at present, must be *difficult*. Our civilisation comprehends great variety and complexity, and this variety and complexity, playing upon a refined sensibility, must produce various and complex results. The poet must become more and more comprehensive, more allusive, more indirect, in order to force, to dislocate if necessary, language to his meaning." A year later Eliot published "The Wasteland," certainly one of the most "difficult," "various," "complex," "allusive," and "indirect" poems in English, in which he "forced" and "dislocated" language in order to accommodate his vision of contemporary Western civilization.

The essay on "The Metaphysical Poets" and "The Wasteland" are undoubtedly important landmarks in the history of the development of the modern poetic sensibility, but we give Eliot more than his due if we insist on regarding them as important revolutionary documents which changed the course of modern poetry. Certainly they created a stir at the time of their publication, continuing to exert a powerful influence at least up until the early 1950's, when Eliot's status as a critic first began to be seriously questioned. The fact remains, however, that the kind of poetry Eliot advocated in "The Metaphysical Poets" and put into effect in "The Wasteland" was not altogether "new," and the widely held notion that the direction of English poetry shifted radically shortly after the end of the first World War is simply not tenable. As Frank Kermode has demonstrated in his important book, *Romantic Image,* in pleading for a return to the mode of poetic vision which he found characteristic of the Metaphysicals, Eliot was in effect recommending support for a kind of poetry currently in existence, for Eliot's description of the Metaphysicals is equally applicable to the late nineteenth-century French Symbolists. In fact, Eliot's summary of those poetic qualities which he found in the Metaphysicals and looked for in the poetry of his own time is remarkably close to the description of the poetry of Stéphane Mallarmé contained in Arthur Symons's *Symbolist Movement in Literature* (1899), a book which did much to clarify the aims of the Symbolists, and exerted a profound

influence on such writers as James Joyce, Ezra Pound, and
Eliot himself. Furthermore, as Joseph E. Duncan has shown,
Eliot's remark that we should effect a return to the way of
the Metaphysicals was anyway rather superfluous, as there
already existed in England a strong revival of interest in
these poets, which had been climaxed by the publication of
Grierson's edition of Donne's poetry for the Oxford University
Press in 1912.

Thus the notion that the "reflective" Victorian poetic was
dramatically checked by Eliot and his followers, who then
introduced a new "intellectual" mode of perception, is simply
not true. Nor must we infer from Eliot's remarks that the
great Victorian poets failed to comprehend the variety and
complexity of their civilization, and that it was left to the
moderns to explore the fundamental problems of human
existence. Browning was far from being a poet who dealt pri-
marily in the kind of smug affirmations which a casual reading
of "Pippa Passes" would lead one to suppose, but instead
scrutinized continually the very foundations of belief and conventions of morality, in his greatest poetry dramatizing the
tension between appearance and reality in what we like to
think of as a characteristically modern way. Tennyson was also
aware that the eternal verities were perhaps neither timeless
nor true, as evidenced by his continued attempts to affirm
some kind of tradition which would prevail amid the collapse
of institutions which had previously appeared to be built on
solid ground.

In short, much of what we tend to regard in twentieth-
century poetry as being distinctly "modern" has its roots firmly
embedded in the latter part of the nineteenth century, and it
is tempting to assert that the division of poetry of the past
hundred years into "Victorian" and "Modern" periods is little
more than the convenience of literary historians. On the other
hand it is clear that such a characteristic "Victorian" poem as
Tennyson's "Idylls of the King" is very different from Eliot's
"Wasteland," a difference extending beyond their respective
modes of expression. If we compare, for example, "The Holy
Grail" episode of the "Idylls" with Eliot's poem, it is evident
that though both poets were distressed by the moral and
spiritual sterility of their respective ages, even going so far as

to utilize the wasteland motif as a common vehicle for their ideas, they reacted to it in different ways. Tennyson apparently believed that God, working through Nature, would see to it that the healing rains would come, irrespective of whether man did anything to deserve his salvation or not, while Eliot implied that redemption would come only as a result of personal self-sacrifice, when man realized that in order to gain the world he must lose it. Tennyson's vision is ultimately optimistic, while Eliot's is hopeful but guarded. The focus in Tennyson's poem is on God; in Eliot's it is on man.

In other words, though we may find clear indications of continuity between Victorian and modern poetry, there was also change. To be sure, all literature is a continuum, but it still moves from one point to another, and if we are to understand its development we should be aware of both aspects, though it is usually the former we need to be reminded of more frequently than the latter. Therefore in entitling this anthology *English Poetry in Transition,* it is intended to remind readers that though there are certain definable characteristics which tend to separate the poetry of the latter part of the nineteenth century from that of the present age, there was no distinct break in the tradition. To insist on such a division, as Helmut Gerber showed in his essay on the Nineties for the English Institute in 1959, is to incur the risk of formulating facile arguments in an effort to prove that during the years covered by this anthology there was either a decline or a rebirth of the poetic sensibility. Certainly there is evidence for both points of view, and a number of writers have put forward persuasive arguments in favor of whichever belief they uphold, but as Gerber has said, "we may . . . after all speak of the last Victorian, but in the same breath we must also speak of the first moderns. This is why we must speak of journeys out, but not out of senile Victorianism into brash but arid Modernism. The transition is from one fertile land into another." Furthermore, lest we may be inclined to view the importance of the 1880–1920 period merely in historical terms, we should remember also that "the transition itself is through a fertile land," and it is this above all which entitles the so-called "Transitional" period to selective study.

The period 1880–1920 we have chosen to label "transitional," but it is not only in retrospect that these years appear as a time of significant change. To many living at the close of the nineteenth century it seemed that the old order was about to give way to a new, and in particular, literature itself was taking on renewed vigor and character. Thus W. B. Yeats in an essay entitled "The Autumn of the Body" (1898) suggested that the arts were about "to take upon their shoulders the burdens that have fallen from the shoulders of the priests," and that they would "lead us back upon our journey by filling our thoughts with the essence of things, and not with things." Henceforth, he said, drawing upon what Symons had written in relation to the French poet Mallarmé, "poetry will . . . be a poetry of essences, separated one from another in little and intense poems." For Yeats, English poetry was about to enter an exciting new era, when the poets themselves would become prophets, directing men's eyes from the material and the mundane to the spiritual and the eternal.

On the other hand, there were others who felt that literature was in decline. Max Nordau for example, in a book translated from German into English under the title *Degeneration* (1892), insisted that late nineteenth-century literature was decadent. "In the civilised world," he wrote, "there obviously prevails a twilight mood," and for all that has been said to the contrary, contemporary writers offer no "ecstatic prophecy," exhibiting instead merely "senseless stammering and the babbling of deranged minds." Furthermore, according to Nordau, what "the ignorant hold up to be the outbursts of gushing, youthful vigour and turbulent constructive impulses are really nothing but the convulsions and spasms of exhaustion."

On the whole, literary history has tended to support Yeats's judgment rather than Nordau's, but during the eighteen-nineties more people subscribed to the theory that English poetry was in decline. This was the view of that arch-traditionalist William Watson, who in "Wordsworth's Grave" complained that "the lyre is loath, / Or powerless now, to give what all men seek!" Far from recognizing the possibility of a reincarnation of Wordsworth's "visionary gleam," he saw instead poetry which either "deadens with ignoble sloth / Or deafens with shrill tumult, loudly weak."

Watson here is referring to the two parallel traditions of late nineteenth-century poetry, which we now label Decadent and Counter-Decadent. Generally speaking, the Decadents followed Tennyson's advice in "The Lotos Eaters," and lived "in the hollow Lotos land," and reclined "on the hills like gods together, careless of mankind," while the Counter-Decadents preferred the brisker code advocated by the same poet's "Ulysses," who found it "dull . . . to pause, to make an end, / To rust unburnished, not to shine in use, / As though to breathe were life." To the first group we usually assign such people as Ernest Dowson and Arthur Symons, who sang of the rapture of bought kisses in poems of tuneful melancholy; Oscar Wilde, who in his life certainly, though to a lesser degree in his poetry, professed abhorrence for all kinds of enthusiastic activity; and Lionel Johnson and Francis Thompson, who, unable to cope with the demands of daily human existence, sought refuge in alcohol or opium and the bosom of the Roman Catholic Church. To the second group it is customary to assign such poets as W. E. Henley, Rudyard Kipling, and Henry Newbolt, who all proclaimed the virtues of the active life, responded to the patriotic demands of Queen and country, and accepted with enthusiasm the technological advances of the modern age.

It would be a mistake, however, to assume that the "Decadents" and the "Counter-Decadents" constituted two separate schools. It is true that the Decadents came to be associated with the Rhymers' Club, a group of young poets who used to meet at irregular intervals at the Cheshire Cheese, while the Counter-Decadents tended to congregate around Henley at Solferino's Restaurant, but they were far from being two mutually exclusive groups. W. B. Yeats, for example, appears to have felt no inconsistency in being associated with both camps simultaneously. Indeed the difficulty of classifying late nineteenth-century poets satisfactorily is well illustrated by Henley himself. In his "Decadent Movement in Literature," an article which appeared in *Harper's New Monthly Magazine* in 1893, Symons actually referred to Henley as a Decadent, a characteristically modern poet to be included in the company of Mallarmé and mentioned in the same breath as Verlaine, a writer to whom many of the Decadents looked for inspiration. However odd Henley's classification in this movement may seem, one can see Symons's point. The squalid realism of the "In Hospital" sequence and parts of "London Voluntaries"; Henley's enthusiasm for the paintings of Whistler; and his application of the techniques of music to his poetry, as evidenced by the symphonic structure of "London Voluntaries"; were all supposedly characteristic of the Decadents. Furthermore, though the Counter-Decadents tended to be closely related to the native English tradition, and the Decadents' cultural sympathies seem to have drawn them more toward France, Henley's early poetry, especially, shows unmistakable signs of French influence.

Nevertheless the general tone, subject matter, and effect of Henley's verse is very different from that of, say, Dowson's. It is true that both poets felt that life was hard, but where Dowson sought "rest," "forgetfulness," "oblivion"—these words continually recur in his poetry—Henley, in the words of his most frequently anthologized poem, thanked "whatever gods may be" for his "unconquerable soul," averring that though his head might become "bloody," it would ever remain "unbowed." Thus though for the sake of convenience we may speak of "Decadents" and "Counter-Decadents," these terms are useful only up to a point. They give a general indication of boundaries, but they may hardly be used to specify the terrain.

However much we may seek to separate the two schools, there was one thing which both the Decadents and the Counter-Decadents seem to have had in common: the desire to find new and interesting ways of expressing themselves. The Decadents tended either to copy the clear, hard, well-sculptured precision of the verse of Gautier and the Parnassians, or the more nebulous poetry of Verlaine with its tuneful languor and pictorial half-tones. Mallarmé also exerted an influence on such poets as Symons and Yeats, but generally speaking it was left to Eliot's generation to exploit the possibilities of the Mallarméan aesthetic. Both Decadents and Counter-Decadents experimented with old French forms such as the *rondeau,* the *ballade,* and the *villanelle,* following the example of the French Parnassians and two of their English disciples, Austin Dobson and Edmund Gosse. Taking their lead from Baudelaire's theory of "les correspondances," expressed in a poem of that name in *Les Fleurs du Mal,* the Decadents in particular exploited the supposed relationships between painting and music on the one hand and poetry on the other; Henley created a new mode of dispassionate, concrete realism in the "In Hospital" sequence; and Kipling looked to the music-hall ballad for inspiration.

Indeed if one were to seek for a unifying principle by which to classify late nineteenth- and early twentieth-century poets, it must be that the majority seem to have had a determination to discover new modes of poetic expression. Even a poet such as Robert Bridges, who hardly qualifies for inclusion in either the Decadent or the Counter-Decadent school, having a closer affinity with Traditionalists such as Watson, reflects the contemporary enthusiasm for technical innovation, for he attempted to free English poetry from traditional, syllabic rhythms by adapting the principles of classical, quantitative meters to English verse. It is true that some poets like Watson persisted in writing in what one might call the Milton-Wordsworth-Tennyson tradition, but when one surveys the poetical scene as a whole, the dominant impulse seems to have been a determination to experiment.

Equally it may be said, however, that in spite of the numerous and frequently successful attempts to discover new and interesting modes of poetic expression, many of the poets writing at the time seem to have had little to say which would appear to warrant such inventive activity. One of the reasons for this was the notion prevailing in some quarters that the justification for writing poetry, or indeed for engaging in any kind of artistic activity, was quite independent of what one had to say. Art was valued for its own sake; if the finished product was "beautiful," this in itself justified its existence. The doctrine of art for art's sake goes at least as far back as Kant, whose notion of "purposiveness without purpose" is generally held to be the germ of the idea, but it first received emphatic expression in France, in the writings of Gautier, who, tired of the vapid platitudes of French Romanticism, declared that art was above political and social considerations, proceeding to demonstrate this dictum by writing novels and poetry which had little relation with either. Walter Pater was mainly responsible for popularizing the art for art's sake theory in England, and though his disciples seem not always to have understood him properly, his name was frequently invoked by those who professed to believe that a work of art should be judged solely in aesthetic terms. Believing that art needed no justification for its existence other than the fact that it was art, there was no incentive for the artist to produce works which evoked anything other than a pleasing aesthetic response. Indeed, to have attempted to do otherwise would have been to create something which, by definition, was inartistic. The artist gave up his social obligations, withdrawing from society into a world of personal reverie, producing art which either reflected his private fantasies or, more simply, his individual technical ingenuity.

Of course the notion of the artist as outsider is at least as old as Plato, but during the early years of the nineteenth century it became especially important. Keats, for example, believed that the artist was different from other people, alienated from society by reason of his purer, more intense vision. Nevertheless both he and the other great Romantic poets were able to convince their readers that their personal, perhaps idiosyncratic vision was not only sound but more truthful than that experienced by other, supposedly more normal people. As the century progressed, however, the personal, individual voice of the poet was hushed, and poetry tended more and more to reflect the hopes, fears, ideas, and intellectual preoccupations of the audience whom the poet was addressing. Thus though Arnold, Browning, and Tennyson all at one time or another felt the desire to express their most private and essentially personal feelings, they stifled this impulse, believing it was the poet's primary duty to describe such things which could be understood and appreciated by all. Personal utterance gave way to public statement; the poet was no longer the outsider; he became instead the acknowledged spokesman for the collective conscience. As long as the poet himself felt keenly about those issues which engaged his contemporaries, Victorian poetry retained its potency and vigor, but when those issues no longer claimed his intense emotional involvement, it degenerated, almost inevitably, into reiteration of well meant but sterile platitudes. Although the publication of such documents as Lyell's *Principles of Geology* and Darwin's *Origin of Species* sorely tried one's religious faith, forcing a reconsideration of the very foundations of one's belief, after his initial shock the average

Victorian, conscious of his country's increasing power and material prosperity, must have felt that in spite of what the scientists had revealed, God was still in his heaven and all was right with the world. Under these circumstances what was the poet to do? He could either trumpet the glories of his age, or turn his back on them altogether, losing himself in a world of art or personal introspection.

In short, at the close of the nineteenth century the poet seems to have been faced with two major alternatives: to be society's outcast or its servant. He had lost his authentic voice. To be sure there were indications that the poet had not entirely forsaken his identity. Lionel Johnson, for example, in a poem such as "Mystic and Cavalier," though giving expression to a profoundly personal dilemma, was nonetheless able to transcend the boundaries of self and communicate a vision more generally relevant, while Kipling on occasions listened to his individual conscience, tempering his optimistic public utterances with a personal note of disquietude. There was also Thomas Hardy, whose poetry eludes classification, and there was W. B. Yeats, certainly one of England's major poets. On the whole, though, in spite of sporadic expressions of unease concerning the growing materialism of the age and the decline of spiritual values, there were relatively few signs that the poets at the turn of the century were able to rise above the articulation of personal reveries or corporate self-congratulation.

Some people, however, professed to see signs of change. In 1912, for example, the year of King George V's coronation, Edward Marsh maintained in his introduction to an anthology of contemporary verse that "English poetry was now once again putting on a new strength and beauty," being about to enter "a new Georgian period which might take rank in due time with the several great poetic ages of the past." Calling his collection simply *Georgian Poetry,* Marsh further maintained that his selection had been made with "no definite aim" in mind, being merely a representative selection of the best work available at the time. Nevertheless, in spite of Marsh's declared avoidance of "definite aim," it was inevitable that this collection and the later ones he edited, as well as those for which J. C. Squire was responsible, should have had a distinctive character. Though strictly speaking there is no more a "Georgian" movement than there are Decadent, Counter-Decadent, and Traditionalist movements, the word "Georgian" does suggest a particular kind of poetry distinguishable from other poetry written at the time. Unlike the poetry of the Decadents, for example, Georgian poetry has little nostalgia, still less wild yearning and preoccupation with sex; unlike the poetry of the Counter-Decadents it avoids national and patriotic themes. There is little poetry in the Georgian anthologies concerned with religion. Stylistically, most of the Georgian poets seem to have avoided self-conscious symbolism, sonorous Victorian rhythms, obscure and bizarre images and phraseology. Above all, the Georgians seem to have been concerned with Nature and rural life, harking back to the Wordsworthian tradition.

The poets whose work seems to approximate most closely to this description are: W. H. Davies, Walter de la Mare, J. C. Squire, A. E. Housman, and Edward Thomas. In a sense Housman was hardly a Georgian, because his volume of poems *A Shropshire Lad* appeared as early as 1896, but his *Last Poems* appeared in 1922, and insofar as his work has clear affinities with the most characteristic poetry of the Georgians—Harold Monro noted in his introduction to *Twentieth-Century Poetry* that Housman was the Georgians' spiritual father—he clearly belongs in their company. Strictly speaking, Thomas was not a Georgian either, because his verses never appeared in the Georgian anthologies. Nevertheless their style and content confirm Thomas's relationship to the movement.

On the other hand, there were poets who were represented in the volumes of *Georgian Poetry* who were at best atypical. The robustness and rapture of G. K. Chesterton sets him apart from the Georgians, and it is perhaps significant that his poetry appeared only in the first of the *Georgian Poetry* anthologies. Chesterton was an admirer of most things medieval, a staunch upholder of the Roman Catholic Church, and an enthusiastic toper of English ale. A group of poets soon gathered round him including Wilfred Rowland Childe, William Kean Seymour, W. R. Titterton, and Hilaire Belloc, their poetry appearing in such journals as the *New Witness* and *G.K.'s Weekly.* More than any of the other poets represented in this anthology,

G. K. Chesterton and his school were propagandists. Believing that the modern world in general and capitalism in particular were destroying personal liberty, they advocated a more equitable distribution of wealth, favoring the ownership of small holdings, in the belief that property gave one a sense of dignity and responsibility.

If Chesterton seems hardly at home among the Georgians, still less does D. H. Lawrence. In spite of his appearance in the Georgian anthologies, Lawrence is more usually associated with the Imagists. The theoretician behind this movement was a young philosopher named T. E. Hulme, who upheld the view that as the old humanist tradition was dead, western art and philosophy had to make a new start. In his essay on "Romanticism and Classicism," later included in a posthumous volume called *Speculations,* he predicted that the poetry of the future would be "dry, hard, and classical," and in an effort to clarify his theory, composed five poems, ironically entitled *The Complete Poetical Works of T. E. Hulme,* in which he endeavored to put his precepts into practice. However, it was F. S. Flint who is usually credited with the more precise formulation of the Imagists' creed, published in his introduction to *Some Imagist Poets* in 1915. As he defined them, the three cardinal principles of Imagism were: to use the language of common speech, but to employ always the exact word, not the nearly exact, nor the merely decorative word; to produce poetry that is hard and clear, and not to deal in generalities, however magnificent and sonorous; and to create new rhythms rather than copy the old, which merely echo old moods. Though Flint was an Englishman and his compatriots D. H. Lawrence and Richard Aldington subscribed to the aesthetic theory upon which Imagism was based, the movement itself was nonetheless more closely associated with American poetry than with British. Ezra Pound, for example, was one of the most enthusiastic proponents of Imagism, and it was he who was responsible for the publication of *Des Imagistes: An Anthology* (1914), and when his interest in the movement began to wane another American, Amy Lowell, furthered the cause, arranging for the publication of several anthologies all entitled *Some Imagist Poets,* which contained the work of mostly American writers:

William Carlos Williams, John Gould Fletcher, H.D., and of course Ezra Pound and Amy Lowell herself.

Although Imagism no more than the poetry written by the G. K. Chesterton school was conceived as a conscious counter-movement to the Georgians, its antipathy toward the Romantic vagueness of the latter sets it squarely in opposition. Similarly, another group of poets opposed—though this time consciously—to the Georgian tradition was that which centered around the Sitwells, Edith, Osbert, and Sacheverell. Unlike the Imagists, they did not subscribe to a carefully worded poetic manifesto, being instead a group of poets whose work began to appear in a journal called *Wheels,* edited by Edith Sitwell herself, which ran through six "cycles" between 1916 and 1921. It is difficult to classify their poetry, but in opposing the tame naturalism and vague Romanticism of the Georgians, they tended to write non-representational, quasi-surrealistic poems which had little relation to life. It was ingenious, frequently amusing, but rarely profound; it was a poetry born out of exasperation and contempt for the kind of poetry which was passing at the time as significant.

Georgianism, the poetry of the G. K. Chesterton school, Imagism, and the non-representational poetry associated with the Sitwells all had their roots firmly embedded in the nineteenth-century tradition. Of the four, the poetry of the Georgians and the Chesterton school are the most obviously native, Georgianism a late and somewhat feeble glimmer of Wordsworthian effulgence, and the Chestertonians reflecting the early nineteenth-century enthusiasm for the ballad and the late nineteenth-century revival of interest in the Middle Ages. Imagism is clearly an extension of the Parnassian tradition, inspired by the Greek and Roman classics, and fortified by the example of Chinese and Japanese poetry, while the non-representational poetry of the Sitwellian circle owes much to French Symbolism and perhaps something to Victorian nonsense verse. It is of course a mistake to see them as four mutually exclusive, independent groups, but they do represent the four main streams of early twentieth-century poetry. Viewed collectively, however, one cannot help remarking that in spite of obvious dissimilarities, and in spite of a few notable individual achievements, a great deal of this poetry is somewhat false and meretricious. It is poetry written for a poetry-reading public, rather than the expression of a man speaking to men. To put it another way, like much of the poetry of the years immediately preceding, though perhaps not to the same degree, a great deal of the poetry of the first two decades of the twentieth century, though technically accomplished and on occasions both brilliant and moving, has comparatively little to say.

From this criticism, however, we must exempt much of the verse written by the so-called "Trench Poets." In August, 1914, England had declared war on Germany, and so began a period which was to change the course of many men's lives, their behavior, their thinking, and in some cases their poetry. The Great War, as it was called, was different from other wars England had fought in, because for the first time in English history war became the responsibility of not just the governing classes but the nation as a whole. With an enthusiasm which transcended class distinctions, Englishmen rushed off to fight for a cause which they believed to be just almost as if they had been starved of idealism, welcoming the opportunity of being baptized anew in the blood of battle.

For the most part they fought bravely, and unlike their compatriots in the Crimean War, according to Tennyson in his "Charge of the Light Brigade," would have had no difficulty in saying who the enemy was and why he had to be destroyed. Quite simply, the Kaiser appeared as a brutal aggressor, a man whose grandiose territorial ambitions constituted a threat to the peace and security of Europe, and it was not only expedient but a moral duty to put him down. Indeed it was perhaps because the average English soldier was so convinced that God was on his side that the subsequent carnage made such a deep impression on him. It was a brutal war. Men had reached the stage of being able to manufacture potent instruments of large-scale destruction, but had not yet devised the means of exterminating whole cities with clean and clinical detachment. Thus though the casualties of the war were high, the number was not sufficiently high to be meaningless; though death was no less a fact in the 1914–1918 war than it was in the war which took place a quarter of a century later, it was more obviously painful and bloody, thanks to the prevailing military strategy of trench warfare.

Therefore, though many a serving-man went off to fight in the early stages of the war full of patriotism and optimistic fervor, as the conflict continued and the devastation spread few were able to avoid speculating on whether or not the war was humanly justifiable. However right the cause, could victory compensate for the widespread misery and horror? Of course not all the poets of the time reacted to the war in this way. Julian Grenfell, for example, seems to have regarded the war merely as an extension of the playing-fields of Eton, being apparently unaware of the profounder issues involved; Rupert Brooke, though more sensitive, was unable to transcend sentimentality. There were others, however, more thoughtful, for whom the war provoked renewed reflection on some of the eternally unanswerable problems which have preoccupied man since he first began to speculate upon the nature of his existence: to this group belong Wilfred Owen, Isaac Rosenberg, Siegfried Sassoon, and Charles Sorley. The Boer War, so far away from England and involving so few of one's friends and family, did not force one to introspection and reassessment of basic values and beliefs; the Great War did. There are few good poems written about the Boer War; there are a number of great ones about the latter.

In the preface to the first Georgian anthology Edward Marsh had maintained that English poetry was once again "putting on new strength and beauty." His words were perhaps a little premature, for in retrospect Georgian poetry seems hardly to warrant such a glowing introduction. His remarks would have had greater relevancy if he had written them a decade or so later, for after the 1914–1918 war there was a revival in English poetry at the center of which was T. S. Eliot. Eliot arrived on the scene at a most propitious moment, coming to poetic maturity when the terrifying realities of the war were fresh in men's minds. Complacency was shattered, and most people were acutely aware of the precariousness and complexity of their situation. It was also fortunate that Eliot came at a time when poetry had at last freed itself from traditional forms, meters, modes of expression, and conventional poetic language. Eliot was himself an important innovator, but it is doubtful if he would have been able to speak so authoritatively in his essay on "The Metaphysical Poets" about what he felt was the most relevant kind of poetry to his civilization, if he had not been heir to that rich period of poetical experimentation which began toward the end of the nineteenth century and continued into the twentieth. It is also doubtful whether Eliot would have been so keenly alive to the necessity of finding a poetic mode adequate to the needs of his generation if the war had not caused such a dramatic upheaval, disrupting the traditional patterns of an imperialist, hierarchical, nominally Christian society. Though Eliot is unquestionably a central figure in the development of modern poetry, his achievement cannot be isolated from that of his immediate predecessors and contemporaries: in codifying the aims of the twentieth-century poet and clarifying his intentions, he pointed the way ahead, but his direction had already been determined by those who preceded him.

English Poetry in Transition
1880 – 1920

Lascelles Abercrombie

LASCELLES ABERCROMBIE (1881-1938) was born at Ashton in
northwest England, the fifth son of nine children. He was educated at Malvern and studied science at Owen's College in
Manchester, but in 1902 decided upon journalism as a career.
His first volume of poems appeared in 1908 and soon afterward he retired to the country, where his best verse was written.
His health was not sufficiently strong for him to be called to
the front during the 1914-1918 war, but he served as an Inspector of Munitions at Liverpool, and in 1919 was appointed
to a lectureship in poetry at the university there, a position
he held for three years. This academic appointment was followed
by others at Leeds and Bedford College, and at Cambridge,
where he delivered the Clark Lectures.

Abercrombie's poetry, though betraying a certain kinship
with Tennyson and Browning, a touch of Hardy whom he in-
tensely admired, and the influence of the metaphysical poets,
is nonetheless original and striking. Unlike so many of his
early twentieth-century contemporaries, he really has something
to say, his problem being to contain his ideas in acceptable
poetic form. In most of his poems we are invited to consider
the tension between the aspiring soul and the instincts of the
healthy, human body, but in striving to communicate this conflict with a passionate intensity characteristic of Donne, too
frequently he degenerates into impassioned rhetoric in which
the earlier poet's dramatic intensity is lacking. Abercrombie
wrote relatively few short poems, believing that the long narrative poem deserved revival, doing what he could to renew
its popularity. As he grew older his poetical output declined,
and he turned to writing about poetry rather than to poetical
composition itself.

Indignation

AN ODE

I

There was an anger among men
In the old days; and it was as a sword
   In the hands of the Spirit then
To hew the ambusht villainy out of his path
And in its thievish lurking kill the fraud.
   And all the greeds of hell kept to their den
When the Spirit in his hands took wrath.
But lately, when there smiting should have been,
   Who has a weapon seen?
The Spirit stands and looks on infamy,
And unashamed the faces of the pit
   Snarl at their enemy,
Finding him wield no insupportable light
And no whirled edge of blaze to hit
Backward their impudence, and hammer them to flight;
   Although ready is he,
Wearing the same righteous steel
Upon his limbs, helmed as he was then
   When he made olden war;
Yet cannot now with foulness fiercely deal.
There is no indignation among men,
   The Spirit has no scimetar.

II

Wilt thou not come again, thou godly sword,
   Into the Spirit's hands?
That he may be a captain of the Lord
   Again, and mow out of our lands
     The crop of wicked men.
   O thou forged anger, sword
   Made of the holy rage
That went out against the old sick fen

Of being and on disorder warr'd
And fought it into fire and white stars,
When God made Heavens out of the unwholesome age
And maladies of existence, into good
Hunting all that liked not to be glad,—
In what armoury art thou now uplaid,
   And is the rust upon thy blade?
These many years unhelpt has stood
The Spirit, weaponless against bad,
Having no sharpness and no heat
Of indignation wherewith to meet
And battle with the vile banners, his great
Beleaguerment of fiends. But to his hands
   Come thou and clear our lands.
Let him exult to feel the weight
Of wrath swinging with his arm abroad,
And the air about him burn'd with a sword.
Let there be fire, and the anger of the Lord.

III

The Mind of Man has been a sacred place,
   And into it the evil race
Would trespass warily, much afraid
Of sorely-felt assaults upon them made
  By statures of great wind that came
  Terribly using a huge flame
   Intolerably white.
But now that wrath comes never out to fight,
The fiendish bands go lording in the day
And openly possess the mind of man.
With meaningless scurries of their insane feet
  They have rutted the helpless ground
  Like baggage-travell'd clay.
And when the climate of man's thought they found
Blue air, a road for immortal lights,—
Days like the house of God, and hosted nights
Held by the champions of eternity,—
  With evil fires the swarms began

To make a weather they could understand
Of yellow dusk and smoky enormous bale
   To grieve over the land
   And make the sunlight fail.
Till a low roof of dirty storm they brought
   To hang upon the mind of man:
Who cannot see that man's huge thought
   Is now a dark calamity?

IV

   But how long shall the Spirit see
The Life of Man, wherein with such delight
He walkt his glebe, and in his ways would sing
   To do his pleasant gardening,
How long see his own especial ground
Vext in a season of disastrous blight,
Trampled and staled and trodden filthily
By troops of insolence, the beasts of hell?
But the Spirit now is built up narrowly,
   And kept within a shameful pound,
   Walled in with folly and stupid greed
     Lest he should come to plead
   Against our ugly wickedness,
Against our wanton dealing of distress,
The forced defilement of humanity,
   The foundries and the furnaces
   That straddle over the human place.
   Nothing comes to rebuke us for
The hearts we wound with laws grievously,
   The souls our commerce clutches
Cunningly into inescapable lime,
Embruted in wicked streets, made debase
   In villainous alleys and foul hutches,
     There trapt in vice and crime,
And for the wrong we did, who made them poor,
Set to pay infamous penalties in jails;
Not even for this the Spirit breaks his pales.
And shall there be no end to life's expense

In mills and yards and factories,
  With no more recompense
Than sleep in warrens and low styes,
  And undelighted food?
Shall still our ravenous and unhandsome mood
Make men poor and keep them poor?—
Either to starve or work in deadly shops
  Where the damn'd wisdom of the wheels
Fearfully fascinates men's wit and steals,
With privy embezzlement that never stops,
The worker's conscience into their spinning roar,—
  Until men are the dead stuff there,
  And the engines are aware?
Shall we not think of Beauty any more
  In our activities?
Or do no better than to God complain?—
I would that to the world would come again
That indignation, that anger of the Lord
  Which once was known among us men.
  For terrible and upright then
The Spirit would stand suddenly out of his ways
  Of crouching grief and tears,
As by a hilt handling the wrathful blaze,
  Having again a sword.
And he would ruin all the mischievous walls
That had been raised up of materials
  Darkly quarried in hell, to hedge
And fence him out of the life of man;
But he with anger's shining edge
Would mightily cut the built iniquities,
Commerce, and all the policies
Of ownership and avarice;
And they would buckle at his stroke,
Perishing into flights of smoke.
Then he with a dreadful song, a sound
To put a howling fear in the bad horde,
Would step again on his own ground,
  He and his indignant sword,
And the golden havoc would begin.
Those foul ghosts encampt in man

Would run from the stabbing light of his blade.
Caught in the anger's burning wheel,
The huge scything of the tempered zeal,
This clumsy unlit shed we have made,
Money, to house our being in,
Would travel like a wind-blown thing.
In that fanning as motes would be,
The sword-thresht fabric of our trade,
Our happy greed, our healthy wrong,
Our villainous prosperity.
And ript out of its cursèd rind
Of laidly duties, that did wring
And clamp in ignominy man's whole mind,
This iron scurf of labour torn away,
Thought would walk again like a sacred king
The shining space of immortality.
  O for that anger in the hands
    Of Spirit! To us, O righteous sword,
      Come thou and clear our lands,
O fire, O indignation of the Lord!

Ceremonial Ode

INTENDED FOR A UNIVERSITY

I

When from Eternity were separate
  The curdled element
And gathered forces, and the world began,—
The Spirit that was shut and darkly blent
Within this being, did the whole distress
With blind desire after spaciousness.
Into this yearning, strictly bound by Fate
And closely natured, came like an open'd grate
  At last the Mind of Man,
Letting the sky in, and a faculty
To light the cell with lost Eternity.

II

So commerce with the Infinite was regained:
    For upward grew Man's ken,
Laying foundations deep in the ancient fen
Where other life helpless and prone remained.
With knowledge painfully quarried and hewn fair,
Platforms of lore, and many a hanging stair
Of strong imagination, Man has raised
His Wisdom like the watch-towers of a town;
    That he, though fastened down
By Fate, be with its cruelty not amazed,
But be of outer vastness greatly aware.

III

This, then, is yours: to build exultingly
    High, and yet more high,
The knowledgeable towers above base wars
And shameful surges reaching up to lay
Dishonouring hands upon your work and drag
Down from uprightness your desires, to lag
Among low places with a common gait;
That so Man's mind, not conquered by his clay,
    May sit above his fate,
Inhabiting the purpose of the stars,
And trade with his Eternity.

Mary and the Bramble

TO MY MOTHER

The great blue ceremony of the air
Did a new morrow for the earth prepare;
The silver troops of mist were almost crept
Back to the streams where through the day they slept;
And, high up on his tower of song, the glad

Galloping wings of a lark already had
A message from the sun, to give bright warning
That he would shortly make a golden morning.
It was a dawn when the year is earliest.
Mary, in her rapt girlhood, from her rest
Came for the hour to wash her soul. Now she
Beheld, with eyes like the rain-shadowed sea,
Of late an urgency disturb the world;
Her thought that, like a curtain wide unfurl'd
With stir of a hurrying throng against it prest,
Seen things flutter'd with spiritual haste
Behind them, as a rush of wingèd zeal
Made with its gusty passage shiver and reel,
Like a loose weaving, all the work of sense.
Surely not always could such vehemence
Of Spirit stay all shrouded in the green
Appearance of earth's knowledgeable mien:
Ay, see this morning trembling like a sail!
Can it still hold the strain? must it not fail
Even now? for lo how it doth thrill and bend!
Will not, as a torn cloth, earth's season rend
Before this shaking wind of Heaven's speed,
And show her God's obediences indeed
Burning along behind it? Never yet
Was such a fever in the frail earth set
By those hid throngs posting behind its veil!

Unfearing were her eyes; yet would they quail
A little when the curtain seemed nigh torn,
The shining weft of kind clear-weather'd morn,
In pressure of near Spirit forcing it.
And as she walkt, the marvel would permit
Scarce any love for the earth's delighted dress.
Through meadows flowering with happiness
Went Mary, feeling not the air that laid
Honours of gentle dew upon her head;
Nor that the sun now loved with golden stare
The marvellous behaviour of her hair,
Bending with finer swerve from off her brow
Than water which relents before a prow:

Till in the shining darkness many a gleam
Of secret bronze-red lustres answered him.

   The Spirit of Life vaunted itself: "Ho ye
Who wear the Heavens, now look down to me!
I too can praise. My dark encumberment
Of earth, whereinto I was hardly sent,
I have up-wielded as the fire wields flame,
And turned it into glory of God's name:
Till now a praise as good as yours I can,
For now my speech, the long-stammer'd being of Man,
Rises into its mightiest, sweetest word."
Not vain his boast: for seemly to the Lord,
Blue-robed and yellow-kerchieft, Mary went.
There never was to God such worship sent
By any angel in the Heavenly ways,
As this that Life had utter'd for God's praise,
This girlhood—as the service that Life said
In the beauty and the manners of this maid.
Never the harps of Heaven played such song
As her grave walking through the grasses long.
Yea, out of Jewry came the proof in her
That the angel Life was God's best worshipper.

   Now in her vision'd walk beside a brake
Is Mary passing, wherein brambles make
A tangled malice, grown to such a riddle
That any grimness crouching in the middle
Were not espied. Bewildered was the place,
Like a brain full of folly and disgrace;
And with its thorny toils it seemed to be
A naughty heart devising cruelty.
Ready it was with all its small keen spite
To catch at anything that walkt upright,
Although a miching weasel safely went
Therethrough. And close to this entanglement,
This little world out of unkindness made,
With eyes beyond her path young Mary strayed.
As an unheeded bramble's reach she crost,
Her breast a spiny sinew did accost

With eager thorns, tearing her dress to seize
And harm her hidden white virginities.
To it she spake, with such a gentle air
That the thing might not choose but answer her.

"What meanest thou, O Bramble,
 So to hurt my breast?
Why is thy sharp cruelty
 Against my heart prest?"

"How can I help, O Mary,
 Dealing wound to thee?
Thou hast Heaven's favour:
 I am mortality."

"If I, who am thy sister,
 Am in Heaven's love,
If it be so, then should it not
 Thee to gladness move?"

"Nay, nay, it moves me only
 Quietly to wait,
Till I can surely seize thy heart
 In my twisting hate."

"Ah, thou hast pierced my paps, bramble,
 Thy thorns are in my blood;
Tell me for why, thou cruel growth,
 Thy malice is so rude."

"Thou art looking, Mary,
 Beyond the world to be:
If I cannot grapple thee down to the world,
 I can injure thee."

"Ah, thy wicked daggers now
 Into my nipple cling:
It is like guilt, so to be held
 In thy harsh fingering."

The little leaves were language still,
And gave their voice to Mary's will;
But till the bramble's word was said,
Thorns clutcht hard upon the maid.
"Yes, like guilt, for guilt am I,
Sin and wrong and misery.
For thy heart guilt is feeling;
Hurt for which there is no healing
Must the bramble do to thee,
If thou wilt not guilty be.
Know'st thou me? These nails of hate
Are the fastenings of the weight
Of substance which thy God did bind
Upon thy upward-meaning mind.
Life has greatly sworn to be
High as the brows of God in thee;
But I am heaviness, and I
Would hold thee down from being high.
Thou thyself by thy straining
Hast made my weight a wicked thing;
Here in the bramble now I sit
And tear thy flesh with the spines of it.
Yet into my desires come,
And like a worshipping bridegroom
I will turn thy life to dream,
All delicious love to seem.
But if in Heaven God shall wear
Before any worship there
Thy Spirit, and Life boasteth this,
Thou must break through the injuries
And shames I will about thee wind,
The hooks and thickets of my kind;
The whole earth's nature will come to be
Full of my purpose against thee:
Yea, worse than a bramble's handling, men
Shall use thy bosom, Mary, then.
And yet I know that by these scars
I make thee better than the stars
For God to wear; and thou wilt ride

On the lusts that have thee tried,
The murders that fell short of thee,
Like charioting in a victory;
Like shafted horses thou wilt drive
The crimes that I on earth made thrive
Against thee, into Heaven to draw
Thy soul out of my heinous law.
But now in midst of my growth thou art,
And I have thee by the heart;
And closer shall I seize on thee
Even than this; a gallows-tree
Shall bear a bramble-coil on high;
Then twisted about thy soul am I,
Then a withe of my will is bound
Strangling thy very ghost around."

Homeward went Mary, nursing fearfully
The bleeding badges of that cruelty.
Now closer spiritual turbulence whirled
Against her filmy vision of the world,
Which was like shaken silk, so gravely leant
The moving of that throng'd astonishment
On the far side: the time was near at hand
When Gabriel with the fiery-flower'd wand
Would part the tissue of her bodily ken,
And to the opening all God's shining men
Would crowd to watch the message that he took
To earthly life: "Hail, Mary, that dost look
Delightful to the Lord; I bid thee know
That answering God's own love thy womb shall throe."

Witchcraft: New Style

The sun drew off at last his piercing fires.
Over the stale warm air, dull as a pond
And moveless in the grey quieted street,
Blue magic of a summer evening glowed.
The sky, that had been dazzling stone all day,
Hollowed in smooth hard brightness, now dissolved

To infinite soft depth, and smoulder'd down
Low as the roofs, dark burning blue, and soared
Clear to that winking drop of liquid silver,
The first exquisite star. Now the half-light
Tidied away the dusty litter parching
Among the cobbles, veiled in the colour of distance
Shabby slates and brickwork mouldering, turn'd
The hunchback houses into patient things
Resting; and golden windows now began.

A little brisk grey slattern of a woman,
Pattering along in her loose-heel'd clogs,
Pusht the brass-barr'd door of a public house.
The spring went hard against her; hand and knee
Shoved their weak best. As the door poised ajar,
Hullabaloo of talking men burst out,
A pouring babble of inflamed palaver;
And overriding it and shouted down,
High words, jeering or passionate, broken like
Crests that leap and stumble in rushing water.
Just as the door went wide and she stept in,
"She cannot do it!" one was bawling out:
A glaring hulk of flesh with a bull's voice.
He finger'd with his neckerchief, and stretcht
His throat to ease the anger of dispute;
Then spat to put a full stop to the matter.
The little woman waited, with one hand
Propping the door, and smiled at the loud man.
They saw her then; and the sight was enough
To gag the speech of every drinker there:
The din fell down like something chopt off short.
Blank they all wheel'd towards her, with their mouths
Still gaping as though full of voiceless words.
She let the door slam to; and all at ease,
Amused, her smile wrinkling about her eyes,
Went forward: they made room for her quick enough.
Her chin just topt the counter; she gave in
Her bottle to the pot-boy, tuckt it back,
Full of bright tawny ale, under her arm,
Rapt down the coppers on the planisht zinc,

And turned: and no word spoken all the while.
   The first voice, in that silent crowd, was hers,
Her light snickering laugh, as she stood there
Pausing, scanning the sawdust at her feet.
Then she switcht round and faced the positive man
Whose strong "She cannot do it!" all still felt
Huskily shouting in their guilty ears.
   "She can't, eh? She can't do it?"—Then she'd heard!
The man, inside his ruddy insolent flesh,
Had hoped she did not hear. His barrel chest
Gave a slight cringe, as though the glint of her eyes
Prickt him. But he stood up to her awkwardly bold,
One elbow on the counter, gripping his mug
Like a man holding on to a post for safety.
THE MAN. You can't do what's not nature: nobody can.
THE WOMAN. And louts like you have nature in your pocket?
THE MAN. I don't say that—
THE WOMAN.   If you kept saying naught,
No one would guess the fool you are.
SECOND MAN.   Almost
My very words!
THE WOMAN.   O you're the knowing man!
The spark among the cinders!
FIRST MAN.   You can't fetch
A free man back, unless he wants to come.
THE WOMAN. Nay, I'll be bound he doesn't want to come!
THIRD MAN. And he won't come: he told me flat he wouldn't.
THE WOMAN. Are you there, too?
THIRD MAN.   And if he does come back
It will be devilry brought him.
THE WOMAN.   I shall bring him;—
To-night.
FIRST MAN. How will he come?
THE WOMAN.   Running: unless
He's broke his leg, and then he'll have to come
Crawling: but he will come.
FIRST MAN.   How do you know
What he may choose to do, three counties off?
THE WOMAN. He choose?
THIRD MAN.   You haven't got him on a lead.

THE WOMAN. Haven't I though!

SECOND MAN.   That's right; it's what I said.

THE WOMAN. Ay, there are brains in your family.

FIRST MAN.   You have
Some sort of pull on him, to draw him home?

THE WOMAN. You may say that: I have hold of his mind.
And I can slack it off or fetch it taut,
And make him dance a score of miles away
An answer to the least twangling thrum
I play on it. He thought he lurkt at last
Safely; and all the while, what has he been?
An eel on the end of a night-line; and it's time
I haul'd him in. You'll see, to-night I'll land him.

THIRD MAN. Bragging's a light job.

THE WOMAN.   You daren't let me take
Your eyes in mine!—Haul, did I say? no need:
I give his mind a twitch, and up he comes
Tumbling home to me. Whatever work he's at,
He drops the thing he holds like red-hot iron
And runs—runs till he falls down like a beast
Pole-axt, and grunts for breath; then up and on,
No matter does he know the road or not:
The strain I put on his mind will keep him going
Right as a homing-pigeon.

FIRST MAN.   Devilry
I call it.

THE WOMAN. And you're welcome.

SECOND MAN.   But the law
Should have a say here.

THE WOMAN.   What, isn't he mine,
My own? There's naught but what I please about it.

THIRD MAN. Why did you let him go?

THE WOMAN.   To fetch him back!
For I enjoy this, mind. There's many a one
Would think, to see me, "There goes misery!
There's a queer starveling for you!"—and I do
A thing that makes me like a saint in glory,
And the life seem to sound in me like a tune
You could never imagine: I can send power
Delighting out of me! O, the mere thought

Has made my blood go smarting in my veins,
Such a flame glowing along it!—And all the same
I'll pay him out for sidling off from me.
But I'll have supper first.
                    When she was gone,
Their talk could scarcely raise itself again
Above a grumble. But at last a cry
Sharp-pitcht came startling in from the street: at once
Their moody talk exploded into flare
Of swearing hubbub, like gunpowder dropt
On embers; mugs were clapt down, out they bolted
Rowdily jostling, eager for the event.
   All down the street the folk throng'd out of doors,
But left a narrow track clear in the middle;
And there a man came running, a tall man
Running desperately and slowly, pounding
Like a machine, so evenly, so blindly;
And regularly his trotting body wagg'd.
Only one foot clatter'd upon the stones;
The other padded in his dogged stride:
The boot was gone, the sock hung frayed in shreds
About his ankle, the foot was blood and earth;
And never a limp, not the least flinch, to tell
The wounded pulp hit stone at every step.
His clothes were tatter'd and his rent skin showed,
Harrowed with thorns. His face was pale as putty,
Thrown far back; clots of drooping spittle foamed
On his moustache, and his hair hung in tails,
Mired with sweat; and sightless in their sockets
His eyeballs turned up white, as dull as pebbles.
Evenly and doggedly he trotted,
And as he went he moaned. Then out of sight
Round a corner he swerved, and out of hearing.

"The law should have a say to that, by God!"

Hilaire Belloc

JOSEPH HILAIRE PIERRE BELLOC (1870–1953), son of a French father and an English mother, was born in France but came to England after his father's death, attending the Oratory School, Edgbaston. He was apprenticed to a farmer in Sussex for a short time, served in the French army, and tried his hand at journalism. In 1892 he went up to Balliol College, Oxford, on a history scholarship, and as a student there received many prizes and distinctions. In 1906 he became a Member of Parliament, and during the following years wrote profusely on a wide variety of subjects. His last years were spent in comparative seclusion, after he suffered a stroke in 1941 which partially paralyzed him.

Belloc was a versatile writer, turning his pen to everything from nonsense verse to sociology, but his most famous book is perhaps *The Path to Rome* (1902), a description of a journey on foot from Toul in the north of France through Switzerland and northern Italy to Rome. As a poet he belongs to the Chesterton school, sharing that writer's social and political beliefs as well as his passion for the English countryside and English ale. His best poetry is colloquial and direct, though also neat and witty, these qualities showing up especially in his epigrams.

Sonnet XIX

Almighty God, whose justice like a sun
Shall coruscate along the floors of Heaven,
Raising what's low, perfecting what's undone,
Breaking the proud and making odd things even.
The poor of Jesus Christ along the street,
In your rain sodden, in your snows unshod,
They have nor hearth, nor sword, nor human meat,
Nor even the bread of men: Almighty God.

The poor of Jesus Christ whom no man hears
Have waited on your vengeance much too long.
Wipe out not tears but blood: our eyes bleed tears.
Come smite our damnéd sophistries so strong
That thy rude hammer battering this rude wrong
Ring down the abyss of twice ten thousand years.

To Dives

Dives, when you and I go down to Hell,
Where scribblers end and millionaires as well,
We shall be carrying on our separate backs
Two very large but very different packs;
And as you stagger under yours, my friend,
Down the dull shore where all our journeys end,
And go before me (as your rank demands)
Towards the infinite flat underlands,
And that dear river of forgetfulness—
Charon, a man of exquisite address
(For, as your wife's progenitors could tell,
They're very strict on etiquette in Hell),
Will, since you are a lord, observe, "My lord,
We cannot take these weighty things aboard!"
Then down they go, my wretched Dives, down—
The fifteen sorts of boots you kept for town;
The hat to meet the Devil in; the plain
But costly ties; the cases of champagne;

The solid watch, and seal, and chain, and charm;
The working model of a Burning Farm
(To give the little Belials); all the three
Biscuits for Cerberus; the guarantee
From Lambeth that the Rich can never burn,
And even promising a safe return;
The admirable overcoat, designed
To cross Cocytus—very warmly lined:
Sweet Dives, you will leave them all behind
And enter Hell as tattered and as bare
As was your father when he took the air
Behind a barrow-load in Leicester Square.
Then turned to me, and noting one that brings
With careless step a mist of shadowy things:
Laughter and memories, and a few regrets,
Some honour, and a quantity of debts,
A doubt or two of sorts, a trust in God
And (what will seem to you extremely odd)
His father's granfer's father's father's name,
Unspoilt, untitled, even spelt the same;
Charon, who twenty thousand times before
Has ferried poets to the ulterior shore,
Will estimate the weight I bear, and cry—
"Comrade!" (He has himself been known to try
His hand at Latin and Italian verse,
Much in the style of Virgil—only worse)
"We let such vain imaginaries pass!"
Then tell me, Dives, which will look the ass—
You, or myself? Or Charon? Who can tell?
They order things so damnably in Hell.

Drinking Dirge

A thousand years ago I used to dine
   In houses where they gave me such regale
Of dear companionship and comrades fine
   That out I went alone beyond the pale;
And riding, laughed and dared the skies malign
   To show me all the undiscovered tale—

But my philosophy's no more divine,
   I put my pleasure in a pint of ale.

And you, my friends, oh! pleasant friends of mine,
   Who leave me now alone, without avail,
On Californian hills you gave me wine,
   You gave me cider-drink in Longuevaille;
If after many years you come to pine
   For comradeship that is an ancient tale—
You'll find me drinking beer in Dead Man's Chine.
   I put my pleasure in a pint of ale.

In many a briny boat I've tried the brine,
   From many a hidden harbour I've set sail,
Steering towards the sunset where there shine
   The distant amethystine islands pale.
There are no ports beyond the far sea-line,
   Nor any halloa to meet the mariner's hail;
I stand at home and slip the anchor-line.
   I put my pleasure in a pint of ale.

Envoi

Prince! Is it true that when you go to dine
   You bring your bottle in a freezing pail?
Why then you cannot be a friend of mine.
   I put my pleasure in a pint of ale.

Ballade of Genuine Concern

A child at Brighton has been left to drown:
A railway train has jumped the line at Crewe:
I haven't got the change for half a crown:
I can't imagine what on earth to do . . .
Three bisons have stampeded from the Zoo,
A German fleet has anchored in the Clyde.
By God the wretched country's up the flue!
The ice is breaking up on every side.

What! Further news? Rhodesian stocks are down?
England, my England, can the news be true!
Cannot the Duke be got to come to town?
Or will not Mr. Hooper pull us through?
And now the Bank is stopping payment too,
The chief cashier has cut his throat and died,
And Scotland Yard has failed to find a clue:
The ice is breaking up on every side.

A raging mob inflamed by Charley Brown
Is tearing up the rails of Waterloo;
They've hanged the Chancellor in wig and gown,
The Speaker, and the Chief Inspector too!
Police! Police! Is this the road to Kew?
I can't keep up: my garter's come untied;
I shall be murdered by the savage crew.
The ice is breaking up on every side.

Envoi

Prince of the Empire, Prince of Timbuctoo,
Prince eight feet round and nearly four feet wide,
Do try to run a little faster, do.
The ice is breaking up on every side.

Ballade of Gentlemanly Feeling and Railway Strikes

Nothing is more ungentlemanly than
   Exaggeration, causing needless pain;
It's worse than spitting, and it stamps a man
   Deservedly with other men's disdain.
   Weigh human actions carefully. Explain
The worst of them with clarity. Mayhap
   There were two sides to that affair of Cain—
And Judas was a tolerable chap!

This sort of recklessness has laid a ban
　　(Most properly!) upon the works of Paine;
And should in decency condemn the clan
　　Of mean detractors, like the half-insane
　　And filthy Swift, Elijah, and again
The hare-brained Dante, with his snarl and yap—
　　No life, however warped, was lived in vain.
And Judas was a tolerable chap.

Benedict Arnold doubtless had a plan
　　For profiting his country: it is plain
That nothing but the voice of slander can
　　Have poisoned such a man as Charlemagne
　　Against the martyred Ganelon in Spain.
We know that Dreyfus fell into a trap—
　　Which also may be true of poor Bazaine—
And Judas was a tolerable chap.

Envoi

Prince, even you are hardly so inane
　　As not to understand the sad mishap
Befallen those who run the railway-train—
　　And Judas was a tolerable chap.

On Mundane Acquaintances

Good morning, Algernon: Good morning, Percy.
Good morning, Mrs. Roebeck. Christ have mercy!

On His Books

When I am dead, I hope it may be said:
His sins were scarlet, but his books were read!

Robert Bridges

ROBERT SEYMOUR BRIDGES (1844–1930) was born in Kent and educated at Eton, Corpus Christi College, Oxford, and St. Bartholomew's Hospital, London. He qualified as a doctor and practiced medicine for fifteen years before devoting himself almost entirely to literature. In 1873 his first volume of poems appeared, which was followed by several more, as well as a number of dramas based on Greek mythology. Though not especially well known, in 1913 he succeeded Alfred Austin as Poet Laureate, writing patriotic poems during the war without succumbing to jingoism, and generally restoring some of the respect for the Laureateship which had been lost in the immediate past. In 1929 he published *The Testament of Beauty,* a long poem written in what he called "loose alexandrines," describing the evolutionary process in terms of man's steady aspiration toward beauty, truth, and love.

Bridges remained aloof from the various poetical movements current during his time, and though his verse occasionally recalls that of the Elizabethans, essentially he belongs to the school of Arnold and Tennyson. His negative attitude to social discontent and his indifference to the humanitarian movements of the time reflect his kinship with middle-class Victorianism, but his conservatism in such matters should not blind us to his numerous experiments in English prosody, particularly his efforts to adapt classical meters to English verse.

London Snow

When men were all asleep the snow came flying,
In large white flakes falling on the city brown,
Stealthily and perpetually settling and loosely lying,
   Hushing the latest traffic of the drowsy town;
Deadening, muffling, stifling its murmurs failing;
Lazily and incessantly floating down and down:
   Silently sifting and veiling road, roof and railing;
Hiding difference, making unevenness even,
Into angles and crevices softly drifting and sailing.
   All night it fell, and when full inches seven
It lay in the depth of its uncompacted lightness,
The clouds blew off from a high and frosty heaven;
   And all woke earlier for the unaccustomed brightness
Of the winter dawning, the strange unheavenly glare:
The eye marvelled—marvelled at the dazzling whiteness;
   The ear hearkened to the stillness of the solemn air;
No sound of wheel rumbling nor of foot falling,
And the busy morning cries came thin and spare.
   Then boys I heard, as they went to school, calling,
They gathered up the crystal manna to freeze
Their tongues with tasting, their hands with snowballing;
   Or rioted in a drift, plunging up to the knees;
Or peering up from under the white-mossed wonder,
"O look at the trees!" they cried, "O look at the trees!"
   With lessened load a few carts creak and blunder,
Following along the white deserted way,
A country company long dispersed asunder:
   When now already the sun, in pale display
Standing by Paul's high dome, spread forth below
His sparkling beams, and awoke the stir of the day.
   For now doors open, and war is waged with the snow;
And trains of sombre men, past tale of number,
Tread long brown paths, as toward their toil they go:
   But even for them awhile no cares encumber
Their minds diverted; the daily word is unspoken,
The daily thoughts of labour and sorrow slumber
At the sight of the beauty that greets them, for the charm they
     have broken.

Nightingales

Beautiful must be the mountains whence ye come,
And bright in the fruitful valleys the streams, wherefrom
      Ye learn your song:
Where are those starry woods? O might I wander there,
   Among the flowers, which in that heavenly air
      Bloom the year long!

Nay, barren are those mountains and spent the streams:
Our song is the voice of desire, that haunts our dreams,
      A throe of the heart,
Whose pining visions dim, forbidden hopes profound,
   No dying cadence nor long sigh can sound,
      For all our art.

Alone, aloud in the raptured ear of men
We pour our dark nocturnal secret; and then,
      As night is withdrawn
From these sweet-springing meads and bursting boughs of May,
   Dream, while the innumerable choir of day
      Welcome the dawn.

Peace Ode

ON CONCLUSION OF THE BOER WAR, JUNE, 1902

Now joy in all hearts with happy auguries,
And praise on all lips: for sunny June cometh
   Chasing the thick warcloud, that outspread
    Sulfurous and sullen over England.

Full thirty moons since unwilling enmity,
Since daily suspense for hideous peril
   Of brethren unrescued, beleaguer'd
    Plague-stricken in cities unprovided,

Had quencht accustom'd gaiety, from the day
When first the Dutchman's implacable folly,
    The country of Shakespeare defying,
        Thought with a curse to appal the nation:

Whose threat to quell their kinsmen in Africa
Anger'd awhile our easy democracy;
    That, reckless and patient of insult,
        Will not abide arrogant defiance:

They called to arms; and war began evilly.
From slily forestor'd, well-hidden armouries,
    And early advantage, the despot
        Stood for a time prevalent against us

Till from the coil of slow-gathering battle
He rancorous, with full moneybags hurried,
    Peddling to European envy
        His traffic of pennyworthy slander.

For since the first keel launch'd upon Ocean
Ne'er had before so mighty an armament
    O'errun the realm of dark Poseidon,
        So resolutely measur'd the waters,

As soon from our ports in diligent passage
O'er half the round world plow'd hither & thither
    The pathless Atlantic, revengeful
        Soldiery pouring on Esperanza:

Nor shows the Argive story of Ilium,
With tale of ancient auxiliar cities,
    So vast a roll of wide alliance
        As, rallying to the aid of England,

Came from the swarming counties accoutering,
And misty highlands of Caledonia,
    With Cambria's half-Celtic offspring,
        And the ever-merry fighting Irish:

Came too the new world's hardy Canadians,
And from remote Australia champions
    Like huntsmen, and from those twin islands
      Lying off antipodal beyond her,

Under the old flag sailing across the sea:
For mighty is blood's empery, where honour
    And freedom ancestral have upbuilt
      Inheritance to a lovely glory.

Thee, France, love I, fair lawgiver and scholar;
Thy lively grace, thy temper illustrious;
    And thee, in all wisdom Diviner,
      Germany, deep melodist immortal;

Nor less have envied soft Italy's spirit,
In marble unveil'd and eloquent colour:
    But best love I England, wer' I not
      Born to her aery should envy also.

Wherefore to-day one gift above every gift
Let us beseech, that God will accord to her
    Always a right judgement in all things;
      Ev'n to celestial excellencies;

And grant us in long peace to accumulate
Joy, and to stablish friendliness and commerce,
    And barter in markets for unpriced
      Beauty, the pearl of unending empire.

There Is a Hill
Beside the Silver Thames

There is a hill beside the silver Thames,
Shady with birch and beech and odorous pine:
And brilliant underfoot with thousand gems
Steeply the thickets to his floods decline.

  Straight trees in every place
  Their thick tops interlace,
And pendant branches trail their foliage fine
  Upon his watery face.

Swift from the sweltering pasturage he flows:
His stream, alert to seek the pleasant shade,
Pictures his gentle purpose, as he goes
Straight to the caverned pool his toil has made.
  His winter floods lay bare
  The stout roots in the air:
His summer streams are cool, when they have played
  Among their fibrous hair.

A rushy island guards the sacred bower,
And hides it from the meadow, where in peace
The lazy cows wrench many a scented flower,
Robbing the golden market of the bees:
  And laden barges float
  By banks of myosote;
And scented flag and golden flower-de-lys
  Delay the loitering boat.

And on this side the island, where the pool
Eddies away, are tangled mass on mass
The water-weeds, that net the fishes cool,
And scarce allow a narrow stream to pass;
  Where spreading crowfoot mars
  The drowning nenuphars,
Waving the tassels of her silken grass
  Below her silver stars.

But in the purple pool there nothing grows,
Not the white water-lily spoked with gold;
Though best she loves the hollows, and well knows
On quiet streams her broad shields to unfold:
  Yet should her roots but try
  Within these deeps to lie,
Not her long reaching stalk could ever hold
  Her waxen head so high.

Sometimes an angler comes, and drops his hook
Within its hidden depths, and 'gainst a tree
Leaning his rod, reads in some pleasant book,
Forgetting soon his pride of fishery;
    And dreams, or falls asleep,
    While curious fishes peep
About his nibbled bait, or scornfully
    Dart off and rise and leap.

And sometimes a slow figure 'neath the trees,
In ancient-fashioned smock, with tottering care
Upon a staff propping his weary knees,
May by the pathway of the forest fare:
    As from a buried day
    Across the mind will stray
Some perishing mute shadow,—and unaware
    He passeth on his way.

Else, he that wishes solitude is safe,
Whether he bathe at morning in the stream:
Or lead his love there when the hot hours chafe
The meadows, busy with a blurring steam;
    Or watch, as fades the light,
    The gibbous moon grow bright,
Until her magic rays dance in a dream,
    And glorify the night.

Where is the bower beside the silver Thames?
O pool and flowery thickets, hear my vow!
O trees of freshest foliage and straight stems,
No sharer of my secret I allow:
    Lest ere I come the while
    Strange feet your shades defile;
Or lest the burly oarsman turn his prow
    Within your guardian isle.

Christmas Eve, 1917

Many happy returns, sweet Babe, of the day!
Didst not thou sow good seed in the world, thy field?
Cam'st thou to save the poor? Thy poor yet pine.
Thousands to-day suffer death-pangs like thine;
Our jewels of life are spilt on the ground as dross;
Ten thousand mothers stand beneath the cross.
Peace to men of goodwill was the angels' song:
Now there is fiercer war, worse filth and wrong.
If thou didst sow good seed, is this the yield?
Shall not thy folk be quell'd in dead dismay?

Nay, with a larger hope we are fed and heal'd
Than e'er was reveal'd to the saints who died so strong;
For while men slept the seed had quicken'd unseen.
England is as a field whereon the corn is green.

Of trial and dark tribulation this vision is born—
Britain as a field green with the springing corn.
While we slumber'd the seed was growing unseen.
Happy returns of the day, dear Babe, we say.

ENGLAND has buried her sins with her fathers' bones.
Thou shalt be throned on the ruin of kingly thrones.
The wish of thine heart is rooted in carnal mind;
For good seed didst thou sow in the world thy field:
It shall ripen in gold and harvest an hundredfold.
Peace shall come as a flood upon all mankind;
Love shall comfort and succour the poor that are pined.

Wherever our gentle children are wander'd and sped,
Simple apostles thine of the world to come,
They carried the living seed of the living Bread,
The angel-song and the gospel of Christendom,
That while the nation slept was springing unseen.

So tho' we be sorely stricken we feel no dread:
Our thousand sons suffer death-pangs like thine:

It shall ripen in gold and harvest an hundredfold:
Peace and Love shall hallow our care and teen,
Shall bind in fellowship all the folk of the earth
To kneel at thy cradle, Babe, and bless thy birth.

Ring we the bells up and down in country and town,
And keep the old feast unholpen of preacher or priest,
Wishing thee happy returns, and thy Mother May,
Ever happier and happier returns, dear CHRIST, of thy day!

Rupert Brooke

RUPERT BROOKE (1887–1915) was born at Rugby, where he later attended school. Afterward he went on to King's College, Cambridge, where he soon established himself as a young scholar of promise, his study of the Elizabethan and Jacobean drama assuring him of a Fellowship at King's in 1911. At the same time Brooke was also attracting attention as a poet, and together with Harold Monro and Edward Marsh was responsible for the launching of the influential Georgian anthologies. At the outbreak of the war Brooke was commissioned with the Royal Naval Division, and in the spring of 1915 sailed to the Aegean as part of the ill-fated Dardanelles expedition. There he contracted septicemia, dying shortly afterward aboard a hospital ship, and was later buried on the island of Scyros.

Though in 1911 Brooke had published a small volume of poems which was well received, and "The Old Vicarage, Grantchester," included in the first volume of *Georgian Poetry,* enhanced his reputation, it is by his war poetry we chiefly remember him. These verses were first published in *New Numbers* in December, 1914, and though at the time they did not attract much attention, after Brooke's death, both Sir Winston Churchill, writing in the London *Times,* and Dean Inge, who chose one of his poems as the text for the Easter sermon in St. Paul's Cathedral, drew attention to them, resulting in their being reprinted in a volume called *1914 and Other Poems,* edited by Edward Marsh. In retrospect, however, it seems not to have been Brooke's merit as a war poet which brought him fame, but the fact that his tragic death, putting an end to a potentially brilliant career, cast an emotional glow over his work, causing many to overrate his poetical talents.

A Channel Passage

The damned ship lurched and slithered. Quiet and quick
  My cold gorge rose; the long sea rolled; I knew
I must think hard of something, or be sick;
  And could think hard of only one thing—*you!*
You, you alone could hold my fancy ever!
  And with you memories come, sharp pain, and dole.
Now there's a choice—heartache or tortured liver!
  A sea-sick body, or a you-sick soul!

Do I forget you? Retchings twist and tie me,
  Old meat, good meals, brown gobbets, up I throw.
Do I remember? Acrid return and slimy,
  The sobs and slobber of a last year's woe.
And still the sick ship rolls. 'Tis hard, I tell ye,
To choose 'twixt love and nausea, heart and belly.

The Old Vicarage, Grantchester

(CAFÉ DES WESTENS, BERLIN, MAY 1912)

Just now the lilac is in bloom,
All before my little room;
And in my flower-beds, I think,
Smile the carnation and the pink;
And down the borders, well I know,
The poppy and the pansy blow . . .
Oh! there the chestnuts, summer through,
Beside the river make for you
A tunnel of green gloom, and sleep
Deeply above; and green and deep
The stream mysterious glides beneath,
Green as a dream and deep as death.
—Oh, damn! I know it! and I know
How the May fields all golden show,
And when the day is young and sweet,
Gild gloriously the bare feet

That run to bathe . . .
$\qquad$ *Du lieber Gott!*
Here am I, sweating, sick, and hot,
And there the shadowed waters fresh
Lean up to embrace the naked flesh.
Temperamentvoll German Jews
Drink beer around;—and *there* the dews
Are soft beneath a morn of gold.
Here tulips bloom as they are told;
Unkempt about those hedges blows
An English unofficial rose;
And there the unregulated sun
Slopes down to rest when day is done,
And wakes a vague unpunctual star,
A slippered Hesper; and there are
Meads towards Haslingfield and Coton
Where *das Betreten*'s not *verboten.*

$\epsilon\iota\theta$ $\gamma\epsilon\upsilon\sigma\iota\mu\eta\upsilon$ . . . would I were
In Grantchester, in Grantchester!—
Some, it may be, can get in touch
With Nature there, or Earth, or such.
And clever modern men have seen
A Faun a-peeping through the green,
And felt the Classics were not dead,
To glimpse a Naiad's reedy head,
Or hear the Goat-foot piping low: . . .
But these are things I do not know.
I only know that you may lie
Day-long and watch the Cambridge sky,
And, flower-lulled in sleepy grass,
Hear the cool lapse of hours pass,
Until the centuries blend and blur
In Grantchester, in Grantchester. . . .
Still in the dawnlit waters cool
His ghostly Lordship swims his pool,
And tries the strokes, essays the tricks,
Long learnt on Hellespont, or Styx.
Dan Chaucer hears his river still

Chatter beneath a phantom mill.
Tennyson notes, with studious eye,
How Cambridge waters hurry by . . .
And in that garden, black and white,
Creep whispers through the grass all night;
And spectral dance, before the dawn,
A hundred Vicars down the lawn;
Curates, long dust, will come and go
On lissom, clerical, printless toe;
And oft between the boughs is seen
The sly shade of a Rural Dean . . .
Till, at a shiver in the skies,
Vanishing with Satanic cries,
The prim ecclesiastic rout
Leaves but a startled sleeper-out,
Grey heavens, the first bird's drowsy calls,
The falling house that never falls.

God! I will pack, and take a train,
And get me to England once again!
For England's the one land, I know,
Where men with Splendid Hearts may go;
And Cambridgeshire, of all England,
The shire for Men who Understand;
And of *that* district I prefer
The lovely hamlet Grantchester.
For Cambridge people rarely smile,
Being urban, squat, and packed with guile;
And Royston men in the far South
Are black and fierce and strange of mouth;
At Over they fling oaths at one,
And worse than oaths at Trumpington,
And Ditton girls are mean and dirty,
And there's none in Harston under thirty,
And folks in Shelford and those parts
Have twisted lips and twisted hearts,
And Barton men make Cockney rhymes,
And Coton's full of nameless crimes,
And things are done you'd not believe
At Madingley, on Christmas Eve.

Strong men have run for miles and miles,
When one from Cherry Hinton smiles;
Strong men have blanched, and shot their wives,
Rather than send them to St. Ives;
Strong men have cried like babes, bydam,
To hear what happened at Babraham.

But Grantchester! ah, Grantchester!
There's peace and holy quiet there,
Great clouds along pacific skies,
And men and women with straight eyes,
Lithe children lovelier than a dream,
A bosky wood, a slumbrous stream,
And little kindly winds that creep
Round twilight corners, half asleep.
In Grantchester their skins are white;
They bathe by day, they bathe by night;
The women there do all they ought;
The men observe the Rules of Thought.
They love the Good; they worship Truth;
They laugh uproariously in youth;
(And when they get to feeling old,
They up and shoot themselves, I'm told) . . .

Ah God! to see the branches stir
Across the moon at Grantchester!
To smell the thrilling-sweet and rotten
Unforgettable, unforgotten
River-smell, and hear the breeze
Sobbing in the little trees.
Say, do the elm-clumps greatly stand
Still guardians of that holy land?
The chestnuts shade, in reverend dream,
The yet unacademic stream?
Is dawn a secret shy and cold
Anadyomene, silver-gold?
And sunset still a golden sea
From Haslingfield to Madingley?
And after, ere the night is born,
Do hares come out about the corn?

Oh, is the water sweet and cool,
Gentle and brown, above the pool?
And laughs the immortal river still
Under the mill, under the mill?
Say, is there Beauty yet to find?
And Certainty? and Quiet kind?
Deep meadows yet, for to forget
The lies, and truths, and pain? . . . oh! yet
Stands the Church clock at ten to three?
And is there honey still for tea?

The Busy Heart

Now that we've done our best and worst, and parted,
   I would fill my mind with thoughts that will not rend.
(O heart, I do not dare go empty-hearted)
   I'll think of Love in books, Love without end;
Women with child, content; and old men sleeping;
   And wet strong ploughlands, scarred for certain grain;
And babes that weep, and so forget their weeping;
   And the young heavens, forgetful after rain;
And evening hush, broken by homing wings;
   And Song's nobility, and Wisdom holy,
That live, we dead. I would think of a thousand things,
   Lovely and durable, and taste them slowly,
One after one, like tasting a sweet food.
I have need to busy my heart with quietude.

Waikiki

Warm perfumes like a breath from vine and tree
   Drift down the darkness. Plangent, hidden from eyes,
   Somewhere an *eukaleli* thrills and cries
And stabs with pain the night's brown savagery.
And dark scents whisper; and dim waves creep to me,
   Gleam like a woman's hair, stretch out, and rise;
   And new stars burn into the ancient skies,
Over the murmurous soft Hawaian sea.

And I recall, lose, grasp, forget again,
　And still remember, a tale I have heard, or known
An empty tale, of idleness and pain,
　Of two that loved—or did not love—and one
Whose perplexed heart did evil, foolishly,
A long while since, and by some other sea.

III. The Dead

Blow out, you bugles, over the rich Dead!
　There's none of these so lonely and poor of old,
　But, dying, has made us rarer gifts than gold.
These laid the world away; poured out the red
Sweet wine of youth; gave up the years to be
　Of work and joy, and that unhoped serene,
　That men call age; and those who would have been,
Their sons, they gave, their immortality.

Blow, bugles, blow! They brought us, for our dearth,
　Holiness, lacked so long, and Love, and Pain.
Honour has come back, as a king, to earth,
　And paid his subjects with a royal wage;
And Nobleness walks in our ways again;
　And we have come into our heritage.

IV. The Dead

These hearts were woven of human joys and cares,
　Washed marvellously with sorrow, swift to mirth.
The years had given them kindness. Dawn was theirs,
　And sunset, and the colours of the earth.
These had seen movement, and heard music; known
　Slumber and waking; loved; gone proudly friended;
Felt the quick stir of wonder; sat alone;
　Touched flowers and furs and cheeks. All this is ended.

There are waters blown by changing winds to laughter
And lit by the rich skies, all day. And after,

Frost, with a gesture, stays the waves that dance
And wandering loveliness. He leaves a white
Unbroken glory, a gathered radiance,
A width, a shining peace, under the night.

The Soldier

If I should die, think only this of me:
That there's some corner of a foreign field
That is for ever England. There shall be
In that rich earth a richer dust concealed;
A dust whom England bore, shaped, made aware,
Gave, once, her flowers to love, her ways to roam,
A body of England's, breathing English air,
Washed by the rivers, blest by suns of home.

And think, this heart, all evil shed away,
A pulse in the eternal mind, no less
Gives somewhere back the thoughts by England
given;
Her sights and sounds; dreams happy as her day;
And laughter, learnt of friends; and gentleness,
In hearts at peace, under an English heaven.

G. K. Chesterton

GILBERT KEITH CHESTERTON (1874–1936) was born in London and educated at St. Paul's School. Because he showed an aptitude for both art and literature he enrolled in the Slade School of Art and also studied English literature at London University at the same time, eventually settling on a career in journalism. He soon became a versatile and prolific writer, publishing over one hundred volumes in his lifetime, including volumes of poems, novels, plays, detective stories, and religious, political, and sociological studies. He was a compulsive man who continually overworked and ate and drank too much, and early in the 1914–1918 war suffered a severe illness which brought him close to death. He recovered, however, and was soon writing as furiously as ever, keeping up the pace almost until his death.

In spite of his bluff exterior and his chronic absent-mindedness, Chesterton was a man deeply concerned with man's place in the world and his relations with God and his fellows. During the Boer War he supported the Boers as a result of his violent anti-Imperialism; he had a firm belief in the importance of property for giving man personal dignity and encouraging a sense of self-realization; and latterly he became a convert to Roman Catholicism. Chesterton's philosophy of life, though appearing in various forms in his numerous published works, was perhaps most explicitly stated in *Orthodoxy* (1908), *What's Wrong with the World?* (1910), and *The Everlasting Man* (1925). As a poet he is best remembered for "The Donkey" and his hearty poems about the English countryside. Though his verse is sometimes noisy, at its best it is direct and unpretentious, revealing great honesty and force.

77

The Donkey

When fishes flew and forests walked
  And figs grew upon thorn,
Some moment when the moon was blood
  Then surely I was born;

With monstrous head and sickening cry
  And ears like errant wings,
The devil's walking parody
  On all four-footed things.

The tattered outlaw of the earth,
  Of ancient crooked will;
Starve, scourge, deride me: I am dumb,
  I keep my secret still.

Fools! For I also had my hour;
  One far fierce hour and sweet:
There was a shout about my ears,
  And palms before my feet.

The Rolling English Road

Before the Roman came to Rye or out to Severn strode,
The rolling English drunkard made the rolling English road.
A reeling road, a rolling road, that rambles round the shire,
And after him the parson ran, the sexton and the squire;
A merry road, a mazy road, and such as we did tread
The night we went to Birmingham by way of Beachy Head.

I knew no harm of Bonaparte and plenty of the Squire,
And for to fight the Frenchman I did not much desire;
But I did bash their baggonets because they came arrayed
To straighten out the crooked road an English drunkard made,
Where you and I went down the lane with ale-mugs in our
    hands,
The night we went to Glastonbury by way of Goodwin Sands.

His sins they were forgiven him; or why do flowers run
Behind him; and the hedges all strengthening in the sun?
The wild thing went from left to right and knew not which was
    which,
But the wild rose was above him when they found him in the
    ditch.
God pardon us, nor harden us; we did not see so clear
The night we went to Bannockburn by way of Brighton Pier.

My friends, we will not go again or ape an ancient rage,
Or stretch the folly of our youth to be the shame of age,
But walk with clearer eyes and ears this path that wandereth,
And see undrugged in evening light the decent inn of death;
For there is good news yet to hear and fine things to be seen,
Before we go to Paradise by way of Kensal Green.

Wine and Water

Old Noah he had an ostrich farm and fowls on the largest
    scale,
He ate his egg with a ladle in an egg-cup big as a pail,
And the soup he took was Elephant Soup and the fish he took
    was Whale,
But they all were small to the cellar he took when he set out
    to sail,
And Noah he often said to his wife when he sat down to dine,
"I don't care where the water goes if it doesn't get into the
    wine."

The cataract of the cliff of heaven fell blinding off the brink
As if it would wash the stars away as suds go down a sink,
The seven heavens came roaring down for the throats of hell to
    drink,
And Noah he cocked his eye and said, "It looks like rain, I
    think,
The water has drowned the Matterhorn as deep as a Mendip
    mine,
But I don't care where the water goes if it doesn't get into
    the wine."

But Noah he sinned, and we have sinned; on tipsy feet we trod,
Till a great big black teetotaller was sent to us for a rod,
And you can't get wine at a P.S.A., or chapel, or Eisteddfod,
For the Curse of Water has come again because of the wrath of
    God,
And water is on the Bishop's board and the Higher Thinker's
    shrine,
But I don't care where the water goes if it doesn't get into the
    wine.

Lepanto

White founts falling in the Courts of the sun,
And the Soldan of Byzantium is smiling as they run;
There is laughter like the fountains in that face of all men
    feared,
It stirs the forest darkness, the darkness of his beard,
It curls the blood-red crescent, the crescent of his lips,
For the inmost sea of all the earth is shaken with his ships.
They have dared the white republics up the capes of Italy,
They have dashed the Adriatic round the Lion of the Sea,
And the Pope has cast his arms abroad for agony and loss,
And called the kings of Christendom for swords about the
    Cross.
The cold Queen of England is looking in the glass;
The shadow of the Valois is yawning at the Mass;
From evening isles fantastical rings faint the Spanish gun,
And the Lord upon the Golden Horn is laughing in the sun.
Dim drums throbbing, in the hills half heard,
Where only on a nameless throne a crownless prince has
    stirred,
Where, risen from a doubtful seat and half attainted stall,
The last knight of Europe takes weapons from the wall,
The last and lingering troubadour to whom the bird has sung,
That once went singing southward when all the world was
    young.
In that enormous silence, tiny and unafraid,
Comes up along a winding road the noise of the Crusade.
Strong gongs groaning as the guns boom far,

Don John of Austria is going to the war,
Stiff flags straining in the night-blasts cold,
In the gloom black-purple, in the glint old-gold,
Torchlight crimson on the copper kettle-drums,
Then the tuckets, then the trumpets, then the cannon, and he
    comes.
Don John laughing in the brave beard curled,
Spurning of his stirrups like the thrones of all the world,
Holding his head up for a flag of all the free.
Love-light of Spain—hurrah!
Death-light of Africa!
Don John of Austria
Is riding to the sea.

Mahound is in his paradise above the evening star,
(*Don John of Austria is going to the war.*)
He moves a mighty turban on the timeless houri's knees,
His turban that is woven of the sunsets and the seas.
He shakes the peacock gardens as he rises from his ease,
And he strides among the tree-tops and is taller than the trees,
And his voice through all the garden is a thunder sent to bring
Black Azrael and Ariel and Ammon on the wing.
Giants and the Genii,
Multiplex of wing and eye,
Whose strong obedience broke the sky
When Solomon was king.

They rush in red and purple from the red clouds of the morn,
From temples where the yellow gods shut up their eyes in scorn;
They rise in green robes roaring from the green hells of the sea
Where fallen skies and evil hues and eyeless creatures be;
On them the sea-valves cluster and the grey sea-forests curl,
Splashed with a splendid sickness, the sickness of the pearl;
They swell in sapphire smoke out of the blue cracks of the
    ground,—
They gather and they wonder and give worship to Mahound.
And he saith, "Break up the mountains where the hermit-folk
    can hide,
And sift the red and silver sands lest bone of saint abide,

And chase the Giaours flying night and day, not giving rest,
For that which was our trouble comes again out of the west.

We have set the seal of Solomon on all things under sun,
Of knowledge and of sorrow and endurance of things done,
But a noise is in the mountains, in the mountains, and I know
The voice that shook our palaces—four hundred years ago:
It is he that saith not 'Kismet'; it is he that knows not Fate;
It is Richard, it is Raymond, it is Godfrey in the gate!
It is he whose loss is laughter when he counts the wager worth,
Put down your feet upon him, that our peace be on the earth."
For he heard drums groaning and he heard guns jar,
(*Don John of Austria is going to the war.*)
Sudden and still—hurrah!
Bolt from Iberia!
Don John of Austria
Is gone by Alcalar.

St Michael's on his Mountain in the sea-roads of the north,
(*Don John of Austria is girt and going forth.*)
Where the grey seas glitter and the sharp tides shift
And the sea-folk labour and the red sails lift.
He shakes his lance of iron and he claps his wings of stone;
The noise is gone through Normandy; the noise is gone alone;
The North is full of tangled things and texts and aching eyes
And dead is all the innocence of anger and surprise,
And Christian killeth Christian in a narrow dusty room,
And Christian dreadeth Christ that hath a newer face of doom,
And Christian hateth Mary that God kissed in Galilee,
But Don John of Austria is riding to the sea.
Don John calling through the blast and the eclipse,
Crying with the trumpet, with the trumpet of his lips,
Trumpet that sayeth ha!
Domino Gloria!
Don John of Austria
Is shouting to the ships.

King Philip's in his closet with the Fleece about his neck,
(*Don John of Austria is armed upon the deck.*)
The walls are hung with velvet that is black and soft as sin,

And little dwarfs creep out of it and little dwarfs creep in.
He holds a crystal phial that has colours like the moon,
He touches, and it tingles, and he trembles very soon,
And his face is as a fungus of a leprous white and grey
Like plants in the high houses that are shuttered from the day,
And death is in the phial and the end of noble work,
But Don John of Austria has fired upon the Turk.
Don John's hunting, and his hounds have bayed—
Booms away past Italy the rumour of his raid.
Gun upon gun, ha! ha!
Gun upon gun, hurrah!
Don John of Austria
Has loosed the cannonade.

The Pope was in his chapel before day or battle broke,
(*Don John of Austria is hidden in the smoke.*)
The hidden room in man's house where God sits all the year,
The secret window whence the world looks small and very dear.
He sees as in a mirror on the monstrous twilight sea
The crescent of the cruel ships whose name is mystery;
They fling great shadows foe-wards, making Cross and Castle
      dark,
They veil the plumèd lions on the galleys of St. Mark;
And above the ships are palaces of brown, black-bearded chiefs,
And below the ships are prisons, where with multitudinous griefs,
Christian captives sick and sunless, all a labouring race repines
Like a race in sunken cities, like a nation in the mines.
They are lost like slaves that swat, and in the skies of morning
      hung
The stairways of the tallest gods when tyranny was young.

They are countless, voiceless, hopeless as those fallen or fleeing
      on
Before the high Kings' horses in the granite of Babylon.
And many a one grows witless in his quiet room in hell
Where a yellow face looks inward through the lattice of his cell,
And he finds his God forgotten, and he seeks no more a sign—
(*But Don John of Austria has burst the battle-line!*)
Don John pounding from the slaughter-painted poop,
Purpling all the ocean like a bloody pirate's sloop,

Scarlet running over on the silvers and the golds,
Breaking of the hatches up and bursting of the holds,
Thronging of the thousands up that labour under sea,
White for bliss and blind for sun and stunned for liberty.
Vivat Hispania!
Domino Gloria!
Don John of Austria
Has set his people free!

Cervantes on his galley sets the sword back in the sheath,
(*Don John of Austria rides homeward with a wreath.*)
And he sees across a weary land a straggling road in Spain,
Up which a lean and foolish knight for ever rides in vain,
And he smiles, but not as Sultans smile, and settles back the
     blade . . .
(*But Don John of Austria rides home from the Crusade.*)

From The Ballad of the White Horse

BOOK VIII   THE SCOURING OF THE HORSE

Far northward and far westward
     The distant tribes drew nigh,
Plains beyond plains, fell beyond fell,
That a man at sunset sees so well,
And the tiny coloured towns that dwell
     In the corners of the sky.

But dark and thick as thronged the host,
     With drum and torch and blade,
The still-eyed King sat pondering,
As one that watches a live thing,
     The scoured chalk; and he said,

"Though I give this land to Our Lady,
     That helped me in Athelney,
Though lordlier trees and lustier sod

And happier hills hath no flesh trod
Than the garden of the Mother of God
 Between Thames side and the sea,

"I know that weeds shall grow in it
 Faster than men can burn;
And though they scatter now and go,
In some far century, sad and slow,
I have a vision, and I know
 The heathen shall return.

"They shall not come with warships,
 They shall not waste with brands,
But books be all their eating,
 And ink be on their hands.

"Not with the humour of hunters
 Or savage skill in war,
But ordering all things with dead words,
Strings shall they make of beasts and birds
 And wheels of wind and star.

"They shall come mild as monkish clerks,
 With many a scroll and pen;
And backward shall ye turn and gaze,
Desiring one of Alfred's days,
 When pagans still were men.

"The dear sun dwarfed of dreadful suns,
 Like fiercer flowers on stalk,
Earth lost and little like a pea
In high heaven's towering forestry,
—These be the small weeds ye shall see
 Crawl, covering the chalk.

"But though they bridge St. Mary's sea,
 Or steal St. Michael's wing—
Though they rear marvels over us,
Greater than great Vergilius
 Wrought for the Roman king;

"By this sign you shall know them,
   The breaking of the sword,
And Man no more a free knight,
   That loves or hates his lord.

"Yea, this shall be the sign of them,
   The sign of the dying fire;
And Man made like a half-wit,
   That knows not of his sire.

"What though they come with scroll and pen,
   And grave as a shaven clerk,
By this sign you shall know them,
   That they ruin and make dark;

"By all men bond to Nothing,
   Being slaves without a lord,
By one blind idiot world obeyed,
   Too blind to be abhorred;

"By terror and the cruel tales
   Of curse in bone and kin,
By weird and weakness winning,
Accursed from the beginning,
By detail of the sinning,
   And denial of the sin;

"By thought a crawling ruin,
   By life a leaping mire,
By a broken heart in the breast of the world,
   And the end of the world's desire;

"By God and man dishonoured,
   By death and life made vain,
Know ye the old barbarian,
   The barbarian come again—

"When is great talk of trend and tide,
   And wisdom and destiny,

Hail that undying heathen
 That is sadder than the sea.

"In what wise men shall smite him,
 Or the Cross stand up again,
Or charity, or chivalry,
My vision saith not; and I see
No more; but now ride doubtfully
 To the battle of the plain."

And the grass-edge of the great down
 Was clean cut as a lawn,
While the levies thronged from near and far,
From the warm woods of the western star,
And the King went out to his last war
 On a tall grey horse at dawn.

And news of his far-off fighting
 Came slowly and brokenly
From the land of the East Saxons,
 From the sunrise and the sea,

From the plains of the white sunrise,
 And sad St. Edmund's crown,
Where the pools of Essex pale and gleam
 Out beyond London Town—

In mighty and doubtful fragments,
 Like faint or fabled wars,
Climbed the old hills of his renown,
Where the bald brow of White Horse Down
 Is close to the cold stars.

But away in the eastern places
 The wind of death walked high,
And a raid was driven athwart the raid,
The sky reddened and the smoke swayed,
 And the tall grey horse went by.

The gates of the great river

Were breached as with a barge,
The walls sank crowded, say the scribes,
And high towers populous with tribes
    Seemed leaning from the charge.

Smoke like rebellious heavens rolled
    Curled over coloured flames,
Mirrored in monstrous purple dreams
    In the mighty pools of Thames.

Loud was the war on London wall,
    And loud in London gates,
And loud the sea-kings in the cloud
Broke through their dreaming gods, and loud
    Cried on their dreadful fates.

And all the while on White Horse Hill
    The horse lay long and wan,
The turf crawled and the fungus crept,
And the little sorrel, while all men slept,
    Unwrought the work of man.

With velvet finger, velvet foot,
    The fierce soft mosses then
Crept on the large white commonweal
All folk had striven to strip and peel,
And the grass, like a great green witch's wheel,
    Unwound the toils of men.

And clover and silent thistle throve,
    And buds burst silently,
With little care for the Thames Valley
    Or what things there might be—

That away on the widening river,
    In the eastern plains for crown
Stood up in the pale purple sky
One turret of smoke like ivory;
And the smoke changed and the wind went by,
    And the King took London Town.

John Davidson

JOHN DAVIDSON (1857–1909) was born in Barrhead, Renfrew-
shire, and received an irregular education interspersed with
work of various kinds before becoming a pupil-teacher at the
Highlanders' Academy, Greenock. The following year he entered Edinburgh University but stayed there only one year
before taking up a series of posts in a number of Scottish
private schools. Eventually he became a clerk in a Glasgow
cotton thread firm, but after being dismissed he moved to
London, determined to make his name as a writer. Although
his early poetry was fairly well received, he was always poor,
and latterly, very ill. In 1909 he ended his life by suicide,
drowning himself in Mount's Bay, Penzance.

Davidson's early verse is vigorous and fresh, but not without
polish and urbanity. As he grew older, however, and realized
that he would never be a literary success, he became increasingly cantankerous and aggressive, pouring out his dissatis-
faction with the world in a series of bitter verse "testaments,"
in which he propounded an eccentric "philosophical science"
based on his reading of Darwin and Nietzsche. Although Davidson maintained that his later verse was a "new poetry, for
the first time in a thousand years," and in spite of its occasional
power, it hardly compares with that which he wrote earlier,
being at its worst little more than the formless outburst of a
hysterical megalomaniac.

A Ballad of a Nun

From Eastertide to Eastertide
   For ten long years her patient knees
Engraved the stones—the fittest bride
   Of Christ in all the diocese.

She conquered every earthly lust;
   The abbess loved her more and more;
And, as a mark of perfect trust,
   Made her the keeper of the door.

High on a hill the convent hung,
   Across a duchy looking down,
Where everlasting mountains flung
   Their shadows over tower and town.

The jewels of their lofty snows
   In constellations flashed at night;
Above their crests the moon arose;
   The deep earth shuddered with delight.

Long ere she left her cloudy bed,
   Still dreaming in the orient land,
On many a mountain's happy head
   Dawn lightly laid her rosy hand.

The adventurous sun took Heaven by storm;
   Clouds scattered largesses of rain;
The sounding cities, rich and warm,
   Smouldered and glittered in the plain.

Sometimes it was a wandering wind,
   Sometimes the fragrance of the pine,
Sometimes the thought how others sinned,
   That turned her sweet blood into wine.

Sometimes she heard a serenade
   Complaining sweetly far away:

She said, "A young man woos a maid";
   And dreamt of love till break of day.

Then would she ply her knotted scourge
   Until she swooned; but evermore
She had the same red sin to purge,
   Poor, passionate keeper of the door!

For still night's starry scroll unfurled,
   And still the day came like a flood:
It was the greatness of the world
   That made her long to use her blood.

In winter-time when Lent drew nigh,
   And hill and plain were wrapped in snow,
She watched beneath the frosty sky
   The nearest city nightly glow.

Like peals of airy bells outworn
   Faint laughter died above her head
In gusts of broken music borne:
   "They keep the Carnival," she said.

Her hungry heart devoured the town:
   "Heaven save me by a miracle!
Unless God sends an angel down,
   Thither I go though it were Hell."

She dug her nails deep in her breast,
   Sobbed, shrieked, and straight withdrew the
      bar:
A fledgling flying from the nest,
   A pale moth rushing to a star.

Fillet and veil in strips she tore;
   Her golden tresses floated wide;
The ring and bracelet that she wore
   As Christ's betrothed, she cast aside.

"Life's dearest meaning I shall probe;
  Lo! I shall taste of love at last!
Away!" She doffed her outer robe,
  And sent it sailing down the blast.

Her body seemed to warm the wind;
  With bleeding feet o'er ice she ran:
"I leave the righteous God behind;
  I go to worship sinful man."

She reached the sounding city's gate;
  No question did the warder ask:
He passed her in: "Welcome, wild mate!"
  He thought her some fantastic mask.

Half-naked through the town she went;
  Each footstep left a bloody mark;
Crowds followed her with looks intent;
  Her bright eyes made the torches dark.

Alone and watching in the street
  There stood a grave youth nobly dressed;
To him she knelt and kissed his feet;
  Her face her great desire confessed.

Straight to his house the nun he led:
  "Strange lady, what would you with me?"
"Your love, your love, sweet lord," she said;
  "I bring you my virginity."

He healed her bosom with a kiss;
  She gave him all her passion's hoard;
And sobbed and murmured ever, "This
  Is life's great meaning, dear, my lord.

"I care not for my broken vow;
  Though God should come in thunder soon,
I am sister to the mountains now,
  And sister to the sun and moon."

Through all the towns of Belmarie
 She made a progress like a queen.
"She is," they said, "whate'er she be,
 The strangest woman ever seen."

"From fairyland she must have come,
 Or else she is a mermaiden."
Some said she was a ghoul, and some
 A heathen goddess born again.

But soon her fire to ashes burned;
 Her beauty changed to haggardness;
Her golden hair to silver turned;
 The hour came of her last caress.

At midnight from her lonely bed
 She rose, and said, "I have had my will."
The old ragged robe she donned, and fled
 Back to the convent on the hill.

Half-naked as she went before,
 She hurried to the city wall,
Unnoticed in the rush and roar
 And splendour of the carnival.

No question did the warder ask:
 Her ragged robe, her shrunken limb,
Her dreadful eyes! "It is no mask;
 It is a she-wolf, gaunt and grim!"

She ran across the icy plain;
 Her worn blood curdled in the blast;
Each footstep left a crimson stain;
 The white-faced moon looked on aghast.

She said between her chattering jaws,
 "Deep peace is mine, I cease to strive;
Oh, comfortable convent laws,
 That bury foolish nuns alive!

"A trowel for my passing-bell,
 A little bed within the wall,
A coverlet of stones; how well
 I there shall keep the Carnival!"

Like tired bells chiming in their sleep,
 The wind faint pearls of laughter bore;
She stopped her ears and climbed the steep,
 And thundered at the convent door.

It opened straight: she entered in,
 And at the wardress' feet fell prone:
"I come to purge away my sin;
 Bury me, close me up in stone."

The wardress raised her tenderly;
 She touched her wet and fast-shut eyes:
"Look, sister; sister, look at me;
 Look; can you see through my disguise?"

She looked and saw her own sad face,
 And trembled, wondering, "Who art thou?"
"God sent me down to fill your place:
 I am the Virgin Mary now."

And with the word, God's mother shone:
 The wanderer whispered, "Mary, hail!"
The vision helped her to put on
 Bracelet and fillet, ring and veil.

"You are sister to the mountains now,
 And sister to the day and night;
Sister to God." And on the brow
 She kissed her thrice, and left her sight.

While dreaming in her cloudy bed,
 Far in the crimson orient land,
On many a mountain's happy head
 Dawn lightly laid her rosy hand.

Thirty Bob a Week

I couldn't touch a stop and turn a screw,
  And set the blooming world a-work for me,
Like such as cut their teeth—I hope, like you—
  On the handle of a skeleton gold key;
I cut mine on a leek, which I eat it every week:
  I'm a clerk at thirty bob as you can see.

But I don't allow it's luck and all a toss;
  There's no such thing as being starred and crossed;
It's just the power of some to be a boss,
  And the bally power of others to be bossed:
I face the music, sir; you bet I ain't a cur;
  Strike me lucky if I don't believe I'm lost!

For like a mole I journey in the dark,
  A-travelling along the underground
From my Pillar'd Halls and broad Suburbean Park,
  To come the daily dull official round;
And home again at night with my pipe all alight,
  A-scheming how to count ten bob a pound.

And it's often very cold and very wet,
  And my missis stitches towels for a hunks;
And the Pillar'd Halls is half of it to let—
  Three rooms about the size of travelling trunks.
And we cough, my wife and I, to dislocate a sigh,
  When the noisy little kids are in their bunks.

But you never hear her do a growl or whine,
  For she's made of flint and roses, very odd;
And I've got to cut my meaning rather fine,
  Or I'd blubber, for I'm made of greens and sod:
So p'r'aps we are in Hell for all that I can tell,
  And lost and damn'd and served up hot to God.

I ain't blaspheming, Mr. Silver-tongue;
  I'm saying things a bit beyond your art:
Of all the rummy starts you ever sprung,

Thirty bob a week's the rummiest start!
With your science and your books and your the'ries about
     spooks,
     Did you ever hear of looking in your heart?

I didn't mean your pocket, Mr., no:
     I mean that having children and a wife,
With thirty bob on which to come and go,
     Isn't dancing to the tabor and the fife:
When it doesn't make you drink, by Heaven! it makes you
     think,
     And notice curious items about life.

I step into my heart and there I meet
     A god-almighty devil singing small,
Who would like to shout and whistle in the street,
     And squelch the passers flat against the wall;
If the whole world was a cake he had the power to take,
     He would take it, ask for more, and eat it all.

And I meet a sort of simpleton beside,
     The kind that life is always giving beans;
With thirty bob a week to keep a bride
     He fell in love and married in his teens:
At thirty bob he stuck; but he knows it isn't luck:
     He knows the seas are deeper than tureens.

And the god-almighty devil and the fool
     That meet me in the High Street on the strike,
When I walk about my heart a-gathering wool,
     Are my good and evil angels if you like.
And both of them together in every kind of weather
     Ride me like a double-seated bike.

That's rough a bit and needs its meaning curled.
     But I have a high old hot un in my mind—
A most engrugious notion of the world,
     That leaves your lightning 'rithmetic behind
I give it at a glance when I say 'There ain't no chance,
     Nor nothing of the lucky-lottery kind.'

And it's this way that I make it out to be:
    No fathers, mothers, countries, climates—none;
Nor Adam was responsible for me,
    Nor society, nor systems, nary one:
A little sleeping seed, I woke—I did, indeed—
    A million years before the blooming sun.

I woke because I thought the time had come;
    Beyond my will there was no other cause;
And everywhere I found myself at home,
    Because I chose to be the thing I was;
And in whatever shape of mollusc or of ape
    I always went according to the laws.

I was the love that chose my mother out;
    I joined two lives and from the union burst;
My weakness and my strength without a doubt
    Are mine alone for ever from the first:
It's just the very same with a difference in the name
    As 'Thy will be done.' You say it if you durst!

They say it daily up and down the land
    As easy as you take a drink, it's true;
But the difficultest go to understand,
    And the difficultest job a man can do,
Is to come it brave and meek with thirty bob a week,
    And feel that that's the proper thing for you.

It's a naked child against a hungry wolf;
    It's playing bowls upon a splitting wreck;
It's walking on a string across a gulf
    With millstones fore-and-aft about your neck;
But the thing is daily done by many a one;
    And we fall, face forward, fighting, on the deck.

In Romney Marsh

As I went down to Dymchurch Wall,
  I heard the South sing o'er the land;
I saw the yellow sunlight fall
  On knolls where Norman churches stand.

And ringing shrilly, taut and lithe,
  Within the wind a core of sound,
The wire from Romney town to Hythe
  Alone its airy journey wound.

A veil of purple vapour flowed
  And trailed its fringe along the Straits;
The upper air like sapphire glowed;
  And roses filled Heaven's central gates.

Masts in the offing wagged their tops;
  The swinging waves pealed on the shore;
The saffron beach, all diamond drops
  And beads of surge, prolonged the roar.

As I came up from Dymchurch Wall,
  I saw above the Downs' low crest
The crimson brands of sunset fall,
  Flicker and fade from out the west.

Night sank: like flakes of silver fire
  The stars in one great shower came down;
Shrill blew the wind; and shrill the wire
  Rang out from Hythe to Romney town.

The darkly shining salt sea drops
  Streamed as the waves clashed on the shore;
The beach, with all its organ stops
  Pealing again, prolonged the roar.

A Cinque Port

Below the down the stranded town,
  What may betide forlornly waits,
With memories of smoky skies,
  When Gallic navies crossed the straits;
When waves with fire and blood grew bright.
And cannon thundered through the night.

With swinging stride the rhythmic tide
  Bore to the harbour barque and sloop;
Across the bar the ship of war,
  In castled stern and lanterned poop,
Came up with conquests on her lee,
The stately mistress of the sea.

Where argosies have wooed the breeze,
  The simple sheep are feeding now;
And near and far across the bar
  The ploughman whistles at the plough;
Where once the long waves washed the shore,
Larks from their lowly lodgings soar.

Below the down the stranded town
  Hears far away the rollers beat;
About the wall the seabirds call;
  The salt wind murmurs through the street;
Forlorn the sea's forsaken bride,
Awaits the end that shall betide.

War Song

In anguish we uplift
  A new unhallowed song:
The race is to the swift;
  The battle to the strong.

Of old it was ordained
   That we, in packs like curs,
Some thirty million trained
   And licensed murderers,

In crime should live and act,
   In cunning folk say sooth
Who flay the naked fact
   And carve the heart of truth.

The rulers cry aloud,
   "We cannot cancel war,
The end and bloody shroud
   Of wrongs the worst abhor,
And order's swaddling band:
   Know that relentless strife
Remains by sea and land
   The holiest law of life.
From fear in every guise,
   From sloth, from lust of pelf,
By war's great sacrifice
   The world redeems itself.
War is the source, the theme
   Of art; the goal, the bent
And brilliant academe
   Of noble sentiment;
The augury, the dawn
   Of golden times of grace;
The true catholicon,
   And blood-bath of the race."

We thirty million trained
   And licensed murderers,
Like zanies rigged, and chained
   By drill and scourge and curse
In shackles of despair
   We know not how to break—
What do we victims care
   For art, what interest take

In things unseen, unheard?
Some diplomat no doubt
Will launch a heedless word,
And lurking war leap out!

We spell-bound armies then,
Huge brutes in dumb distress,
Machines compact of men
Who once had consciences,
Must trample harvests down—
Vineyard, and corn and oil;
Dismantle town by town,
Hamlet and homestead spoil
Of each appointed path,
Till lust of havoc light
A blood-red blaze of wrath
In every frenzied sight.

In many a mountain-pass,
Or meadow green and fresh,
Mass shall encounter mass
Of shuddering human flesh;
Opposing ordnance roar
Across the swaths of slain,
And blood in torrents pour
In vain—always in vain,
For war breeds war again!

The shameful dream is past,
The subtle maze untrod:
We recognize at last
That war is not of God.
Wherefore we now uplift
Our new unhallowed song:
The race is to the swift,
The battle to the strong.

Insomnia

He awakened quivering on a golden rack
Inlaid with gems: no sign of change, no fear
Or hope of death came near;
Only the empty ether hovered black
About him stretched upon his living bier,
Of old by Marlin's Master deftly wrought:
Two Seraphim of Gabriel's helpful race
In that far nook of space
With iron levers wrenched and held him taut.

The Seraph at his head was Agony;
Delight, more terrible, stood at his feet:
Their sixfold pinions beat
The darkness, or were spread immovably,
Poising the rack, whose jewelled fabric meet
To strain a god, did fitfully unmask
With olive light of chrysoprases dim
The smiling Seraphim
Implacably intent upon their task.

From The Testament of a Prime Minister

. . . The trump
Of doom exhaled a long-enduring sigh,
A sigh, no louder, heard and felt throughout
The quaking earth; and in the zenith reared,
The great white throne and Him that sat thereon
Illumined space insufferably bright.
Against His glance the star-strewn firmament,
As evanescent as a wreath of mist
At sunrise, perished utterly. The dead
Before the throne awaited judgement. Books
Were opened and another book which is
The book of life; and all the dead were judged
Out of the matters written in the books
According to their actions. On the right,

When the eternal sentence was pronounced,
I saw the great ones of the earth appear
Magnificently confident of heaven—
The kings, the conquerors, the wise, the bold.
The rich, the proud, and all the lusty lives
That took their power and pleasure in the world
"Enter, ye blessëd, enter!"—from the throne
The high decree. "Inherit now the realm
Prepared for you from the beginning, ye
That used the world I made superb in strength,
Unparagoned in beauty—ye that loved
The haughty morning and the radiant night,
That stored the brilliant hours with generous strife,
With sweet repose, with passion, and with joy,
Glorying and revelling in the gifts I gave.
Created of the self-same stuff as I,
And all My suns and systems, Matter, strained
From the great staple of the Universe
Throughout millenniums of elaborate choice,
Conscious, self-conscious, free to know, to think,
To do, all ye that had my world in charge,
And set yourselves to fill it with delight,
With noble wars, with beauty and with wealth,
With hope for man, with hope for life, with life,
And ever and always life, partake with Me
To all eternity the joys of heaven."

Upon the left—shuddering I saw it so—
The Son of Man and His elect appeared,
Apostles, martyrs, votarists, virgins, saints.
The poor in spirit, the mourners and the meek,
And they that hungered after righteousness,
The merciful and all the pure in heart,
Peacemakers and the salt of the earth I saw
Upon the left in sore amazement stand.
"Depart from Me, ye cursëd"—from the throne
The dread decree—"into eternal fire;
Deniers, slanderers, fools that turned to scorn
The perfect world I made superb in strength,
Unparagoned in beauty; ye that stained

The haughty morning and the radiant night,
Seasons and tides with liturgies and forms,
With cries and intercessions, prayers and tears,
Ashamed to use the glory I had given;
Ye rancorous poisoners of life that found
Temptation only where I offered joy,
My splendid world a charnel-house, and Me
A God of infelicity and woe,
A God of everything unfit to live,
Hating My gifts of intellect, of pride,
Of strength and freedom. Of the self-same stuff
As I and all My suns and galaxies,
The purest Matter, sifted forth and strained
From the great staple of the Universe
Throughout millenniums of elaborate choice,
Conscious, self-conscious, free to know, to think,
To do, having My world in charge, ye set
Yourselves to drain it of delight, of love,
Of beauty, passion, power, supplied the void
With lust, revenge, distress, corruption, hate,
And made My will to life a will to death.
Ye hypocrites, that with a holy lie
Tarnished the cleanliness immaculate
Of human generation, soiling life
On to the end from his pellucid fount
And origin divine, beholding earth
A leprous crust of Sin, depart from Me
Into eternal fire prepared for them
That make my will to live a will to die."

W. H. Davies

WILLIAM HENRY DAVIES (1871–1940), one of the most characteristic poets of the Georgian movement, was born at Newport, Monmouthshire. Brought up by his grandfather, a publican, Davies had little formal schooling, and in his early 'teens was apprenticed to a picture-frame maker. He soon gave this up and went on the road, tramping about England and the United States, where he lost his right foot while attempting to jump a freight train, finally returning to England where he began to write about his experiences.

Davies's most popular book is probably *The Autobiography of a Super-tramp* (1907), a prose account of his early life on the road, but his poetry, made up chiefly of brief lyrics reflecting his love of nature and his keen appreciation of the human comedy, though unsophisticated and occasionally banal, is sometimes fresh and spontaneous. His main fault is that he sometimes makes a too self-conscious attempt to achieve simplicity, resulting in verse which is plainly dull.

School's Out

Girls scream,
    Boys shout;
Dogs bark,
    School's out.

Cats run,
    Horses shy;
Into trees
    Birds fly.

Babes wake
    Open-eyed;
If they can,
    Tramps hide.

Old man,
    Hobble home;
Merry mites,
    Welcome.

The Sluggard

A jar of cider and my pipe,
    In summer, under shady tree;
A book of one that made his mind
    Live by its sweet simplicity:
Then must I laugh at kings who sit
    In richest chambers, signing scrolls;
And princes cheered in public ways,
    And stared at by a thousand fools.

Let me be free to wear my dreams,
    Like weeds in some mad maiden's hair,
When she doth think the earth has not
    Another maid so rich and fair;
And proudly smiles on rich and poor,

The queen of all fair women then:
So I, dressed in my idle dreams,
Will think myself the king of men.

Leisure

What is this life if, full of care,
We have no time to stand and stare.

No time to stand beneath the boughs
And stare as long as sheep or cows.

No time to see, when woods we pass,
Where squirrels hide their nuts in grass.

No time to see, in broad daylight,
Streams full of stars, like skies at night.

No time to turn at Beauty's glance,
And watch her feet, how they can dance.

No time to wait till her mouth can
Enrich that smile her eyes began.

A poor life this if, full of care,
We have no time to stand and stare.

The Hospital Waiting-Room

We wait our turn, as still as mice,
For medicine free, and free advice:
Two mothers, and their little girls
So small—each one with flaxen curls—
And I myself, the last to come.
Now as I entered that bare room,
I was not seen or heard; for both
The mothers—one in finest cloth,
With velvet blouse and crocheted lace,

Lips painted red, and powdered face;
The other ragged, whose face took
Its own dull, white, and wormy look—
Exchanged a hard and bitter stare.
And both the children, sitting there,
Taking example from that sight,
Made ugly faces, full of spite.
This woman said, though not a word
From her red painted lips was heard—
"Why have I come to this, to be
In such a slattern's company?"
The ragged woman's look replied—
"If you can dress with so much pride,
Why are you here, so neat and nice,
For medicine free, and free advice?"
And I, who needed richer food,
Not medicine, to help my blood;
Who could have swallowed then a horse,
And chased its rider round the course,
Sat looking on, ashamed, perplexed,
Until a welcome voice cried—"Next!"

The Inquest

I took my oath I would inquire,
    Without affection, hate, or wrath,
Into the death of Ada Wright—
    So help me God! I took that oath.

When I went out to see the corpse,
    The four months' babe that died so young,
I judged it was seven pounds in weight,
    And little more than one foot long.

One eye, that had a yellow lid,
    Was shut—so was the mouth, that smiled;
The left eye open, shining bright—
    It seemed a knowing little child.

For as I looked at that one eye,
   It seemed to laugh, and say with glee:
"What caused my death you'll never know—
   Perhaps my mother murdered me."

When I went into court again,
   To hear the mother's evidence—
It was a love-child, she explained.
   And smiled, for our intelligence.

"Now, Gentlemen of the Jury," said
   The coroner—"this woman's child
By misadventure met its death."
   "Aye, aye," said we. The mother smiled.

And I could see that child's one eye
   Which seemed to laugh, and say with glee:
"What caused my death you'll never know—
   Perhaps my mother murdered me."

I Am the Poet Davies, William

I am the Poet Davies, William,
   I sin without a blush or blink:
I am a man that lives to eat;
   I am a man that lives to drink.

My face is large, my lips are thick,
   My skin is coarse and black almost;
But the ugliest feature is my verse,
   Which proves my soul is black and lost.

Thank heaven thou didst not marry me,
   A poet full of blackest evil;
For how to manage my damned soul
   Will puzzle many a flaming devil.

One Thing Wanting

"Your life was hard with mangling clothes,
You scrubbed our floors for years;
But now, your children are so good,
That you can rest your poor old limbs,
And want for neither drink nor meat."
"It's true," she said, and laughed for joy;
And still her voice, with all her years,
Could make a song-bird wonder if
A rival sweetness challenged him.
But soon her face was full of trouble:
"If only I could tear," she said,
"My sister Alice out of her grave—
Who taunted me when I was poor—
And make her understand these words:
'See, I have everything I want,
My children, Alice, are so good'—
If I could only once do that,
There's nothing else I want on earth."

All in June

A week ago I had a fire,
    To warm my feet, my hands and face;
Cold winds, that never make a friend,
    Crept in and out of every place.

Today, the fields are rich in grass,
    And buttercups in thousands grow;
I'll show the World where I have been—
    With gold-dust seen on either shoe.

Till to my garden back I come,
    Where bumble-bees, for hours and hours,
Sit on their soft, fat, velvet bums,
    To wriggle out of hollow flowers.

Walter de la Mare

WALTER DE LA MARE (1873–1956) was born at Charlton, Kent, attended St. Paul's Choir School, and became a clerk in the Anglo-American Oil Company. His first book of verse, *Songs of Childhood,* appeared in 1902 under the name of Walter Ramal, but in subsequent volumes he reverted to the use of his own name. He was a prolific author, publishing several collections of verse, as well as some fanciful novels and short stories, critical essays, and introductory tributes to living writers, but it was some time before he could give up his clerical position and become a full-time professional writer.

De la Mare may best be described as a late survival of the Romantic Movement, most of his poetry evoking a fairy world far removed from modern civilization, or investigating the mystery at the heart of experience. Sometimes he gives us merely self-indulgent dreams, but at their best his poems have an intensity which saves them from mawkishness.

Evening

When twilight darkens, and one by one,
The sweet birds to their nests have gone,
When to green banks the glow-worms bring
Pale lamps to brighten evening;
Then stirs in his thick sleep the owl
Through the dewy air to prowl.

Hawking the meadow swiftly he flits,
While the small mouse a-trembling sits
With tiny eye of fear upcast
Until his brooding shape be past,
Hiding her where the moonbeams beat,
Casting black shadows in the wheat.

Now all is still: the field-man is
Lapped deep in slumbering silentness.
Not a leaf stirs, but clouds on high
Pass in dim flocks across the sky,
Puffed by a breeze too light to move
Aught but these wakeful sheep above.

O, what an arch of light now spans
These fields by night no longer Man's!
Their ancient Master is abroad,
Walking beneath the moonlight cold:
His presence is the stillness, He
Fills earth with wonder and mystery.

Sea-Magic

TO R. I.

My heart faints in me for the distant sea.
  The roar of London is the roar of ire
  The lion utters in his old desire
For Libya out of dim captivity.

The long bright silver of Cheapside I see,
  Her gilded weathercocks on roof and spire
  Exulting eastward in the western fire;
All things recall one heart-sick memory:—

Ever the rustle of the advancing foam,
  The surges' desolate thunder, and the cry
  As of some lone babe in the whispering sky;
Ever I peer into the restless gloom
  To where a ship clad dim and loftily
Looms steadfast in the wonder of her home.

Drugged

Inert in his chair,
In a candle's guttering glow;
His bottle empty,
His fire sunk low;
With drug-sealed lids shut fast,
Unsated mouth ajar,
This darkened phantasm walks
Where nightmares are:

In a frenzy of life and light,
Crisscross—a menacing throng—
They gibe, they squeal at the stranger,
Jostling along,
Their faces cadaverous grey:
While on high from an attic stare
Horrors, in beauty apparelled,
Down the dark air.

A stream gurgles over its stones,
The chambers within are afire.
Stumble his shadowy feet
Through shine, through mire;
And the flames leap higher.
In vain yelps the wainscot mouse;
In vain beats the hour;

Vacant, his body must drowse
Until daybreak flower—

Staining these walls with its rose,
And the draughts of the morning shall stir
Cold on cold brow, cold hands.
And the wanderer
Back to flesh house must return.
Lone soul—in horror to see,
Than dream more meagre and awful,
Reality.

The Feckless Dinner-Party

"Who are we waiting for?" "*Soup* burnt?" . . . Eight—
  "Only the tiniest party.—Us!"
"Darling! Divine!" "Ten minutes late—"
  "And my digest—" "I'm *rav*enous!"

" 'Toomes'?"—"Oh, he's new." "Looks crazed, I guess."
  " 'Married'—*Again!*" "Well; more or less!"

"Dinner is *served!*" " 'Dinner is served'!"
  "Is served?" "Is served." "Ah, yes."

"Dear Mr. Prout, will you take down
  The Lilith in leaf-green by the fire?
Blanche Ogleton? . . ." "How coy a frown!—
  Hasn't she borrowed *Eve's* attire?"
"Morose Old Adam!" "Charmed—I vow."
  "Come then, and meet her now."

"Now, Dr. Mallus—would you please?—
  Our daring poetess, Delia Seek?"
"The lady with the bony knees?"
  "And—*entre nous*—less song than beak."
"Sharing her past with Simple Si—"
  "*Bare* facts! He'll blush!" "Oh, fie!"

"And *you,* Sir Nathan—false but fair!—
  That fountain of wit, Aurora Pert."
"More wit than It, poor dear! But there . . ."
  "Pitiless Pacha! *And* such a flirt!"
" 'Flirt'! *Me?*" "Who else?" "You here. . . . Who can . . . ?"
  "In*corr*igible man!"

"And now, Mr. Simon—little me!—
  Last and—" "By no means least!" "Oh, come!
What naughty, naughty flattery!
  Honey!—I *hear* the creature hum!"
"Sweets for the sweet, *I* always say!"
  " 'Always'? . . . We're last." *"This* way?" . . .

"No, sir; straight on, please." "I'd have vowed!—
  I came the other . . ." "It's queer; I'm sure . . ."
"What frightful pictures!" "Fiends!" "The *crowd!*"
  "Such nudes!" "I can't endure . . ."

"Yes, *there* they go." "Heavens! *Are* we right?"
  "Follow up closer!" " 'Prout'?—sand-blind!"
"This endless . . ." "Who's turned down the light?"
  "Keep calm! They're close behind."

"Oh! Dr. Mallus; what dismal stairs!"
  "I hate these old Victor . . ." "Dry rot!"
"Darker and darker!" "Fog!" "The air's . . ."
  "Scarce breathable!" "Hell!" *"What?"*

"The banister's gone!" "It's deep; keep close!"
  "We're going down and down!" "What fun!"
"Damp! Why, my shoes . . ." "It's slimy . . . Not *moss!"*
  "I'm freezing cold!" "Let's run."

". . . Behind us. I'm giddy. . . ." "The catacombs . . ."
  "That shout!" "Who's there?" "I'm *alone!"* "Stand back!"
"She said, Lead . . ." "Oh!" "Where's Toomes?" *"Toomes!"*
      "Toomes!"
  "Stifling!" "My skull will crack!"

"Sir Nathan! *Ai!*" "I *say! Toomes!* Prout!"
  "Where? Where?" " 'Our silks and fine array' . . ."
"She's mad." "I'm dying!" "Oh, let me *out!*"
  "My God! We've lost our way!" . . .

And now how sad-serene the abandoned house,
Whereon at dawn the spring-tide sunbeams beat;
And time's slow pace alone is ominous,
And naught but shadows of noonday therein meet;
Domestic microcosm, only a Trump could rouse:
And, pondering darkly, in the silent rooms,
He who misled them all—the butler, Toomes.

Silence

With changeful sound life beats upon the ear;
  Yet, striving for release,
  The most seductive string's
    Sweet jargonings,
    The happiest throat's
  Most easeful, lovely notes
Fall back into a veiling silentness.

Ev'n 'mid the rumour of a moving host,
  Blackening the clear green earth,
  Vainly 'gainst that thin wall
    The trumpets call,
    Or with loud hum
  The smoke-bemuffled drum:
From that high quietness no reply comes forth.

When, all at peace, two friends at ease alone
  Talk out their hearts—yet still,
  Between the grace-notes of
    The voice of love
    From each to each
  Trembles a rarer speech,
And with its presence every pause doth fill.

Unmoved it broods, this all-encompassing hush
  Of one who stooping near,
  No smallest stir will make
    Our fear to wake;
    But yet intent
  Upon some mystery bent
Hearkens the lightest word we say, or hear.

The Dove

How often, these hours, have I heard the monotonous crool of a
    dove—
Voice low, insistent, obscure, since its nest it has hid in a grove—
Flowers of the linden wherethrough the hosts of the honeybees
    rove.
And I have been busily idle: no problems; nothing to prove;
No urgent foreboding; but only life's shallow habitual groove:
Then why, if I pause to listen, should the languageless note of a
    dove
So dark with disquietude seem? And what is it sorrowing of?

Moonlight

The far moon maketh lovers wise
  In her pale beauty trembling down,
Lending curved cheeks, dark lips, dark eyes,
  A strangeness not her own.
And, though they shut their lids to kiss,
  In starless darkness peace to win,
Even on that secret world from this
  Her twilight enters in.

The Quarry

You hunted me with all the pack,
  Too blind, too blind, to see

By no wild hope of force or greed
  Could you make sure of me.

And like a phantom through the glades,
  With tender breast aglow,
The goddess in me laughed to hear
  Your horns a-roving go.

She laughed to think no mortal ever
  By dint of mortal flesh
The very Cause that was the Hunt
  One moment could enmesh:

That though with captive limbs I lay,
  Stilled breath and vanquished eyes,
He that hunts Love with horse and hound
  Hunts out his heart and eyes.

The Listeners

"Is there anybody there?" said the Traveller,
  Knocking on the moonlit door;
And his horse in the silence champed the grasses
  Of the forest's ferny floor:
And a bird flew up out of the turret,
  Above the Traveller's head:
And he smote upon the door again a second time;
  "Is there anybody there?" he said.
But no one descended to the Traveller;
  No head from the leaf-fringed sill
Leaned over and looked into his grey eyes,
  Where he stood perplexed and still.
But only a host of phantom listeners
  That dwelt in the lone house then
Stood listening in the quiet of the moonlight
  To that voice from the world of men:
Stood thronging the faint moonbeams on the dark stair,
  That goes down to the empty hall,

Hearkening in an air stirred and shaken
　By the lonely Traveller's call.
And he felt in his heart their strangeness,
　Their stillness answering his cry,
While his horse moved, cropping the dark turf,
　'Neath the starred and leafy sky;
For he suddenly smote on the door, even
　Louder, and lifted his head:—
"Tell them I came, and no one answered,
　That I kept my word," he said.
Never the least stir made the listeners,
　Though every word he spake
Fell echoing through the shadowiness of the still house
　From the one man left awake:
Ay, they heard his foot upon the stirrup.
　And the sound of iron on stone,
And how the silence surged softly backward,
　When the plunging hoofs were gone.

Austin Dobson

HENRY AUSTIN DOBSON (1840-1921) was born in Plymouth and educated at Beaumarris School, a private school in Coventry, and the Gymnase at Strasbourg. At the age of sixteen he decided against following his father's profession of engineer, entering the Board of Trade as a clerk, where he was later joined by Edmund Gosse. Although employed as a full-time clerk, Dobson still found sufficient time from his clerical duties to study, and it was not long before he began making a name for himself as a poet, essayist, and biographer. He was a shy and inhibited man, something of a prude, a person who wished for little more than to live unobtrusively with his ten children in Ealing, a conventional suburb of London.

Dobson's early work was largely in verse, and only later did he devote most of his attention to prose, writing biographies of many eighteenth-century literary figures and editing their most famous works. His poetry is heavily influenced by the French Parnassians, Banville's "Petite Traitise" attracting his attention in 1874, and also by Horace, whom Tennyson advised him to study in 1877. His verse makes no pretension toward profundity. It is precise, elegant, and unoriginal, perhaps best described by Dobson himself when he wrote:

> Let others prate of problems and of powers;
> I bring but fancies born of idle hours,
> That striving only after Art and Ease,
> Have scarcely more of moral than the flowers
> And little else of mission than to please.

Ars Victrix

(IMITATED FROM THÉOPHILE GAUTIER)

Yes; when the ways oppose—
    When the hard means rebel,
Fairer the work out-grows,—
    More potent far the spell.

O Poet, then, forbear
    The loosely-sandalled verse,
Choose rather thou to wear
    The buskin—strait and terse;

Leave to the tiro's hand
    The limp and shapeless style.
See that thy form demand
    The labour of the file.

Sculptor, do thou discard
    The yielding clay,—consign
To Paros marble hard
    The beauty of thy line;—

Model thy Satyr's face
    For bronze of Syracuse;
In the veined agate trace
    The profile of thy Muse.

Painter, that still must mix
    But transient tints anew,
Thou in the furnace fix
    The firm enamel's hue;

Let the smooth tile receive
    Thy dove-drawn Erycine;
Thy Sirens blue at eve
    Coiled in a wash of wine.

All passes. ART alone
Enduring stays to us;
The Bust outlasts the throne,—
The Coin, Tiberius:

Even the gods must go,
Only the lofty Rhyme
Not countless years o'erthrow,—
Not long array of time.

Paint, chisel, then, or write;
But that the work surpass,
With the hard fashion fight,—
With the resisting mass.

The Ballad of Prose and Rhyme

When the ways are heavy with mire and rut,
In November fogs, in December snows,
When the North Wind howls, and the doors are shut,—
There is place and enough for the pains of prose;
But whenever a scent from the whitethorn blows,
And the jasmine stars at the casement climb,
And a Rosalind-face at the lattice shows,
Then hey!—for the ripple of laughing rhyme!

When the brain gets dry as an empty nut,
When the reason stands on its squarest toes,
When the mind (like a beard) has a "formal cut,"—
There is place and enough for the pains of prose;
But whenever the May-blood stirs and glows,
And the young year draws to the "golden prime,"
And Sir Romeo sticks in his ear a rose,—
Then hey!—for the ripple of laughing rhyme!

In a theme where the thoughts have a pedant-strut,
In a changing quarrel of "Ayes" and "Noes,"
In a starched procession of "If" and "But,"—

There is place and enough for the pains of prose;
  But whenever a soft glance softer grows
And the light hours dance to the trysting-time,
  And the secret is told "that no one knows,"—
Then hey!—for the ripple of laughing rhyme!

Envoy

In the work-a-day world,—or its needs and woes,
There is place and enough for the pains of prose;
But whenever the May-bells clash and chime,
Then hey!—for the ripple of laughing rhyme!

On a Fan That Belonged
to the Marquise De Pompadour

Chicken-skin, delicate, white,
  Painted by Carlo Vanloo,
Loves in a riot of light,
  Roses and vaporous blue;
  Hark to the dainty *frou-frou!*
Picture above, if you can,
  Eyes that could melt as the dew,—
This was the Pompadour's fan!

See how they rise at the sight,
  Thronging the *Oeil de Boeuf* through,
Courtiers as butterflies bright,
  Beauties that Fragonard drew,
  Talon-rouge, falbala, queue,
Cardinal, Duke,—to a man,
  Eager to sigh or to sue,—
This was the Pompadour's fan!

The Ballad of Imitation

"C'est imiter quelqu'un que de planter des choux."
—ALFRED DE MUSSET

If they hint, O Musician, the piece that you played
  Is nought but a copy of Chopin or Spohr;
That the ballad you sing is but merely "conveyed"
  From the stock of the Arnes and the Purcells of yore;
  That there's nothing, in short, in the words or the score
That is not as out-worn as the "Wandering Jew,"
  Make answer—Beethoven could scarcely do more—
That the man who plants cabbages imitates, too!

If they tell you, Sir Artist, your light and your shade
  Are simply adapted from other men's lore;
That—plainly to speak of a "spade" as a "spade"—
  You've "stolen" your grouping from three or from four;
  That (however the writer the truth may deplore),
'Twas Gainsborough painted *your* "Little Boy Blue";
  Smile only serenely—though cut to the core—
For the man who plants cabbages imitates, too!

And you too, my Poet, be never dismayed
  If they whisper your Epic—"Sir Eperon d'Or"—
Is nothing but Tennyson thinly arrayed
  In a tissue that's taken from Morris's store;
  That no one, in fact, but a child could ignore
That you "lift" or "accommodate" all that you do;
  Take heart—though your Pegasus' withers be sore—
For the man who plants cabbages imitates, too!

POSTSCRIPTUM—And you, whom we all so adore,
  Dear Critics, whose verdicts are always so new!—
One word in your ear. There were Critics before . . .
  And the man who plants cabbages imitates, too!

The Ballad of the Bore

"Garrulus hunc quando consumet cunque."
—Hor. Sat. I. ix. 33.

I see him come from far,
    And, sick with hopelessness,
Invoke some kindly star,—
    I see him come, no less.
    Is there no sure recess
Where hunted men may lie?
    Ye gods, it is too hard!
I feel his glittering eye,—
    Defend us from The Bard!

He knows nor let nor bar:
    With ever nearing stress,
Like Juggernaut his car,
    I see him onward press;
    He waves a huge MS.;
He puts evasion by,
    He stands—as one on guard,
And reads—how volubly!—
    Defend us from The Bard!

He reads—of Fates that mar,
    Of Woes beyond redress,
Of all the Moons that are,
    Of Maids that never bless
    (As one, indeed, might guess);
Of Vows, of Hopes too high,
    Of Dolours by the yard
That none believe (nor buy),—
    Defend us from The Bard!

Envoy

PRINCE PHOEBUS, all must die,
　Or well—or evil—starred,
　Or whole of heart or scarred;
But why in this way—why?
　Defend us from The Bard!

Ernest Dowson

ERNEST CHRISTOPHER DOWSON (1867–1900) was born in Kent, and though after an irregular schooling in England and France he went up to Oxford, he left without taking a degree. He worked for a while in the Limehouse dock owned by his family, but spent most of his time in London with literary friends. He was a member of the Rhymers' Club, contributing to both of its anthologies, and was tacitly recognized by the other members as the one person among them most likely to achieve literary eminence. Unfortunately the Dowson family fortune steadily declined, and soon Ernest was obliged to live by his pen. He withdrew to France where his health, never very robust and impaired by his heavy drinking and irregular habits, rapidly deteriorated. He returned to England suffering from tuberculosis, and died in the modest, Catford home of his friend and later biographer of Wilde, Robert Sherard.

Though Dowson made his mark as a poet of short, graceful lyrics which owed much to the example of contemporary French poetry, notably that of Verlaine, he also wrote a number of short stories which were collected under the title of *Dilemmas* (1895), translated several works from the French, collaborated with Arthur Moore on two novels, and composed a one-act play called *The Pierrot of the Minute,* now chiefly remembered for the illustrations by Aubrey Beardsley which accompanied its publication. His poem "Non Sum Qualis Eram Bonae Sub Regno Cynarae," or "Cynara" as it is more usually known, is perhaps one of the best known and most characteristic poems of the Decadents.

Nuns of
the Perpetual Adoration

Calm, sad, secure; behind high convent walls,
    These watch the sacred lamp, these watch and pray:
And it is one with them when evening falls,
    And one with them the cold return of day.

These heed not time; their nights and days they make
    Into a long, returning rosary,
Whereon their lives are threaded for Christ's sake;
    Meekness and vigilance and chastity.

A vowed patrol, in silent companies,
    Life-long they keep before the living Christ.
In the dim church, their prayers and penances
    Are fragrant incense to the Sacrificed.

Outside, the world is wild and passionate;
    Man's weary laughter and his sick despair
Entreat at their impenetrable gate:
    They heed no voices in their dream of prayer.

They saw the glory of the world displayed;
    They saw the bitter of it, and the sweet;
They knew the roses of the world should fade,
    And be trod under by the hurrying feet.

Therefore they rather put away desire,
    And crossed their hands and came to sanctuary
And veiled their heads and put on coarse attire:
    Because their comeliness was vanity.

And there they rest; they have serene insight
    Of the illuminating dawn to be:
Mary's sweet Star dispels for them the night,
    The proper darkness of humanity.

Calm, sad, secure; with faces worn and mild:
  Surely their choice of vigil is the best?
Yea! for our roses fade, the world is wild;
  But there, beside the altar, there, is rest.

To One in Bedlam

With delicate, mad hands, behind his sordid bars,
Surely he hath his posies, which they tear and twine;
Those scentless wisps of straw, that miserably line
His strait, caged universe, whereat the dull world stares,

Pedant and pitiful. O, how his rapt gaze wars
With their stupidity! Know they what dreams divine
Lift his long, laughing reveries like enchaunted wine,
And make his melancholy germane to the stars?

O lamentable brother! if those pity thee,
Am I not fain of all thy lone eyes promise me;
Half a fool's kingdom, far from men who sow and reap,
All their days, vanity? Better than mortal flowers,
Thy moon-kissed roses seem: better than love or sleep,
The star-crowned solitude of thine oblivious hours!

Ad Manus Puellae

I was always a lover of ladies' hands!
  Or ever mine heart came here to tryst,
For the sake of your carved white hands' commands:
  The tapering fingers, the dainty wrist;
  The hands of a girl were what I kissed.

I remember an hand like a *fleur-de-lys*
  When it slid from its silken sheath, her glove;
With its odours passing ambergris:
  And that was the empty husk of a love.
  Oh, how shall I kiss your hands enough?

They are pale with the pallor of ivories;
　　But they blush to the tips like a curled sea-shell:
What treasure, in kingly treasuries,
　　Of gold, and spice for the thurible,
　　Is sweet as her hands to hoard and tell?

I know not the way from your finger-tips,
　　Nor how I shall gain the higher lands,
The citadel of your sacred lips:
　　I am captive still of my pleasant bands,
　　The hands of a girl, and most your hands.

Non Sum Qualis Eram Bonae
Sub Regno Cynarae

Last night, ah, yesternight, betwixt her lips and mine
There fell thy shadow, Cynara! thy breath was shed
Upon my soul between the kisses and the wine;
And I was desolate and sick of an old passion,
　　Yea, I was desolate and bowed my head:
I have been faithful to thee, Cynara! in my fashion.

All night upon mine heart I felt her warm heart beat,
Night-long within mine arms in love and sleep she lay;
Surely the kisses of her bought red mouth were sweet;
But I was desolate and sick of an old passion,
　　When I awoke and found the dawn was gray:
I have been faithful to thee, Cynara! in my fashion.

I have forgot much, Cynara! gone with the wind,
Flung roses, roses riotously with the throng,
Dancing, to put thy pale, lost lilies out of mind;
But I was desolate and sick of an old passion,
　　Yea, all the time, because the dance was long:
I have been faithful to thee, Cynara! in my fashion.

I cried for madder music and for stronger wine,
But when the feast is finished and the lamps expire,

Then falls thy shadow, Cynara! the night is thine;
And I am desolate and sick of an old passion,
   Yea, hungry for the lips of my desire:
I have been faithful to thee, Cynara! in my fashion.

Beata Solitudo

What land of Silence,
   Where pale stars shine
On apple-blossom
   And dew-drenched vine,
   Is yours and mine?

The silent valley
   That we will find,
Where all the voices
   Of humankind
   Are left behind.

There all forgetting,
   Forgotten quite,
We will repose us,
   With our delight
   Hid out of sight.

The world forsaken,
   And out of mind
Honour and labour,
   We shall not find
   The stars unkind.

And men shall travail,
   And laugh and weep;
But we have vistas
   Of gods asleep,
   With dreams as deep.

A land of Silence,
   Where pale stars shine

On apple-blossoms
And dew-drenched vine,
Be yours and mine!

Terre Promise

Even now the fragrant darkness of her hair
Had brushed my cheek; and once, in passing by,
Her hand upon my hand lay tranquilly:
What things unspoken trembled in the air!

Always I know, how little severs me
From mine heart's country, that is yet so far;
And must I lean and long across a bar,
That half a word would' shatter utterly?

Ah might it be, that just by touch of hand,
Or speaking silence, shall the barrier fall;
And she shall pass, with no vain words at all,
But droop into mine arms, and understand!

Carthusians

Through what long heaviness, assayed in what strange fire,
    Have these white monks been brought into the way of peace,
Despising the world's wisdom and the world's desire,
    Which from the body of this death bring no release?

Within their austere walls no voices penetrate;
    A sacred silence only, as of death, obtains;
Nothing finds entry here of loud or passionate;
    This quiet is the exceeding profit of their pain.

From many lands they came, in divers fiery ways
    Each knew at last the vanity of earthly joys;
And one was crowned with thorns, and one was crowned with
        bays,
    And each was tired at last of the world's foolish noise.

It was not theirs with Dominic to preach God's holy wrath,
　　They were too stern to bear sweet Francis' gentle sway;
Theirs was a higher calling and a steeper path,
　　To dwell alone with Christ, to meditate and pray.

A cloistered company, they are companionless,
　　None knoweth here the secret of his brother's heart:
They are but come together for more loneliness,
　　Whose bond is solitude and silence all their part.

O beatific life! Who is there shall gainsay,
　　Your great refusal's victory, your little loss,
Deserting vanity for the more perfect way,
　　The sweeter service of the most dolorous Cross.

Ye shall prevail at last! Surely ye shall prevail!
　　Your silence and austerity shall win at last:
Desire and mirth, the world's ephemeral lights shall fail,
　　The sweet star of your queen is never overcast.

We fling up flowers and laugh, we laugh across the wine;
　　With wine we dull our souls and careful strains of art;
Our cups are polished skulls round which the roses twine:
　　None dares to look at Death who leers and lurks apart.

Move on, white company, whom that has not sufficed!
　　Our viols cease, our wine is death, our roses fail:
Pray for our heedlessness, O dwellers with the Christ!
　　Though the world fall apart, surely ye shall prevail.

James Elroy Flecker

JAMES ELROY FLECKER (1884–1915) was born in London and educated at Uppingham and Trinity College, Oxford, before going into the Consular Service. In 1910 he was posted to the Levant, where he spent most of his time in Beirut. Soon after his appointment his health began to fail; he contracted tuberculosis; and he died in Switzerland a couple of years later.

Although Flecker is usually accorded a brief mention in histories of twentieth-century literature by reason of his two verse dramas, *Hassan* and *Don Juan,* his poetry is frequently ignored. Though included in the recent Penguin anthology of Georgian poetry, his place in twentieth-century poetry is perhaps best understood if we consider him as a late Decadent, for his melancholy tone, his nostalgia, his allegiance to the doctrine of art for art's sake, and his admiration for the French Parnassians, all point to his kinship with the *fin-de-siècle*.

To a Poet a Thousand Years Hence

I who am dead a thousand years,
  And wrote this sweet archaic song,
Send you my words for messengers
  The way I shall not pass along.

I care not if you bridge the seas,
  Or ride secure the cruel sky,
Or build consummate palaces
  Of metal or of masonry.

But have you wine and music still,
  And statues and a bright-eyed love,
And foolish thoughts of good and ill,
  And prayers to them who sit above?

How shall we conquer? Like a wind
  That falls at eve our fancies blow,
And old Maeonides the blind
  Said it three thousand years ago.

O friend unseen, unborn, unknown,
  Student of our sweet English tongue,
Read out my words at night, alone:
  I was a poet, I was young.

Since I can never see your face,
  And never shake you by the hand,
I send my soul through time and space
  To greet you. You will understand.

Tenebris Interlucentem

A linnet who had lost her way
Sang on a blackened bough in hell,
Till all the ghosts remembered well
The trees, the wind, the golden day.

At last they knew that they had died
When they heard music in that land,
And someone there stole forth a hand
To draw a brother to his side.

A Ship, an Isle, a Sickle Moon

A ship, an isle, a sickle moon—
With few but with how splendid stars
The mirrors of the sea are strewn
Between their silver bars!

* * *

An isle beside an isle she lay,
The pale ship anchored in the bay,
While in the young moon's port of gold
A star-ship—as the mirrors told—
Put forth its great and lonely light
To the unreflecting Ocean, Night.
And still, a ship upon her seas,
The isle and the island cypresses
Went sailing on without the gale:
And still there moved the moon so pale,
A crescent ship without a sail!

In Hospital

Would I might lie like this, without the pain,
    For seven years—as one with snowy hair,
Who in the high tower dreams his dying reign—

    Lie here and watch the walls—how grey and bare,
The metal bed-post, the uncoloured screen,
    The mat, the jug, the cupboard, and the chair;

And served by an old woman, calm and clean,
    Her misted face familiar, yet unknown,
Who comes in silence, and departs unseen,

And with no other visit, lie alone,
Nor stir, except I had my food to find
    In that dull bowl Diogenes might own.

And down my window I would draw the blind,
    And never look without, but, waiting, hear
A noise of rain, a whistling of the wind.

And only know that flame-foot Spring is near
By trilling birds, or by the patch of sun
    Crouching behind my curtain. So, in fear,

Noon-dreams should enter, softly, one by one,
    And throng about the floor, and float and play
And flicker on the screen, while minutes run—

The last majestic minutes of the day—
And with the mystic shadows, Shadow grows.
    Then the grey square of wall should fade away,

And glow again, and open, and disclose
    The shimmering lake in which the planets swim
And all that lake a dewdrop on a rose.

Brumana

Oh shall I never never be home again?
Meadows of England shining in the rain
Spread wide your daisied lawns: your ramparts green
With briar fortify, with blossom screen
Till my far morning—and O streams that slow
And pure and deep through plains and playlands go,
For me your love and all your kingcups store,
And—dark militia of the southern shore,
Old fragrant friends—preserve me the last lines
Of that long saga which you sung me, pines,
When, lonely boy, beneath the chosen tree
I listened, with my eyes upon the sea.

O traitor pines, you sang what life has found
The falsest of fair tales.
Earth blew a far-horn prelude all around,
That native music of her forest home,
While from the sea's blue fields and syren dales
Shadows and light noon-spectres of the foam
Riding the summer gales
On aery viols plucked an idle sound.
Hearing you sing, O trees,
Hearing you murmur, "There are older seas,
That beat on vaster sands,
Where the wise snailfish move their pearly towers
To carven rocks and sculptured promont'ries,"
Hearing you whisper, "Lands
Where blaze the unimaginable flowers."

Beneath me in the valley waves the palm,
Beneath, beyond the valley, breaks the sea;
Beneath me sleep in mist and light and calm
Cities of Lebanon, dream-shadow-dim,
Where Kings of Tyre and Kings of Tyre did rule
In ancient days in endless dynasty,
And all around the snowy mountains swim
Like mighty swans afloat in heaven's pool.

But I will walk upon the wooded hill
Where stands a grove, O pines, of sister pines,
And when the downy twilight droops her wing
And no sea glimmers and no mountain shines
My heart shall listen still.
For pines are gossip pines the wide world through
And full of runic tales to sigh or sing.
'Tis ever sweet through pines to see the sky
Mantling a deeper gold or darker blue.
'Tis ever sweet to lie
On the dry carpet of the needles brown,
And though the fanciful green lizard stir
And windy odours light as thistledown

Breathe from the lavdanon and lavender,
Half to forget the wandering and pain,
Half to remember days that have gone by,
And dream and dream that I am home again.

F. S. Flint

FRANK STEWART FLINT (1885–1960) was born in London, the son of a commercial traveler, and educated at a local school until the age of fourteen. For a time he held a series of odd jobs, but at nineteen he became a typist in the Civil Service, at the same time studying Latin and French at a workingmen's school. He became an exceptionally good linguist and translator, having taught himself no less than ten languages, and eventually was appointed Chief of the Overseas Section, Statistics Division, of the Civil Service.

Flint's first volume of poems, *In the Net of the Stars* (1909), was a collection of highly derivative love lyrics, but with *Cadences* (1915) he proclaimed his allegiance to the Imagist movement. Indeed, it may fairly be said that Flint was the most significant of the British proponents of Imagism in its purest form. Together with T. E. Hulme and Harold Monro he belonged to the group which used to meet in a Soho restaurant to discuss the new poetry, and when the movement was under way, he theorized about its aims and commented upon the work of his fellow Imagists. Flint's poetry is the work of his early years. As he grew older he wrote verse hardly at all, concentrating on his translations and professional duties, latterly avoiding all contact with his former literary associates.

Poems in Unrhymed Cadence

I

London, my beautiful,
It is not the sunset
Nor the pale green sky
Shimmering through the curtain
Of the silver birch,
Nor the quietness;
It is not the hopping
Of the little birds
Upon the lawn,
Nor the darkness
Stealing over all things
That moves me.

But as the moon creeps slowly
Over the tree-tops
Among the stars,
I think of her
And the glow her passing
Sheds on men.
London, my beautiful,
I will climb
Into the branches
To the moonlit tree-tops,
That my blood may be cooled
By the wind.

II

Under the lily shadow
And the gold
And the blue and mauve
That the whin and the lilac
Pour down on the water,
The fishes quiver.

Over the green cold leaves
And the rippled silver
And the tarnished copper
Of its neck and beak,
Toward the deep black water
Beneath the arches,
The swan floats slowly.

Into the dark of the arch the swan floats
And the black depth of my sorrow
Bears a white rose of flame.

III   IN THE GARDEN

The grass is beneath my head;
And I gaze
At the thronging stars
In the aisles of night.

They fall . . . they fall. . . .
I am overwhelmed,
And afraid.

Each little leaf of the aspen
Is caressed by the wind,
And each is crying.

And the perfume
Of invisible roses
Deepens the anguish.

Let a strong mesh of roots
Feed the crimson of roses
Upon my heart;
And then fold over the hollow
Where all the pain was.

Edmund Gosse

Sir Edmund Gosse (1849–1928), son of Philip Gosse, the famous Victorian marine biologist, was born in Hackney, London, but moved to South Devon shortly afterward. He was brought up in an atmosphere of strict religiosity (his parents belonged to the Plymouth Brethren), and it was not until he was sixteen that he began to read for pleasure, literary works having been debarred from him by his father, who believed that all literature other than religious writing was frivolous and immoral. In 1865 Charles Kingsley obtained a job for him as a cataloguer in the British Museum, a position which he held for ten years. During this time he began to make a name for himself as a literary critic. Gosse was responsible for introducing Ibsen to the English public, and by 1885 his literary reputation was such that he was appointed Clark Lecturer at Cambridge University, a position he held for five years. From 1904–1914 he was librarian at the House of Lords, and in 1907 he published his best work, *Father and Son,* an autobiographical novel describing his childhood. From 1918 to 1928 he contributed literary articles to *The Sunday Times;* in 1925 he was knighted; and by the time of his death he had received numerous honorary degrees from universities in England and abroad.

Gosse's poetry is elegant, and for the most part genteel, but without much depth. His most obvious literary debt is to the French Parnassians and occasionally to the Metaphysicals, especially to the poetry of Donne.

The Shepherdess

She walks—the lady of my delight—
   A shepherdess of sheep.
Her flocks are thoughts. She keeps them white;
   She guards them from the steep;
She feeds them on the fragrant height,
   And folds them in for sleep.

She roams maternal hills and bright,
   Dark valleys safe and deep.
Into that tender breast at night
   The chastest stars may peep.
She walks—the lady of my delight—
   A shepherdess of sheep.

She holds her little thoughts in sight,
   Though gay they run and leap.
She is so circumspect and right;
   She has her soul to keep.
She walks—the lady of my delight—
   A shepherdess of sheep.

In the Grass

Oh! flame of grass, shot upward from the earth,
   Keen with a thousand quivering sunlit fires,
   Green with the sap of satisfied desires
And sweet fulfilment of your pale sad birth,
Behold! I clasp you as a lover might,
   Roll on you, bathing in the noonday sun,
   And, if it might be, I would fain be one
With all your odour, mystery, and light,
             Oh flame of grass!

For here, to chasten my untimely gloom,
   My lady took my hand and spoke my name;
   The sun was on her gold hair like a flame;

The bright wind smote her forehead like perfume;
   The daisies darkened at her feet; she came,
As spring comes, scattering incense on your bloom
         Oh flame of grass!

Lying in the Grass

TO THOMAS HARDY

Between two russet tufts of summer grass,
I watch the world through hot air as through glass,
And by my face sweet lights and colours pass.

Before me, dark against the fading sky,
I watch three mowers mowing, as I lie:
With brawny arms they sweep in harmony.

Brown English faces by the sun burnt red,
Rich glowing colour on bare throat and head,
My heart would leap to watch them, were I dead!

And in my strong young living as I lie,
I seem to move with them in harmony,—
A fourth is mowing, and that fourth am I.

The music of the scythes that glide and leap,
The young men whistling as their great arms sweep,
And all the perfume and sweet sense of sleep,

The weary butterflies that droop their wings,
The dreamy nightingale that hardly sings,
And all the lassitude of happy things,

Is mingling with the warm and pulsing blood
That gushes through my veins a languid flood
And feeds my spirit as the sap a bud.

Behind the mowers, on the amber air,

A dark-green beech-wood rises, still and fair,
A white path winding up it like a stair.

And see that girl, with pitcher on her head,
And clean white apron on her gown of red,—
Her even-song of love is but half-said:

She waits the youngest mower. Now he goes;
Her cheeks are redder than a wild blush-rose;
They climb up where the deepest shadows close.

But though they pass and vanish, I am there;
I watch his rough hands meet beneath her hair,
Their broken speech sounds sweet to me like prayer.

Ah! now the rosy children come to play,
And romp and struggle with the new-mown hay;
Their clear high voices sound from far away.

They know so little why the world is sad,
They dig themselves warm graves and yet are glad;
Their muffled screams and laughter make me mad!

I long to go and play among them there;
Unseen, like wind, to take them by the hair,
And gently make their rosy cheeks more fair.

The happy children! full of frank surprise,
And sudden whims and innocent ecstasies;
What godhead sparkles from their liquid eyes!

No wonder round those urns of mingled clays
That Tuscan potters fashioned in old days,
And coloured like the torrid earth ablaze,

We find the little gods and loves portrayed,
Through ancient forests wandering undismayed,
Or gathered, whispering, in some pleasant glade.

They knew, as I do now, what keen delight

A strong man feels to watch the tender flight
Of little children playing in his sight.

I do not hunger for a well-stored mind,
I only wish to live my life, and find
My heart in unison with all mankind.

My life is like the single dewy star
That trembles on the horizon's primrose-bar,—
A microcosm where all things living are.

And if, among the noiseless grasses, Death
Should come behind and take away my breath,
I should not rise as one who sorroweth;

For I should pass, but all the world would be
Full of desire and young delight and glee,
And why should men be sad through loss of me?

The light is dying; in the silver blue
The young moon shines from her bright window through:
The mowers all are gone, and I go too.

Impression

In these restrained and careful times
Our knowledge petrifies our rhymes;
Ah! for that reckless fire men had
When it was witty to be mad.

When wild conceits were piled in scores,
And lit by flaring metaphors,
When all was crazed and out of tune,—
Yet throbbed with music of the moon.

If we could dare to write as ill
As some whose voices haunt us still,
Even we, perchance, might call our own
Their deep enchanting undertone.

We are too diffident and nice,
Too learned and too over-wise,
Too much afraid of faults to be
The flutes of bold sincerity.

For as this sweet life passes by,
We blink and nod with critic eye;
We've no words rude enough to give
Its charm so frank and fugitive.

The green and scarlet of the Park,
The undulating streets at dark,
The brown smoke blown across the blue,
This coloured city we walk through,—

The pallid faces full of pain,
The field-smell of the passing wain,
The laughter, longing, perfume, strife,
The daily spectacle of life;—

Ah! how shall this be given to rhyme,
By rhymesters of a knowing time?
Ah! for the age when verse was glad,
Being godlike, to be bad and mad.

Revelation

Unto the silver night
    She brought with her pale hand
The topaz lanthorn-light,
And darted splendour o'er the land;
    Around her in a band,
Ringstraked and pied, the great soft moths came flying,
    And flapping with their mad wings, fann'd
The flickering flame, ascending, falling, dying.

Behind the thorny pink
    Close wall of blossom'd may,
I gazed thro' one green chink

And saw no more than thousands may,—
    Saw sweetness, tender and gay,—
Saw full rose lips as rounded as the cherry,
    Saw braided locks more dark than bay,
And flashing eyes decorous, pure, and merry.

    With food for furry friends
      She pass'd, her lamp and she,
    Till eaves and gable-ends
Hid all that saffron sheen from me:
      Around my rosy tree
Once more the silver-starry night was shining,
    With depths of heaven, dewy and free,
And crystals of a carven moon declining.

    Alas! for him who dwells
      In frigid air of thought,
    When warmer light dispels
The frozen calm his spirit sought;
      By life too lately taught
He sees the ecstatic Human from his stealing;
    Reels from the joy experience brought,
And dares not clutch what Love was half revealing.

Renouncement

I must not think of thee; and, tired yet strong,
I shun the thought that lurks in all delight—
The thought of thee—and in the blue heaven's height,
And in the sweetest passage of a song.
Oh, just beyond the fairest thoughts that throng
This breast, the thought of thee waits, hidden yet bright;
But it must never, never come in sight;
I must stop short of thee the whole day long.
But when sleep comes to close each difficult day,
When night gives pause to the long watch I keep,
And all my bonds I needs must loose apart,
Must doff my will as raiment laid away—
With the first dream that comes with the first sleep
I run, I run, I am gathered to thy heart.

Julian Grenfell

JULIAN HENRY GRENFELL (1888–1915), son of William Henry Grenfell, afterward first baron Desborough, was educated at Eton and Balliol College, Oxford. In 1910 he obtained a commission in the First Royal Dragoons, but died from wounds received while fighting in the 1914–1918 war, being awarded the Distinguished Service Order for gallantry. Grenfell was one of the more admirable of the products of the British public-school system, a good athlete, an admirer of the Stoic philosophers, aristocratic, brave, and when the occasion arose, capable of self-sacrifice.

Grenfell's poem "Into Battle," written one month before his death, is one of the best known poems of the 1914–1918 war, though perhaps not one of the best. The rest of his poetry is considerably inferior, being mostly in a lighter vein.

Into Battle

The naked earth is warm with spring,
   And with green grass and bursting trees
Leans to the sun's gaze glorying,
   And quivers in the sunny breeze;
And life is colour and warmth and light,
   And a striving evermore for these;
And he is dead who will not fight;
   And who dies fighting has increase.

The fighting man shall from the sun
   Take warmth, and life from the glowing earth;
Speed with the light-foot winds to run,
   And with the trees to newer birth;
And find, when fighting shall be done,
   Great rest, and fullness after dearth.

All the bright company of Heaven
   Hold him in their high comradeship,
The Dog-Star, and the Sisters Seven,
   Orion's Belt and sworded hip.

The woodland trees that stand together,
   They stand to him each one a friend;
They gently speak in the windy weather;
   They guide to valley and ridge's end.

The kestrel hovering by day,
   And the little owls that call by night,
Bid him be swift and keen as they,
   As keen of ear, as swift of sight.

The blackbird sings to him, "Brother, brother,
   If this be the last song you shall sing,
Sing well, for you may not sing another;
   Brother, sing."

In dreary, doubtful, waiting hours,
  Before the brazen frenzy starts,
The horses show him nobler powers;
  O patient eyes, courageous hearts!

And when the burning moment breaks,
  And all things else are out of mind,
And only joy of battle takes
  Him by the throat, and makes him blind,

Through joy and blindness he shall know,
  Not caring much to know, that still
Nor lead nor steel shall reach him, so
  That it be not the Destined Will.

The thundering line of battle stands,
  And in the air death moans and sings;
But Day shall clasp him with strong hands,
  And Night shall fold him in soft wings.

Thomas Hardy

THOMAS HARDY (1840–1928) was born at Higher Bockhampton, Dorset, the son of a builder. He was educated at various local schools, and at the age of sixteen was placed with an ecclesiastical architect in Dorchester. He continued his architectural studies in London in 1862, returning home five years later as a result of ill health. Around 1870 Hardy was able to devote his time almost entirely to literature, and before 1910 had produced a number of major novels most of which were set in his native Wessex. In 1910 he received the Order of Merit, and was later awarded several honorary degrees by various British universities. He died at the age of eighty-eight at Max Gate, his home for over forty years.

Though Hardy is remembered chiefly as a novelist, he regarded his poetry as equally important. Most of it was published in his later years, though much of it had been written when he was still a comparatively young man. His greatest poetical achievement is *The Dynasts,* published in three parts in 1903, 1906, and 1908, a long epic poem about Napoleon in which Hardy set forth his philosophy of the "Immanent Will" working itself out in human affairs. His poetry has frequently been called pessimistic, though the poet himself referred to it as "distinctly melioristic," and it cannot be denied that his vision is generally gloomy. He speculates upon the absurdity of human existence in a world which seems "God-forgotten," but he is able also to communicate his genuine love of the English countryside without dwelling overmuch on the romantic and the picturesque. Hardy's poetry is dramatic rather than pictorial, traditional in form and expression, the only traceable influences on it being Browning and perhaps Donne.

Nature's Questioning

When I look forth at dawning, pool,
    Field, flock, and lonely tree,
    All seem to gaze at me
Like chastened children sitting silent in a school;

    Their faces dulled, constrained, and worn,
        As though the master's ways
        Through the long teaching days
Had cowed them till their early zest was overborne.

    Upon them stirs in lippings mere
        (As if once clear in call,
        But now scarce breathed at all)—
"We wonder, ever wonder, why we find us here!

    "Has some Vast Imbecility,
        Mighty to build and blend,
        But impotent to tend,
Framed us in jest, and left us now to hazardry?

    "Or come we of an Automaton
        Unconscious of our pains? . . .
        Or are we live remains
Of Godhead dying downwards, brain and eye now gone?

    "Or is it that some high Plan betides,
        As yet not understood,
        Of Evil stormed by Good,
We the Forlorn Hope over which Achievement strides?"

    Thus things around. No answerer I . . .
        Meanwhile the winds, and rains,
        And Earth's old glooms and pains
Are still the same, and Life and Death are neighbours nigh.

Drummer Hodge

I

They throw in Drummer Hodge, to rest
    Uncoffined—just as found:
His landmark is a kopje-crest
    That breaks the veldt around;
And foreign constellations west
    Each night above his mound.

II

Young Hodge the Drummer never knew—
    Fresh from his Wessex home—
The meaning of the broad Karoo,
    The Bush, the dusty loam,
And why uprose to nightly view
    Strange stars amid the gloam.

III

Yet portion of that unknown plain
    Will Hodge for ever be;
His homely Northern breast and brain
    Grow to some Southern tree,
And strange-eyed constellations reign
    His stars eternally.

At a Lunar Eclipse

Thy shadow, Earth, from Pole to Central Sea,
Now steals along upon the Moon's meek shine
In even monochrome and curving line
Of imperturbable serenity.

How shall I link such sun-cast symmetry
With the torn troubled form I know as thine,
That profile, placid as a brow divine,
With continents of moil and misery?

And can immense Mortality but throw
So small a shade, and Heaven's high human scheme
Be hemmed within the coasts yon arc implies?

Is such the stellar gauge of earthly show,
Nation at war with nation, brains that teem,
Heroes, and women fairer than the skies?

The Lacking Sense

SCENE.—*A sad-coloured landscape, Waddon Vale*

I

"O Time, whence comes the Mother's moody look amid her
     labours,
As of one who all unwittingly has wounded where she loves?
  Why weaves she not her world-webs to according lutes and
     tabors,
With nevermore this too remorseful air upon her face,
     As of angel fallen from grace?"

II

—"Her look is but her story: construe not its symbols keenly:
  In her wonderworks yea surely has she wounded where she
     loves.
The sense of ills misdealt for blisses blanks the mien most
     queenly,
  Self-smitings kill self-joys; and everywhere beneath the sun
     Such deeds her hands have done."

III

—"And how explains thy ancient Mind her crimes upon her
   creatures,
   These fallings from her fair beginnings, woundings where she
      loves,
Into her would-be perfect motions, modes, effects, and features
   Admitting cramps, black humours, wan decay, and baleful
      blights,
         Distress into delights?"

IV

—"Ah! knowest thou not her secret yet, her vainly veiled
   deficience,
   Whence it comes that all unwittingly she wounds the lives she
      loves?
That sightless are those orbs of hers?—which bar to her
   omniscience
   Brings those fearful unfulfilments, that red ravage through her
      zones
         Whereat all creation groans.

V

"She whispers it in each pathetic strenuous slow endeavour,
   When in mothering she unwittingly sets wounds on what she
      loves;
Yet her primal doom pursues her, faultful, fatal is she ever;
   Though so deft and nigh to vision is her facile finger-touch
         That the seers marvel much.

VI

"Deal, then, her groping skill no scorn, no note of malediction;
   Not long on thee will press the hand that hurts the lives it
      loves;

And while she plods dead-reckoning on, in darkness of affliction,
  Assist her where thy creaturely dependence can or may,
      For thou art of her clay."

God-Forgotten

I towered far, and lo! I stood within
  The presence of the Lord Most High,
Sent thither by the sons of Earth, to win
    Some answer to their cry.

—"The Earth, sayest thou? The Human race?
  By Me created? Sad its lot?
Nay: I have no remembrance of such place:
    Such world I fashioned not."—

—"O Lord, forgive me when I say
  Thou spakest the word that made it all."—
"The Earth of men—let me bethink me. . . . Yea!
    I dimly do recall

"Some tiny sphere I built long back
  (Mid millions of such shapes of mine)
So named . . . It perished, surely—not a wrack
    Remaining, or a sign?

"It lost my interest from the first,
  My aims therefor succeeding ill;
Haply it died of doing as it durst?"—
    "Lord, it existeth still."—

"Dark, then, its life! For not a cry
  Of aught it bears do I now hear;
Of its own act the threads were snapt whereby
    Its plaints had reached mine ear.

"It used to ask for gifts of good,
  Till came its severance, self-entailed,

When sudden silence on that side ensued,
    And has till now prevailed.

"All other orbs have kept in touch;
    Their voicings reach me speedily:
Thy people took upon them overmuch
    In sundering them from me!

"And it is strange—though sad enough—
    Earth's race should think that one whose call
Frames, daily, shining spheres of flawless stuff
    Must heed their tainted ball! . . .

"But sayest it is by pangs distraught,
    And strife, and silent suffering?—
Sore grieved am I that injury should be wrought
    Even on so poor a thing!

"Thou shouldst have learnt that *Not to Mend*
    For Me could mean but *Not to Know:*
Hence, Messengers! and straightway put an end
    To what men undergo." . . .

Homing at dawn, I thought to see
    One of the Messengers standing by.
—Oh, childish thought! . . . Yet often it comes to me
    When trouble hovers nigh.

An August Midnight

I

A shaded lamp and a waving blind,
And the beat of a clock from a distant floor:
On this scene enter—winged, horned, and spined—
A longlegs, a moth, and a dumbledore;
While 'mid my page there idly stands
A sleepy fly, that rubs its hands . . .

II

Thus meet we five, in this still place,
At this point of time, at this point in space.
—My guests besmear my new-penned line,
Or bang at the lamp and fall supine.
"God's humblest, they!" I muse. Yet why?
They know Earth-secrets that know not I.

The Darkling Thrush

I leant upon a coppice gate
    When Frost was spectre-gray,
And Winter's dregs made desolate
    The weakening eye of day.
The tangled bine-stems scored the sky
    Like strings of broken lyres,
And all mankind that haunted nigh
    Had sought their household fires.

The land's sharp features seemed to be
    The Century's corpse outleant,
His crypt the cloudy canopy,
    The wind his death-lament.
The ancient pulse of germ and birth
    Was shrunken hard and dry,
And every spirit upon earth
    Seemed fervourless as I.

At once a voice arose among
    The bleak twigs overhead
In a full-hearted evensong
    Of joy illimited;
An aged thrush, frail, gaunt, and small,
    In blast-beruffled plume,
Had chosen thus to fling his soul
    Upon the growing gloom.

So little cause for carolings
    Of such ecstatic sound
Was written on terrestrial things
    Afar or nigh around,
That I could think there trembled through
    His happy good-night air
Some blessed Hope, whereof he knew
    And I was unaware.

Reminiscences of a Dancing Man

I

Who now remembers Almack's balls—
    Willis's sometime named—
In those two smooth-floored upper halls
    For faded ones so famed?
Where as we trod to trilling sound
The fancied phantoms stood around,
    Or joined us in the maze,
Of the powdered Dears from Georgian years,
Whose dust lay in sightless sealed-up biers,
    The fairest of former days.

II

Who now remembers gay Cremorne,
    And all its jaunty jills,
And those wild whirling figures born
    Of Jullien's grand quadrilles?
With hats on head and morning coats
There footed to his prancing notes
    Our partner-girls and we;
And the gas-jets winked, and the lustres clinked,
And the platform throbbed as with arms enlinked
    We moved to the minstrelsy.

III

Who now recalls those crowded rooms
    Of old yclept "The Argyle,"
Where to the deep Drum-polka's booms
    We hopped in standard style?
Whither have danced those damsels now!
Is Death the partner who doth moue
    Their wormy chaps and bare?
Do their spectres spin like sparks within
The smoky halls of the Prince of Sin
    To a thunderous Jullien air?

The Minute Before Meeting

The grey gaunt days dividing us in twain
Seemed hopeless hills my strength must faint to climb,
But they are gone; and now I would detain
The few clock-beats that part us; rein back Time,

And live in close expectance never closed
In change for far expectance closed at last,
So harshly has expectance been imposed
On my long need while these slow blank months passed.

And knowing that what is now about to be
Will all *have been* in O, so short a space!
I read beyond it my despondency
When more dividing months shall take its place,
Thereby denying to this hour of grace
A full-up measure of felicity.

New Year's Eve

"I have finished another year," said God,
    "In grey, green, white, and brown;
I have strewn the leaf upon the sod,

Sealed up the worm within the clod,
    And let the last sun down."

"And what's the good of it?" I said,
    "What reasons made you call
From formless void this earth we tread,
When nine-and-ninety can be read
    Why nought should be at all?

"Yea, Sire: why shaped you us, 'who in
    This tabernacle groan'—
If ever a joy be found herein,
Such joy no man had wished to win
    If he had never known!"

Then he: "My labours—logicless—
    You may explain; not I:
Sense-sealed I have wrought, without a guess
That I evolved a Consciousness
    To ask for reasons why.

"Strange that ephemeral creatures who
    By my own ordering are,
Should see the shortness of my view,
Use ethic tests I never knew,
    Or made provision for!"

He sank to raptness as of yore,
    And opening New Year's Day
Wove it by rote as theretofore,
And went on working evermore
    In his unweeting way.

Channel Firing

That night your great guns, unawares,
    Shook all our coffins as we lay,
And broke the chancel window-squares,
    We thought it was the Judgment-day

And sat upright. While drearisome
Arose the howl of wakened hounds:
The mouse let fall the altar-crumb,
The worms drew back into the mounds,

The glebe cow drooled. Till God called, "No;
It's gunnery practice out at sea
Just as before you went below;
The world is as it used to be:

"All nations striving strong to make
Red war yet redder. Mad as hatters
They do no more for Christés sake
Than you who are helpless in such matters.

"That this is not the judgment-hour
For some of them's a blessed thing,
For if it were they'd have to scour
Hell's floor for so much threatening. . . .

"Ha, ha. It will be warmer when
I blow the trumpet (if indeed
I ever do; for you are men,
And rest eternal sorely need)."

So down we lay again. "I wonder,
Will the world ever saner be,"
Said one, "than when He sent us under
In our indifferent century!"

And many a skeleton shook his head.
"Instead of preaching forty year,"
My neighbour Parson Thirdly said,
"I wish I had stuck to pipes and beer."

Again the guns disturbed the hour,
Roaring their readiness to avenge,
As far inland as Stourton Tower,
And Camelot, and starlit Stonehenge.

Under the Waterfall

"Whenever I plunge my arm, like this,
In a basin of water, I never miss
The sweet sharp sense of a fugitive day
Fetched back from its thickening shroud of gray.
      Hence the only prime
      And real love-rhyme
      That I know by heart,
      And that leaves no smart,
Is the purl of a little valley fall
About three spans wide and two spans tall
Over a table of solid rock,
And into a scoop of the self-same block;
The purl of a runlet that never ceases
In stir of kingdoms, in wars, in peaces;
With a hollow boiling voice it speaks
And has spoken since hills were turfless peaks."

"And why gives this the only prime
Idea to you of a real love-rhyme?
And why does plunging your arm in a bowl
Full of spring water, bring throbs to your soul?"

"Well, under the fall, in a crease of the stone,
Though where precisely none ever has known,
Jammed darkly, nothing to show how prized,
And by now with its smoothness opalized,
      Is a drinking-glass:
      For, down that pass
      My lover and I
      Walked under a sky
Of blue with a leaf-wove awning of green,
In the burn of August, to paint the scene,
And we placed our basket of fruit and wine
By the runlet's rim, where we sat to dine;
And when we had drunk from the glass together,
Arched by the oak-copse from the weather,
I held the vessel to rinse in the fall,

Where it slipped, and sank, and was past recall,
Though we stooped and plumbed the little abyss
With long bared arms. There the glass still is.
And, as said, if I thrust my arm below
Cold water in basin or bowl, a throe
From the past awakens a sense of that time,
And the glass we used, and the cascade's rhyme.
The basin seems the pool, and its edge
The hard smooth face of the brook-side ledge,
And the leafy pattern of china-ware
The hanging plants that were bathing there.
"By night, by day, when it shines or lours,
There lies intact that chalice of ours,
And its presence adds to the rhyme of love
Persistently sung by the fall above.
No lip has touched it since his and mine
In turns therefrom sipped lovers' wine."

The Blinded Bird

So zestfully canst thou sing?
And all this indignity,
With God's consent, on thee!
Blinded ere yet a-wing
By the red-hot needle thou,
I stand and wonder how
So zestfully thou can sing!

Resenting not such wrong,
Thy grievous pain forgot,
Eternal dark thy lot,
Groping thy whole life long,
After that stab of fire;
Enjailed in pitiless wire;
Resenting not such wrong!

Who hath charity? This bird.
Who suffereth long and is kind,
Is not provoked, though blind

And alive ensepulchred?
Who hopeth, endureth all things?
Who thinketh no evil, but sings?
Who is divine? This bird.

The Ballet

They crush together—a rustling heap of flesh—
Of more than flesh, a heap of souls; and then
  They part, enmesh,
  And crush together again,
Like the pink petals of a too sanguine rose
  Frightened shut just when it blows.

Though all alike in their tinsel livery,
And indistinguishable at a sweeping glance,
  They muster, maybe,
  As lives wide in irrelevance;
A world of her own has each one underneath,
  Detached as a sword from its sheath.

Daughters, wives, mistresses; honest or false, sold, bought;
Hearts of all sizes; gay, fond, gushing, or penned,
  Various in thought
  Of lover, rival, friend;
Links in a one-pulsed chain, all showing one smile,
  Yet severed so many a mile!

In Time of
"The Breaking of Nations"

I

Only a man harrowing clods
  In a slow silent walk
With an old horse that stumbles and nods
  Half asleep as they stalk.

II

Only thin smoke without flame
    From the heaps of couch-grass:
Yet this will go onward the same
    Though Dynasties pass.

III

Yonder a maid and her wight
    Come whispering by:
War's annals will cloud into night
    Ere their story die.

Weathers

I

This is the weather the cuckoo likes,
    And so do I;
When showers betumble the chestnut spikes,
    And nestlings fly:
And the little brown nightingale bills his best,
And they sit outside at "The Travellers' Rest,"
And maids come forth sprig-muslin drest,
And citizens dream of the south and west,
    And so do I.

II

This is the weather the shepherd shuns,
    And so do I;
When beeches drip in browns and duns,
    And thresh, and ply;
And hill-hid tides throb, throe on throe,
And meadow rivulets overflow,

And drops on gate-bars hang in a row,
And rooks in families homeward go,
And so do I.

Snow in the Suburbs

Every branch big with it,
Bent every twig with it;
Every fork like a white web-foot;
Every street and pavement mute:
Some flakes have lost their way, and grope back upward, when
Meeting those meandering down they turn and descend again.
The palings are glued together like a wall,
And there is no waft of wind with the fleecy fall.

A sparrow enters the tree,
Whereon immediately
A snow-lump thrice his own slight size
Descends on him and showers his head and eyes.
And overturns him,
And near inurns him,
And lights on a nether twig, when its brush
Starts off a volley of other lodging lumps with a rush.

The steps are a blanched slope,
Up which, with feeble hope,
A black cat comes, wide-eyed and thin;
And we take him in.

At Wynyard's Gap

SHE *(on horseback)*

The hounds pass here?

HE *(on horseback)*

They did an hour ago,
Just in full cry, and went down-wind, I saw,

Towards Pen Wood, where they may kill, and draw
A second time, and bear towards the Yeo.

She

How vexing! And I've crept along unthinking.

He

Ah!—lost in dreams. Fancy to fancy linking!

She *(more softly)*

Not that, quite. . . . Now, to settle what I'll do.

He

Go home again. But have you seen the view
From the top there? Not? It's really worth your while.—
You must dismount, because there is a stile.

> *They dismount, hitch their horses, and climb a few-score
> yards from the road.*

There you see half South Wessex,—combe, and glen,
And down, to Lewsdon Hill and Pilsdon Pen.

She

Yes. It is fine. And I, though living out there
By Crewkerne, never knew it. *(She turns her head)* Well, I declare,
Look at the horses!—How shall I catch my mare?

> *The horses have got loose and scampered off.*

Now that's your fault, through leading me up here!
You must have known 'twould happen—

He

No, my dear!

She

I'm not your dear.

HE *(blandly)*

But you can't help being so,
If it comes to that. The fairest girl I've seen
Is of course dear—by her own fault, I mean.

SHE *(quickly)*

What house is that we see just down below?

HE

Oh—that's the inn called "Wynyard's Gap."—I'll go
While you wait here, and catch those brutes. Don't stir.

He goes. She waits.

SHE

What a handsome man. Not local, I'll aver.

He comes back.

HE

I met a farmer's labourer some way on;
He says he'll bring them to us here anon,
If possible before the day is dim.
Come down to the inn: there we can wait for him.

They descend slowly in that direction.

SHE

What a lonely inn. Why is there such a one?

HE

For us to wait at. Thus 'tis things are done.

SHE

Thus things are done? Well—what things do you mean?

HE

Romantic things. Meetings unknown, unseen.

SHE

But ours is accident, and needn't have been,
And isn't what I'd plan with a stranger, quite,
Particularly at this time—nearly night.

HE

Nor I. But still, the tavern's loneliness
Is favourable for lovers in distress,
When they've eloped, for instance, and are in fear
Of being pursued. No one would find them here.

    He goes to speak to the labourer approaching; and returns.

He says the horses long have passed the combe,
And cannot be overtaken. They'll go home.

SHE

And what's to be done? And it's beginning to rain.
'Tis always so. One trouble brings a train!

HE

It seems to me that here we'd better stay
And rest us till some vehicle comes this way:
In fact, we might put up here till the morning:
The floods are high, and night-farers have warning.

SHE

Put up? Do you think so!

HE

                  I incline to such,
My *dear* (do you mind?)

SHE

Yes.—Well *(more softly),* I don't much,
If I seem like it. But I ought to tell you
One thing. I'm married. Being so, it's well you—

He

Oh, so am I. *(A silence, he regarding her)* I note a charming
    thing—
You stand so stock-still that your ear-ring shakes
At each pulsation which the vein there makes.

She

Does it? Perhaps because it's flustering
To be caught thus! *(In a murmur)* Why did we chance to meet
    here!

He

God knows! Perhaps to taste a bitter-sweet here.—
Still, let us enter. Shelter we must get:
The night is darkening and is growing wet.
So, anyhow, you can treat me as a lover
Just for this once. To-morrow 'twill be over!

> *They reach the inn. The door is locked, and they discern a
> board marked "To Let." While they stand stultified a
> van is seen drawing near, with passengers.*

She

Ah, here's an end of it! The Crewkerne carrier.

He

So cynic circumstance erects its barrier!

She *(mischievously)*

To your love-making, which would have grown stronger,
No doubt, if we had stayed on here much longer?

> *The carrier comes up. Her companion reluctantly hails him.*

He

Yes. . . . And in which you might have shown some ruth,
Had but the inn been open!—Well, forsooth,
I'm sorry it's not. Are you? Now, dear, the truth!

SHE *(with gentle evasiveness)*

I am—almost. But best 'tis thus to be.
For—dear one—there I've said it!—you can see
That both at one inn (though roomed separately,
Of course)—so lone, too—might have been unfit,
Perfect as 'tis for lovers, I admit.

HE *(after a sigh)*

Carrier! A lift for my wife, please.

SHE *(in quick undertones)*

Wife? But nay—

HE *(continuing)*

Her horse has thrown her and has gone astray:
See she gets safe to Crewkerne. I've to stay.

CARRIER

I will, sir! I'm for Crookhorn straight away.

HE *(to her, aloud)*

Right now, dear. I shall soon be home. Adieu! *(Kisses her.)*

SHE *(whispering confusedly)*

You shouldn't! Pretending you are my husband, too!
I now must act the part of wife to you!

HE *(whispering)*

Yes, since I've kissed you, dear. You see it's done
To silence tongues as we're found here alone
At night, by gossipers, and seem as shown
Staying together!

SHE *(whispering)*

Then must I, too, kiss?

He

Yes: a mere matter of form, you know,
To check all scandal. People will talk so!

She

I'd no idea it would reach to this! *(Kisses him.)*
What makes it worse is, I'm ashamed to say,
I've a young baby waiting me at home!

He

Ah—there you beat me!—But, my dearest, play
The wife to the end, and don't give me away,
Despite the baby, since we've got so far,
And what we've acted feel we almost are!

She *(sighing)*

Yes. 'Tis so! And my conscience has gone dumb!

(Aloud)

'Bye, dear, awhile! I'll sit up till you come.
(In a whisper)
Which means Good-bye for ever, truly heard!
Upon to-night be silent!

He

Never a word,
Till Pilsdon Pen by Marshwood wind is stirred!

He hands her up. Exeunt omnes.

Drinking Song

Once on a time when thought began
    Lived Thales: he
    Was said to see
Vast truths that mortals seldom can;

It seems without
A moment's doubt
That everything was made for man.

Chorus.

Fill full your cups: feel no distress
That thoughts so great should now be less!

Earth mid the sky stood firm and flat,
    He held, till came
    A sage by name
Copernicus, and righted that.
    We trod, he told,
    A globe that rolled
Around a sun it warmed it at.

Chorus.

Fill full your cups: feel no distress;
'Tis only one great thought the less!

But still we held, as time flew by
    And wit increased,
    Ours was, at least,
The only world whose rank was high:
    Till rumours flew
    From folk who knew
Of globes galore about the sky.

Chorus.

Fill full your cups: feel no distress;
'Tis only one great thought the less!

And that this earth, our one estate,
    Was no prime ball,
    The best of all,
But common, mean; indeed, tenth-rate:
    And men, so proud,
    A feeble crowd,
Unworthy any special fate.

Chorus.

Fill full your cups: feel no distress;
'Tis only one great thought the less!

Then rose one Hume, who could not see,
    If earth were such,
    Required were much
To prove no miracles could be:
    "Better believe
    The eyes deceive
Than that God's clockwork jolts," said he.

Chorus.

Fill full your cups: feel no distress;
'Tis only one great thought the less!

Next this strange message Darwin brings,
    (Though saying his say
    In a quiet way);
We all are one with creeping things;
    And apes and men
    Blood-brethren,
And likewise reptile forms with stings.

Chorus.

Fill full your cups: feel no distress;
'Tis only one great thought the less!

And when this philosoph had done
    Came Doctor Cheyne:
    Speaking plain he
Proved no virgin bore a son.
    "Such tale, indeed,
    Helps not our creed,"
He said. "A tale long known to none."

Chorus.

Fill full your cups: feel no distress;
'Tis only one great thought the less!

And now comes Einstein with a notion—
        Not yet quite clear
        To many here—
That's there's no time, no space, no motion,
        Nor rathe nor late,
        Nor square nor straight,
But just a sort of bending-ocean.

Chorus.

Fill full your cups: feel no distress;
'Tis only one great thought the less!

So here we are, in piteous case:
        Like butterflies
        Of many dyes
Upon an Alpine glacier's face:
        To fly and cower
        In some warm bower
Our chief concern in such a place.

Chorus.

Fill full your cups: feel no distress
At all our great thoughts shrinking less:
We'll do a good deed nevertheless!

W. E. Henley

WILLIAM ERNEST HENLEY (1849–1903) was born in Gloucester and attended the Crypt Grammar School in that town; there he became first a boyish admirer and later a close friend of the Victorian schoolmaster-poet T. E. Brown. At the age of twelve he was found to have tuberculosis of the bone, which necessitated the amputation of a foot. He was about to lose the other one too but fortunately entered the Edinburgh Infirmary in 1874, where he came under the care of Lister, the discoverer of antiseptic surgery, who managed to save it. He was discharged from hospital in 1875 and became a journalist in Edinburgh, later moving to London where he eventually became editor of the influential Tory magazine *The National Observer*. In 1894 he retired from journalism, exhausted both physically and emotionally after a life of continual pain and the recent loss of his only child, Margaret. Four years later, however, he was working once more, this time as editor of the *Monthly Review*. He died after an injury received while boarding a train.

Henley's fame rests almost as securely on his literary criticism and his editing of standard texts of famous British authors as on his poetry. His verse is most frequently somber, expressing a belief in stoic endurance and death as a release from suffering rather than as the beginning of a new life. It is direct and forceful, though on occasion descending to bombast and jingoism, and his most significant technical achievement is probably his skillful use of impressionistic free verse, as in "London Voluntaries," anticipating the poetic mode of Eliot and some of his contemporaries.

From In Hospital

I   ENTER PATIENT

The morning mists still haunt the stony street;
The northern summer air is shrill and cold;
And lo, the Hospital, grey, quiet, old,
Where Life and Death like friendly chafferers meet.
Thro' the loud spaciousness and draughty gloom
A small, strange child—so agèd yet so young!—
Her little arm besplinted and beslung,
Precedes me gravely to the waiting-room.
I limp behind, my confidence all gone.
The grey-haired soldier-porter waves me on,
And on I crawl, and still my spirits fail:
A tragic meanness seems so to environ
These corridors and stairs of stone and iron,
Cold, naked, clean—half-workhouse and half-jail.

IV   BEFORE

Behold me waiting—waiting for the knife.
A little while, and at a leap I storm
The thick, sweet mystery of chloroform,
The drunken dark, the little death-in-life.
The gods are good to me: I have no wife,
No innocent child, to think of as I near
The fateful minute; nothing all-too dear
Unmans me for my bout of passive strife.
Yet am I tremulous and a trifle sick,
And, face to face with chance, I shrink a little:
My hopes are strong, my will is something weak.
Here comes the basket? Thank you. I am ready.
But, gentlemen my porters, life is brittle:
You carry Caesar and his fortunes—steady!

VI   AFTER

Like as a flamelet blanketed in smoke,
So through the anaesthetic shows my life;
So flashes and so fades my thought, at strife
With the strong stupor that I heave and choke
And sicken at, it is so foully sweet.
Faces look strange from space—and disappear.
Far voices, sudden loud, offend my ear—
And hush as sudden. Then my senses fleet:
All were a blank, save for this dull, new pain
That grinds my leg and foot; and brokenly
Time and the place glimpse on to me again;
And, unsurprised, out of uncertainty,
I wake—relapsing—somewhat faint and fain,
To an immense, complacent dreamery.

XXIV   SUICIDE

Staring corpselike at the ceiling,
    See his harsh, unrazored features,
    Ghastly brown against the pillow,
    And his throat—so strangely bandaged!

Lack of work and lack of victuals,
    A debauch of smuggled whisky,
    And his children in the workhouse
    Made the world so black a riddle

That he plunged for a solution;
    And, although his knife was edgeless,
    He was sinking fast towards one,
    When they came, and found, and saved him.

Stupid now with shame and sorrow,
    In the night I hear him sobbing.
    But sometimes he talks a little.
    He has told me all his troubles.

In his broad face, tanned and bloodless,
    White and wild his eyeballs glisten;
    And his smile, occult and tragic,
    Yet so slavish, makes you shudder.

XXVIII   DISCHARGED

Carry me out
Into the wind and the sunshine,
Into the beautiful world.

O, the wonder, the spell of the streets!
The stature and strength of the horses,
The rustle and echo of footfalls,
The flat roar and rattle of wheels!
A swift tram floats huge on us . . .
It's a dream?
The smell of the mud in my nostrils
Blows brave—like a breath of the sea!

As of old,
Ambulant, undulant drapery,
Vaguely and strangely provocative,
Flutters and beckons. O, yonder—
Is it?—the gleam of a stocking!
Sudden, a spire
Wedged in the mist! O, the houses,
The long lines of lofty, grey houses,
Cross-hatched with shadow and light!
These are the streets. . . .
Each is an avenue leading
Whither I will!

Free . . . !
Dizzy, hysterical, faint,
I sit, and the carriage rolls on with me
Into the wonderful world.

Ballade of
A Toyokuni Colour-Print

TO W. A.

Was I a Samurai renowned,
Two-sworded, fierce, immense of bow?
A histrion angular and profound?
A priest? a porter?—Child, although
I have forgotten clean, I know
That in the shade of Fujisan,
What time the cherry-orchards blow,
I loved you once in old Japan.

As here you loiter, flowing-gowned
And hugely sashed, with pins a-row
Your quaint head as with flamelets crowned,
Demure, inviting—even so,
When merry maids in Miyako
To feel the sweet o' the year began,
And green gardens to overflow,
I loved you once in old Japan.

Clear shine the hills; the rice-fields round
Two cranes are circling; sleepy and slow,
A blue canal the lake's blue bound
Breaks at the bamboo bridge; and lo!
Touched with the sundown's spirit and glow,
I see you turn, with flirted fan,
Against the plum-tree's bloomy snow. . . .
I loved you once in old Japan!

Envoy

Dear, 'twas a dozen lives ago;
But that I was a lucky man
The Toyokuni here will show:
I loved you—once—in old Japan.

Ballade of Dead Actors

I. M.

EDWARD JOHN HENLEY (1861-1898)

Where are the passions they essayed,
And where the tears they made to flow?
Where the wild humours they portrayed
For laughing worlds to see and know?
Othello's wrath and Juliet's woe?
Sir Peter's whims and Timon's gall?
And Millamant and Romeo?
Into the night go one and all.

Where are the braveries, fresh or frayed?
The plumes, the armours—friend and foe?
The cloth of gold, the rare brocade,
The mantles glittering to and fro?
The pomp, the pride, the royal show?
The cries of war and festival?
The youth, the grace, the charm, the glow?
Into the night go one and all.

The curtain falls, the play is played:
The Beggar packs beside the Beau;
The Monarch troops, and troops the Maid;
The Thunder huddles with the Snow.
Where are the revellers high and low?
The clashing swords? The lover's call?
The dancers gleaming row on row?
Into the night go one and all.

Envoy

Prince, in one common overthrow
The Hero tumbles with the Thrall:
As dust that drives, as straws that blow,
Into the night go one and all.

London Voluntaries

I Grave

St. Margaret's bells,
Quiring their innocent, old-world canticles,
Sing in the storied air,
All rosy-and-golden, as with memories
Of woods at evensong, and sands and seas
Disconsolate for that the night is nigh.
O, the low, lingering lights! The large last gleam
(Hark! how those brazen choristers cry and call!)
Touching these solemn ancientries, and there,
The silent River ranging tide-mark high
And the callow, grey-faced Hospital,
With the strange glimmer and glamour of a dream!
The Sabbath peace is in the slumbrous trees,
And from the wistful, the fast-widowing sky
(Hark! how those plangent comforters call and cry!)
Falls as in August plots late roseleaves fall.
The sober Sabbath stir—
Leisurely voices, desultory feet!—
Comes from the dry, dust-coloured street,
Where in their summer frocks the girls go by,
And sweethearts lean and loiter and confer,
Just as they did an hundred years ago,
Just as an hundred years to come they will:—
When you and I, Dear Love, lie lost and low,
And sweet-throats none our welkin shall fulfil,
Nor any sunset fade serene and slow;
But, being dead, we shall not grieve to die.

II Andante con moto

Forth from the dust and din,
The crush, the heat, the many-spotted glare,
The odour and sense of life and lust aflare,
The wrangle and jangle of unrests,

Let us take horse, Dear Heart, take horse and win—
As from swart August to the green lap of May—
To quietness and the fresh and fragrant breasts
Of the still, delicious night, not yet aware
In any of her innumerable nests
Of that first sudden plash of dawn,
Clear, sapphirine, luminous, large,
Which tells that soon the flowing springs of day
In deep and ever deeper eddies drawn
Forward and up, in wider and wider way,
Shall float the sands, and brim the shores,
On this our lith of the World, as round it roars
And spins into the outlook of the Sun
(The Lord's first gift, the Lord's especial charge),
With light, with living light, from marge to marge
Until the course He set and staked be run.

Through street and square, through square and street,
Each with his home-grown quality of dark
And violated silence, loud and fleet,
Waylaid by a merry ghost at every lamp,
The hansom wheels and plunges. Hark, O, hark,
Sweet, how the old mare's bit and chain
Ring back a rough refrain
Upon the marked and cheerful tramp
Of her four shoes! Here is the Park,
And O, the languid midsummer wafts adust,
The tired midsummer blooms!
O, the mysterious distances, the glooms
Romantic, the august
And solemn shapes! At night this City of Trees
Turns to a tryst of vague and strange
And monstrous Majesties,
Let loose from some dim underworld to range
These terrene vistas till their twilight sets:
When, dispossessed of wonderfulness, they stand
Beggared and common, plain to all the land
For stooks of leaves! And lo! the Wizard Hour,
His silent, shining sorcery winged with power!
Still, still the streets, between their carcanets

Of linking gold, are avenues of sleep.
But see how gable ends and parapets
In gradual beauty and significance
Emerge! And did you hear
That little twitter-and-cheep,
Breaking inordinately loud and clear
On this still, spectral, exquisite atmosphere?
'Tis a first nest at matins! And behold
A rakehell cat—how furtive and acold!
A spent witch homing from some infamous dance—
Obscene, quick-trotting, see her tip and fade
Through shadowy railings into a pit of shade!
And now! a little wind and shy,
The smell of ships (that earnest of romance),
A sense of space and water, and thereby
A lamplit bridge touching the troubled sky,
And look, O, look! a tangle of silver gleams
And dusky lights, our River and all his dreams,
His dreams that never save in our deaths can die.

What miracle is happening in the air,
Charging the very texture of the gray
With something luminous and rare?
The night goes out like an ill-parcelled fire,
And, as one lights a candle, it is day.
The extinguisher, that perks it like a spire
On the little formal church, is not yet green
Across the water: but the house-tops nigher,
The corner-lines, the chimneys—look how clean,
How new, how naked! See the batch of boats,
Here at the stairs, washed in the fresh-sprung beam!
And those are barges that were goblin floats,
Black, hag-steered, fraught with devilry and dream!
And in the piles the water frolics clear,
The ripples into loose rings wander and flee,
And we—we can behold that could but hear
The ancient River singing as he goes,
New-mailed in morning, to the ancient Sea.
The gas burns lank and jaded in its glass:
The old Ruffian soon shall yawn himself awake,

And light his pipe, and shoulder his tools, and take
His hobnailed way to work!

                    Let us too pass—
Pass ere the sun leaps and your shadow shows—
Through these long, blindfold rows
Of casements staring blind to right and left,
Each with his gaze turned inward on some piece
Of life in death's own likeness—Life bereft
Of living looks as by the Great Release—
Pass to an exquisite night's more exquisite close!

Reach upon reach of burial—so they feel,
These colonies of dreams! And as we steal
Homeward together, but for the buxom breeze,
Fitfully frolicking to heel
With news of dawn-drenched woods and tumbling seas,
We might—thus awed, thus lonely that we are—
Be wandering some dispeopled star,
Some world of memories and unbroken graves,
So broods the abounding Silence near and far:
Till even your footfall craves
Forgiveness of the majesty it braves.

III   Scherzando

Down through the ancient Strand
The spirit of October, mild and boon
And sauntering, takes his way
This golden end of afternoon,
As though the corn stood yellow in all the land,
And the ripe apples dropped to the harvest-moon.

Lo! the round sun, half-down the western slope—
Seen as along an unglazed telescope—
Lingers and lolls, loth to be done with day:
Gifting the long, lean, lanky street
And its abounding confluences of being
With aspects generous and bland;

Making a thousand harnesses to shine
As with new ore from some enchanted mine,
And every horse's coat so full of sheen
He looks new-tailored, and every 'bus feels clean,
And never a hansom but is worth the feeing;
And every jeweller within the pale
Offers a real Arabian Night for sale;
And even the roar
Of the strong streams of toil, that pause and pour
Eastward and westward, sounds suffused—
Seems as it were bemused
And blurred, and like the speech
Of lazy seas on a lotus-haunted beach—
With this enchanted lustrousness,
This mellow magic, that (as a man's caress
Brings back to some faded face, beloved before,
A heavenly shadow of the grace it wore
Ere the poor eyes were minded to beseech)
Old things transfigures, and you hail and bless
Their looks of long-lapsed loveliness once more:
Till Clement's, angular and cold and staid,
Gleams forth in glamour's very stuffs arrayed;
And Bride's, her aëry, unsubstantial charm
Through flight on flight of springing, soaring stone
Grown flushed and warm,
Laughs into life full-mooded and fresh-blown;
And the high majesty of Paul's
Uplifts a voice of living light, and calls—
Calls to his millions to behold and see
How goodly this his London Town can be!

For earth and sky and air
Are golden everywhere,
And golden with a gold so suave and fine
The looking on it lifts the heart like wine.
Trafalgar Square
(The fountains volleying golden glaze)
Shines like an angel-market. High aloft
Over his couchant Lions, in a haze
Shimmering and bland and soft,

A dust of chrysoprase,
Our Sailor takes the golden gaze
Of the saluting sun, and flames superb,
As once he flamed it on his ocean round.
The dingy dreariness of the picture-place,
Turned very nearly bright,
Takes on a luminous transiency of grace,
And shows no more a scandal to the ground.
The very blind man pottering on the kerb,
Among the posies and the ostrich feathers
And the rude voices touched with all the weathers
Of the long, varying year,
Shares in the universal alms of light.

The windows, with their fleeting, flickering fires,
The height and spread of frontage shining sheer,
The quiring signs, the rejoicing roofs and spires—
'Tis El Dorado—El Dorado plain,
The Golden City! And when a girl goes by,
Look! as she turns her glancing head,
A call of gold is floated from her ear!
Golden, all golden! In a golden glory,
Long-lapsing down a golden coasted sky,
The day, not dies but seems
Dispersed in wafts and drifts of gold, and shed
Upon a past of golden song and story
And memories of gold and golden dreams.

IV   Largo e mesto

Out of the poisonous East,
Over a continent of blight,
Like a maleficent Influence released
From the most squalid cellarage of hell,
The Wind-Fiend, the abominable—
The Hangman Wind that tortures temper and light—
Comes slouching, sullen and obscene,
Hard on the skirts of the embittered night;
And in a cloud unclean

Of excremental humours, roused to strife
By the operation of some ruinous change,
Wherever his evil mandate run and range,
Into a dire intensity of life,
A craftsman at his bench, he settles down
To the grim job of throttling London Town.

So, by a jealous lightlessness beset
That might have oppressed the dragons of old time
Crunching and groping in the abysmal slime,
A cave of cut-throat thoughts and villainous dreams,
Hag-rid and crying with cold and dirt and wet,
The afflicted City, prone from mark to mark
In shameful occultation, seems
A nightmare labyrinthine, dim and drifting,
With wavering gulfs and antic heights, and shifting,
Rent in the stuff of a material dark,
Wherein the lamplight, scattered and sick and pale,
Shows like the leper's living blotch of bale:
Uncoiling monstrous into street on street
Paven with perils, teeming with mischance,
Where man and beast go blindfold and in dread,
Working with oaths and threats and faltering feet
Somewhither in the hideousness ahead;
Working through wicked airs and deadly dews
That make the laden robber grin askance
At the good places in his black romance,
And the poor, loitering harlot rather choose
Go pinched and pined to bed
Than lurk and shiver and curse her wretched way
From arch to arch, scouting some threepenny prey.

Forgot his dawns and far-flushed afterglows,
His green garlands and windy eyots forgot,
The old Father-River flows,
His watchfires cores of menace in the gloom,
As he came oozing from the Pit, and bore,
Sunk in his filthily transfigured sides,
Shoals of dishonoured dead to tumble and rot
In the squalor of the universal shore:

His voices sounding through the gruesome air
As from the Ferry where the Boat of Doom
With her blaspheming cargo reels and rides:
The while his children, the brave ships,
No more adventurous and fair,
Nor tripping it light of heel as home-bound brides,
But infamously enchanted,
Huddle together in the foul eclipse,
Or feel their course by inches desperately,
As through a tangle of alleys murder-haunted,
From sinister reach to reach out—out—to sea.

And Death the while—
Death with his well-worn, lean, professional smile,
Death in his threadbare working trim—
Comes to your bedside, unannounced and bland,
And with expert, inevitable hand
Feels at your windpipe, fingers you in the lung,
Or flicks the clot well into the labouring heart:
Thus signifying unto old and young,
However hard of mouth or wild of whim,
'Tis time—'tis time by his ancient watch—to part
From books and women and talk and drink and art.
And you go humbly after him
To a mean suburban lodging: on the way
To what or where
Not Death, who is old and very wise, can say:
And you—how should you care
So long as, unreclaimed of hell,
The Wind-Fiend, the insufferable,
Thus vicious and thus patient, sits him down
To the black job of burking London Town?

V   Allegro maëstoso

Spring winds that blow
As over leagues of myrtle-blooms and may;
Bevies of spring clouds trooping slow,
Like matrons heavy bosomed and aglow

With the mild and placid pride of increase! Nay,
What makes this insolent and comely stream
Of appetence, this freshet of desire
(Milk from the wild breasts of the wilful Day!),
Down Piccadilly dance and murmur and gleam
In genial wave on wave and gyre on gyre?
Why does that nymph unparalleled splash and churn
The wealth of her enchanted urn
Till, over-billowing all between
Her cheerful margents, grey and living green,
It floats and wanders, glittering and fleeing,
An estuary of the joy of being?
Why should the lovely leafage of the Park
Touch to an ecstasy the act of seeing?
—Sure, sure my paramour, my Bride of Brides,
Lingering and flushed, mysteriously abides
In some dim, eye-proof angle of odorous dark,
Some smiling nook of green-and-golden shade,
In the divine conviction robed and crowned
The globe fulfils his immemorial round
But as the marrying-place of all things made!

There is no man, this deifying day,
But feels the primal blessing in his blood.
There is no woman but disdains—
The sacred impulse of the May
Brightening like sex made sunshine through her veins—
To vail the ensigns of her womanhood.
None but, rejoicing, flaunts them as she goes,
Bounteous in looks of her delicious best,
On her inviolable quest:
These with their hopes, with their sweet secrets those,
But all desirable and frankly fair,
As each were keeping some most prosperous tryst,
And in the knowledge went imparadised!
For look! a magical influence everywhere,
Look how the liberal and transfiguring air
Washes this inn of memorable meetings,
This centre of ravishments and gracious greetings,
Till, through its jocund loveliness of length

A tidal-race of lust from shore to shore,
A brimming reach of beauty met with strength,
It shines and sounds like some miraculous dream,
Some vision multitudinous and agleam,
Of happiness as it shall be evermore!

Praise God for giving
Through this His messenger among the days
His word the life He gave is thrice-worth living!
For Pan, the bountiful, imperious Pan—
Not dead, not dead, as impotent dreamers feigned,
But the gay genius of a million Mays
Renewing his beneficent endeavour!—
Still reigns and triumphs, as he hath triumphed and reigned
Since in the dim blue dawn of time
The universal ebb-and-flow began,
To sound his ancient music, and prevails,
By the persuasion of his mighty rhyme,
Here in this radiant and immortal street
Lavishly and omnipotently as ever
In the open hills, the undissembling dales,
The laughing-places of the juvenile earth.
For lo! the wills of man and woman meet,
Meet and are moved, each unto each endeared,
As once in Eden's prodigal bowers befell,
To share his shameless, elemental mirth
In one great act of faith: while deep and strong,
Incomparably nerved and cheered,
The enormous heart of London joys to beat
To the measures of his rough, majestic song;
The lewd, perennial, overmastering spell
That keeps the rolling universe ensphered,
And life, and all for which life lives to long,
Wanton and wondrous and for ever well.

To James McNeill Whistler

Under a stagnant sky,
Gloom out of gloom uncoiling into gloom,

The River, jaded and forlorn,
Welters and wanders wearily—wretchedly—on;
Yet in and out among the ribs
Of the old skeleton bridge, as in the piles
Of some dead lake-built city, full of skulls,
Worm-worn, rat-riddled, mouldy with memories,
Lingers to babble to a broken tune
(Once, O, the unvoiced music of my heart!)
So melancholy a soliloquy
It sounds as it might tell
The secret of the unending grief-in-grain,
The terror of Time and Change and Death,
That wastes this floating, transitory world.

What of the incantation
That forced the huddled shapes on yonder shore
To take and wear the night
Like a material majesty?
That touched the shafts of wavering fire
About this miserable welter and wash—
(River, O River of Journeys, River of Dreams!)—
Into long, shining signals from the panes
Of an enchanted pleasure-house,
Where life and life might live life lost in life
For ever and evermore?

O Death! O Change! O Time!
Without you, O, the insufferable eyes
Of these poor Might-Have-Beens,
These fatuous, ineffectual Yesterdays!

What Have I Done for You,
England, My England?

What have I done for you,
    England, my England?
What is there I would not do,
    England, my own?

With your glorious eyes austere,
As the Lord were walking near,
Whispering terrible things and dear
    As the Song on your bugles blown,
       England—
    Round the world on your bugles blown!

Where shall the watchful Sun,
    England, my England,
Match the master-work you've done,
    England, my own?
When shall he rejoice agen
Such a breed of mighty men
As come forward, one to ten,
    To the Song on your bugles blown,
       England—
    Down the years on your bugles blown?

Ever the faith endures,
    England, my England:—
"Take and break us: we are yours,
    "England, my own!
"Life is good, and joy runs high
"Between English earth and sky:
"Death is death; but we shall die
    "To the Song on your bugles blown,
       "England—
    "To the stars on your bugles blown!"

They call you proud and hard,
    England, my England:
You with worlds to watch and ward,
    England, my own!
You whose mailed hand keeps the keys
Of such teeming destinies
You could know nor dread nor ease
    Were the Song on your bugles blown,
       England,
    Round the Pit on your bugles blown!

Mother of Ships whose might,
England, my England,
Is the fierce old Sea's delight,
England, my own,
Chosen daughter of the Lord,
Spouse-in-Chief of the ancient sword,
There's the menace of the Word
In the Song on your bugles blown,
England—
Out of heaven on your bugles blown!

Invictus

Out of the night that covers me,
Black as the pit from pole to pole,
I thank whatever gods may be
For my unconquerable soul.

In the fell clutch of circumstance
I have not winced nor cried aloud:
Under the bludgeonings of chance
My head is bloody, but unbow'd.

Beyond this place of wrath and tears
Looms but the Horror of the shade,
And yet the menace of the years
Finds and shall find me unafraid.

It matters not how strait the gate,
How charged with punishments the scroll,
I am the master of my fate:
I am the captain of my soul.

A. E. Housman

ALFRED EDWARD HOUSMAN (1859–1936) was born in rural
Worcestershire, the eldest of a family of seven, and was educated at Bromsgrove School, where he won a scholarship to
St. John's College, Oxford. He failed "Greats," but after a
long interlude as a clerk in the Patent Office he became Professor of Latin at London University in 1892 and later Professor
of Latin at Cambridge. In spite of his late start, Housman
became one of the most respected classicists of his time, his
emendations to the Latin poet Manilius being regarded as the
standard commentary even today.

Housman was foremost a scholar and his devotion to poetry
sporadic, only two volumes of his verse being published during
his lifetime with a third appearing posthumously. The content
of his poetry is almost invariably pessimistic, frequently ironic;
stylistically he is traditional, almost conservative. In contrast
to many of his contemporaries, Housman's poetry is spare,
unadorned, and direct, its great achievement being its com-
bination of direct statement and passionate intensity, expressed
with extreme austerity and economy of diction.

LEAVE your home behind, lad,
  And reach your friends your hand,
And go, and luck with you
  While Ludlow tower shall stand.

Oh, come you home of Sunday
  When Ludlow streets are still
And Ludlow bells are calling
  To farm and lane and mill,

Or come you home of Monday
  When Ludlow market hums
And Ludlow chimes are playing
  "The conquering hero comes,"

Come you home a hero,
  Or come not home at all,
The lads you leave will mind you
  Till Ludlow tower shall fall.

And you will list the bugle
  That blows in lands of morn,
And make the foes of England
  Be sorry you were born.

And you till trump of doomsday
  On lands of morn may lie,
And make the hearts of comrades
  Be heavy where you die.

Leave your home behind you,
  Your friends by field and town:
Oh, town and field will mind you
  Till Ludlow tower is down.

On MOONLIT heath and lonesome bank
   The sheep beside me graze;
And yon the gallows used to clank
   Fast by the four cross ways.

A careless shepherd once would keep
   The flocks by moonlight there,
And high amongst the glimmering sheep
   The dead man stood on air.

They hang us now in Shrewsbury jail:
   The whistles blow forlorn,
And trains all night groan on the rail
   To men that die at morn.

There sleeps in Shrewsbury jail to-night,
   Or wakes, as may betide,
A better lad, if things went right,
   Than most that sleep outside.

And naked to the hangman's noose
   The morning clocks will ring
A neck God made for other use
   Than strangling in a string.

And sharp the link of life will snap,
   And dead on air will stand
Heels that held up as straight a chap
   As treads upon the land.

So here I'll watch the night and wait
   To see the morning shine,
When he will hear the stroke of eight
   And not the stroke of nine;

And wish my friend as sound a sleep
   As lads' I did not know,
That shepherded the moonlit sheep
   A hundred years ago.

ON YOUR midnight pallet lying,
    Listen, and undo the door:
Lads that waste the light in sighing
    In the dark should sigh no more;
Night should ease a lover's sorrow;
Therefore, since I go to-morrow,
    Pity me before.

In the land to which I travel,
    The far dwelling, let me say—
Once, if here the couch is gravel,
    In a kinder bed I lay,
And the breast the darnel smothers
Rested once upon another's
    When it was not clay.

WHEN I was one-and-twenty
    I heard a wise man say,
"Give crowns and pounds and guineas
    But not your heart away;
Give pearls away and rubies
    But keep your fancy free."
But I was one-and-twenty,
    No use to talk to me.

When I was one-and-twenty
    I heard him say again,
"The heart out of the bosom
    Was never given in vain;
'Tis paid with sighs a plenty
    And sold for endless rue."
And I am two-and-twenty,
    And oh, 'tis true, 'tis true.

With rue my heart is laden
  For golden friends I had,
For many a rose-lipt maiden
  And many a lightfoot lad.

By brooks too broad for leaping
  The lightfoot boys are laid;
The rose-lipt girls are sleeping
  In fields where roses fade.

"Terence, this is stupid stuff:
You eat your victuals fast enough;
There can't be much amiss, 'tis clear,
To see the rate you drink your beer.
But oh, good Lord, the verse you make,
It gives a chap the belly-ache.
The cow, the old cow, she is dead;
It sleeps well, the horned head:
We poor lads, 'tis our turn now
To hear such tunes as killed the cow.
Pretty friendship 'tis to rhyme
Your friends to death before their time
Moping melancholy mad:
Come, pipe a tune to dance to, lad."

  Why, if 'tis dancing you would be,
There's brisker pipes than poetry.
Say, for what were hop-yards meant,
Or why was Burton built on Trent?
Oh many a peer of England brews
Livelier liquor than the Muse,
And malt does more than Milton can
To justify God's ways to man.
Ale, man, ale's the stuff to drink
For fellows whom it hurts to think:

Look into the pewter pot
To see the world as the world's not.
And faith, 'tis pleasant till 'tis past:
The mischief is that 'twill not last.
Oh I have been to Ludlow fair
And left my necktie God knows where,
And carried half way home, or near,
Pints and quarts of Ludlow beer:
Then the world seemed none so bad,
And I myself a sterling lad;
And down in lovely muck I've lain,
Happy till I woke again.
Then I saw the morning sky:
Heigho, the tale was all a lie;
The world, it was the old world yet,
I was I, my things were wet,
And nothing now remained to do
But begin the game anew.

Therefore, since the world has still
Much good, but much less good than ill,
And while the sun and moon endure
Luck's a chance, but trouble's sure,
I'd face it as a wise man would,
And train for ill and not for good.
'Tis true, the stuff I bring for sale
Is not so brisk a brew as ale:
Out of a stem that scored the hand
I wrung it in a weary land.
But take it: if the smack is sour,
The better for the embittered hour;
It should do good to heart and head
When your soul is in my soul's stead;
And I will friend you, if I may
In the dark and cloudy day.

There was a king reigned in the East:
There, when kings will sit to feast,
They get their fill before they think
With poisoned meat and poisoned drink.

He gathered all that springs to birth
From the many-venomed earth;
First a little, thence to more,
He sampled all her killing store;
And easy, smiling, seasoned sound,
Sate the king when healths went round.
They put arsenic in his meat
And stared aghast to watch him eat;
They poured strychnine in his cup
And shook to see him drink it up:
They shook, they stared as white's their shirt:
Them it was their poison hurt.
—I tell the tale that I heard told.
Mithridates, he died old.

HER strong enchantments failing,
   Her towers of fear in wreck,
Her limbecks dried of poisons
   And the knife at her neck,

The Queen of air and darkness
   Begins to shrill and cry,
"O young man, O my slayer,
   To-morrow you shall die."

O Queen of air and darkness,
   I think 'tis truth you say,
And I shall die to-morrow;
   But you will die to-day.

THE chestnut casts his flambeaux, and the flowers
   Stream from the hawthorn on the wind away,
The doors clap to, the pane is blind with showers.
   Pass me the can, lad; there's an end of May.

There's one spoilt spring to scant our mortal lot,
   One season ruined of our little store.
May will be fine next year as like as not:
   Oh ay, but then we shall be twenty-four.

We for a certainty are not the first
   Have sat in taverns while the tempest hurled
Their hopeful plans to emptiness, and cursed
   Whatever brute and blackguard made the world.

It is in truth iniquity on high
   To cheat our sentenced souls of aught they crave,
And mar the merriment as you and I
   Fare on our long fool's-errand to the grave.

Iniquity it is; but pass the can.
   My lad, no pair of kings our mothers bore;
Our only portion is the estate of man:
   We want the moon, but we shall get no more.

If here to-day the cloud of thunder lours
   To-morrow it will hie on far behests;
The flesh will grieve on other bones than ours
   Soon, and the soul will mourn in other breasts.

The troubles of our proud and angry dust
   Are from eternity, and shall not fail.
Bear them we can, and if we can we must.
   Shoulder the sky, my lad, and drink your ale.

Parta Quies

Good-night; ensured release,
Imperishable peace
   Have these for yours,
While sea abides, and land,
And earth's foundations stand,
   And heaven endures.

When earth's foundations flee,
Nor sky, nor land, nor sea
   At all is found,
Content you, let them burn:
It is not your concern;
   Sleep on, sleep sound.

T. E. Hulme

THOMAS ERNEST HULME (1883–1917) was born at Endon, North Staffordshire, and attended the High School at Newcastle-under-Lyme before entering St. John's College, Cambridge. In 1904 he was sent down for taking part in a brawl, whereupon he followed his own intellectual inclinations in London for a couple of years, traveled in Canada and on the Continent, and was eventually re-admitted to Cambridge largely as a result of the recommendation he received from the French philosopher Bergson. He did not stay long at Cambridge, however, but proceeded to Berlin, where he studied German philosophy and psychology, then returned to London, where he soon became the center of a group of young intellectuals among whom were T. S. Eliot and Ezra Pound. He fought in the 1914–1918 war, was wounded in the spring of 1915, but returned to the front a few months later. He was killed near Nieupont in September, 1917.

Hulme was a philosopher rather than a poet, translating both Bergson and Sorel into English, but he also wrote some verse in an effort to exemplify the new kind of "hard, dry, and classical" poetry which he felt was appropriate to his civilization. It is this verse, no more than five poems in all, which he ironically entitled *The Complete Poetry of T. E. Hulme,* which qualifies him for inclusion in this anthology.

Autumn

A touch of cold in the Autumn night—
I walked abroad,
And saw the ruddy moon lean over a hedge
Like a red-faced farmer.
I did not stop to speak, but nodded,
And round about were the wistful stars
With white faces like town children.

The Embankment

(THE FANTASIA OF A FALLEN GENTLEMAN
ON A COLD AND BITTER NIGHT.)

Once, in finesse of fiddles found I ecstasy,
In a flash of gold heels on the hard pavement.
Now see I
That warmth's the very stuff of poesy.
Oh, God, make small
The old star-eaten blanket of the sky,
That I may fold it round me and in comfort lie.

Lionel Johnson

LIONEL PIGOT JOHNSON (1867–1902), born in Kent and educated at Winchester and New College, Oxford, achieved success both as a critic and as a poet. His *Art of Thomas Hardy* (1894) was widely praised, and his first volume of poetry published a year later also received favorable attention, but during the latter part of the eighteen-nineties he became noticeably alcoholic and increasingly withdrawn. Toward the end of his life his work rapidly declined, and in 1902 he died, supposedly after falling off a bar-stool in a pub in Fleet Street, London.

Johnson converted to Roman Catholicism in 1891 and later, largely as a result of his friendship with W. B. Yeats, became an active member of the Irish Literary Society, his poetry reflecting both these interests. Stylistically Johnson was a Parnassian. His "Note Upon the Practice and Theory of Verse at the Present Time Obtaining in France," published in Volume VI of *The Hobby Horse,* made clear his admiration for the meticulous precision of that school, and implied that English verse could profit from its example. Ezra Pound was an admirer of Johnson, especially insofar as he seemed to anticipate the Imagists, editing Johnson's *Collected Poems* for the Bodley Head in 1915.

By the Statue of
King Charles at Charing Cross

TO WILLIAM WATSON

Sombre and rich, the skies;
Great glooms, and starry plains.
Gently the night wind sighs;
Else a vast silence reigns.

The splendid silence clings
Around me: and around
The saddest of all kings
Crowned, and again discrowned.

Comely and calm, he rides
Hard by his own Whitehall:
Only the night wind glides:
No crowds, nor rebels, brawl.

Gone, too, his Court: and yet,
The stars his courtiers are:
Stars in their stations set;
And every wandering star.

Alone he rides, alone,
The fair and fatal king:
Dark night is all his own,
That strange and solemn thing.

Which are more full of fate:
The stars; or those sad eyes?
Which are more still and great:
Those brows; or the dark skies?

Although his whole heart yearn
In passionate tragedy:
Never was face so stern
With sweet austerity.

Vanquished in life, his death
By beauty made amends:
The passing of his breath
Won his defeated ends.

Brief life, and hapless? Nay:
Through death, life grew sublime.
Speak after sentence? Yea:
And to the end of time.

Armoured he rides, his head
Bare to the stars of doom:
He triumphs now, the dead,
Beholding London's gloom.

Our wearier spirit faints,
Vexed in the world's employ:
His soul was of the saints;
And art to him was joy.

King, tried in fires of woe!
Men hunger for thy grace:
And through the night I go,
Loving thy mournful face.

Yet, when the city sleeps;
When all the cries are still:
The stars and heavenly deeps
Work out a perfect will.

Mystic and Cavalier

TO HERBERT PERCY HORNE

Go from me: I am one of those, who fall.
What! hath no cold wind swept your heart at all,
In my sad company? Before the end,
    Go from me, dear my friend!

Yours are the victories of light: your feet
Rest from good toil, where rest is brave and sweet.
But after warfare in a mourning gloom,
    I rest in clouds of doom.

Have you not read so, looking in these eyes?
Is it the common light of the pure skies,
Lights up their shadowy depths? The end is set:
    Though the end be not yet.

When gracious music stirs, and all is bright,
And beauty triumphs through a courtly night;
When I too joy, a man like other men:
    Yet, am I like them, then?

And in the battle, when the horsemen sweep
Against a thousand deaths, and fall on sleep:
Who ever sought that sudden calm, if I
    Sought not? Yet, could not die.

Seek with thine eyes to pierce this crystal sphere:
Canst read a fate there, prosperous and clear?
Only the mists, only the weeping clouds:
    Dimness, and airy shrouds.

Beneath, what angels are at work? What powers
Prepare the secret of the fatal hours?
See! the mists tremble, and the clouds are stirred:
    When comes the calling word?

The clouds are breaking from the crystal ball,
Breaking and clearing: and I look to fall.
When the cold winds and airs of portent sweep,
    My spirit may have sleep.

O rich and sounding voices of the air!
Interpreters and prophets of despair:
Priests of a fearful sacrament! I come,
    To make with you mine home.

The Dark Angel

Dark Angel, with thine aching lust
To rid the world of penitence:
Malicious Angel, who still dost
My soul such subtile violence!

Because of thee, no thought, no thing,
Abides for me undesecrate:
Dark Angel, ever on the wing,
Who never reachest me too late!

When music sounds, then changest thou
Its silvery to a sultry fire:
Nor will thine envious heart allow
Delight untortured by desire.

Through thee, the gracious Muses turn
To Furies, O mine Enemy!
And all the things of beauty burn
With flames of evil ecstasy.

Because of thee, the land of dreams
Becomes a gathering place of fears:
Until tormented slumber seems
One vehemence of useless tears.

When sunlight glows upon the flowers,
Or ripples down the dancing sea:
Thou, with thy troop of passionate powers,
Beleaguerest, bewilderest, me.

Within the breath of autumn woods,
Within the winter silences:
Thy venomous spirit stirs and broods,
O Master of impieties!

The ardour of red flame is thine,
And thine the steely soul of ice:

Thou poisonest the fair design
Of nature, with unfair device.

Apples of ashes, golden bright;
Waters of bitterness, how sweet!
O banquet of a foul delight,
Prepared by thee, dark Paraclete!

Thou art the whisper in the gloom,
The hinting tone, the haunting laugh:
Thou art the adorner of my tomb,
The minstrel of mine epitaph.

I fight thee, in the Holy Name!
Yet, what thou dost, is what God saith:
Tempter! should I escape thy flame,
Thou wilt have helped my soul from Death:

The second Death, that never dies,
That cannot die, when time is dead:
Live Death, wherein the lost soul cries,
Eternally uncomforted.

Dark Angel, with thine aching lust!
Of two defeats, of two despairs:
Less dread, a change to drifting dust,
Than thine eternity of cares.

Do what thou wilt, thou shalt not so,
Dark Angel! triumph over me:
Lonely, unto the Lone I go;
Divine, to the Divinity.

To a Passionist

Clad in a vestment wrought with passion-flowers;
Celebrant of one Passion; called by name
Passionist: is thy world, one world with ours?
Thine, a like heart? Thy very soul, the same?

Thou pleadest an eternal sorrow: we
Praise the still changing beauty of this earth.
Passionate good and evil, thou dost see:
Our eyes behold the dreams of death and birth.

We love the joys of men: we love the dawn,
Red with the sun, and with the pure dew pearled
Thy stern soul feels, after the sun withdrawn,
How much pain goes to perfecting the world.

Canst thou be right? Is thine the very truth?
Stands then our life in so forlorn a state?
Nay, but thou wrongest us: thou wrong'st our youth,
Who dost our happiness compassionate.

And yet! and yet! O royal Calvary!
Whence divine sorrow triumphed through years past:
Could ages bow before mere memory?
Those passion-flowers must blossom, to the last.

Purple they bloom, the splendour of a King:
Crimson they bleed, the sacrament of Death:
About our thrones and pleasaunces they cling,
Where guilty eyes read, what each blossom saith.

The Church of a Dream

TO BERNHARD BERENSON

Sadly the dead leaves rustle in the whistling wind,
Around the weather-worn, gray church, low down the vale:
The Saints in golden vesture shake before the gale;
The glorious windows shake, where still they dwell enshrined;
Old Saints by long dead, shrivelled hands, long since designed:
There still, although the world autumnal be, and pale,
Still in their golden vesture the old saints prevail;
Alone with Christ, desolate else, left by mankind.

Only one ancient Priest offers the Sacrifice,
Murmuring holy Latin immemorial:
Swaying with tremulous hands the old censer full of spice,
In gray, sweet incense clouds; blue, sweet clouds mystical:
To him, in place of men, for he is old, suffice
Melancholy remembrances and vesperal.

The Destroyer of a Soul

I hate you with a necessary hate.
First, I sought patience: passionate was she:
My patience turned in very scorn of me,
That I should dare forgive a sin so great,
As this, through which I sit disconsolate;
Mourning for that live soul, I used to see;
Soul of a saint, whose friend I used to be:
Till you came by! a cold, corrupting, fate.

Why come you now? You, whom I cannot cease
With pure and perfect hate to hate? Go, ring
The death-bell with a deep, triumphant toll!
Say you, my friend sits by me still? Ah, peace!
Call you this thing my friend? this nameless thing?
This living body, hiding its dead soul?

Our Lady of the Snows

UPON READING THE POEM OF THAT NAME IN THE
UNDERWOODS OF MR. STEVENSON.

Far from the world, far from delight,
Distinguishing not day from night;
Vowed to one sacrifice of all
The happy things, that men befall;
Pleading one sacrifice, before
Whom sun and sea and wind adore;

Far from earth's comfort, far away,
We cry to God, we cry and pray
For men, who have the common day.
Dance, merry world! and sing: but we,
Hearing, remember Calvary:
Get gold, and thrive you! but the sun
Once paled; and the centurion
Said: *This dead man was God's own Son.*
Think you, we shrink from common toil,
Works of the mart, works of the soil;
That, prisoners of strong despair,
We breathe this melancholy air;
Forgetting the dear calls of race,
And bonds of house, and ties of place;
That, cowards, from the field we turn,
And heavenward, in our weakness, yearn?
Unjust! unkind! while you despise
Our lonely years, our mournful cries:
You are the happier for our prayer;
The guerdon of our souls, you share.
Not in such feebleness of heart,
We play our solitary part;
Not fugitives of battle, we
Hide from the world, and let things be:
But rather, looking over earth,
Between the bounds of death and birth;
And sad at heart, for sorrow and sin,
We wondered, where might help begin.
And on our wonder came God's choice,
A sudden light, a clarion voice,
Clearing the dark, and sounding clear:
And we obeyed: behold us, here!
In prison bound, but with your chains:
Sufferers, but of alien pains.
Merry the world, and thrives apace,
Each in his customary place:
Sailors upon the carrying sea,
Shepherds upon the pasture lea,
And merchants of the town; and they,

Who march to death, the fighting way;
And there are lovers in the spring,
With those, who dance, and those, who sing:
The commonwealth of every day,
Eastward and westward, far away.
Once the sun paled; once cried aloud
The Roman, from beneath the cloud:
This day the Son of God is dead!
Yet heed men, what the Roman said?
They heed not: we then heed for them,
The mindless of Jerusalem;
Careless, they live and die: but we
Care, in their stead, for Calvary.
O joyous men and women! strong,
To urge the wheel of life along,
With strenuous arm, and cheerful strain,
And wisdom of laborious brain:
We give our life, our heart, our breath,
That you may live to conquer death;
That, past your tomb, with souls in health,
Joy may be yours, and blessed wealth;
Through vigils of the painful night,
Our spirits with your tempters fight:
For you, for you, we live alone,
Where no joy comes, where cold winds moan:
Nor friends have we, nor have we foes;
Our Queen is of the lonely Snows.
Ah! and sometimes, our prayers between,
Come sudden thoughts of what hath been:
Dreams! And from dreams, once more we fall
To prayer: *God save, Christ keep, them all.*
And thou, who knowest not these things,
Hearken, what news our message brings!
Our toils, thy joy of life forgot:
Our lives of prayer forget thee not.

Ninety-Eight

TO R. BARRY O'BRIEN

Who fears to speak of Ninety-Eight?
He, who despairs of Ireland still:
Whose paltry soul finds nothing great
In honest failure: he, whose will,
Feeble and faint in days of gloom,
Takes old defeat for final doom.

Who fears to speak of Ninety-Eight?
The man, who fears to speak of death:
Who clings and clasps the knees of fate,
And whimpers with his latest breath:
Who hugs his comfort to his heart,
And dares not play a Christian part.

Who fears to speak of Ninety-Eight?
The renegade, who sells his trust:
Whose love has rottened into hate,
Whose hopes have withered into dust:
He, who denies, and deems it mad,
The faith, his nobler boyhood had.

Who fears to speak of Ninety-Eight?
The enemy of Ireland fears!
For Ireland undegenerate
Keeps yet the spirit of old years:
He sees, in visions of the night,
A nation arming for the right.

Who fears to speak of Ninety-Eight?
Not he, who hates a poisonous peace:
For, while the days of triumph wait,
And till the days of sorrow cease,
He, with the Lord of Hosts his friend,
Will fight for Ireland to the end.

Let sword cross sword, or thought meet thought:
One fire of battle thrills them both.
Deliverance only can be wrought
By warfare without stay or sloth:
And by your prayers at Heaven's high gate,
True hearts, that beat in Ninety-Eight!

Nihilism

TO SAMUEL SMITH

Among immortal things not made with hands:
Among immortal things, dead hands have made:
Under the Heavens, upon the Earth, there stands
Man's life, my life: of life I am afraid.

Where silent things, and unimpassioned things,
Where things of nought, and things decaying, are:
I shall be calm soon, with the calm death brings.
The skies are gray there, without any star.

Only the rest! the rest! Only the gloom,
Soft and long gloom! The pausing from all thought!
My life, I cannot taste: the eternal tomb
Brings me the peace, which life has never brought.

For all the things I do, and do not well;
All the forced drawings of a mortal breath:
Are as the hollow music of a bell,
That times the slow approach of perfect death.

Rudyard Kipling

RUDYARD KIPLING (1865–1936) was born in Bombay, India, but educated in England. He returned to India and became a journalist, his first stories appearing in the local newspapers around 1885, his first volume of verse appearing one year later. As his fame increased he moved to London, married an American, and moved with her to Brattleboro, Vermont, where she had some property. In 1896 Kipling returned to England, and in 1900 he served as a correspondent during the Boer War. During the 1914–1918 war he turned to anti-German propaganda, becoming a near fanatic in his patriotism. In 1907 he received the Nobel Prize for Literature, and in 1933 was elected foreign associate of the French Academy. His later years he passed uneventfully in rural Sussex, dying in London in 1936.

Kipling's fame is as dependent on his fiction as on his verse, probably the former finding more sympathetic readers than the latter. In both he preaches a code of stoicism, political conservatism, and the importance of Great Britain's imperialist mission. Many of his contemporaries believed that his poetry hardly deserved that name, but in recent years T. S. Eliot in particular has drawn attention to Kipling's variety and ingenuity, giving him credit for helping to free English poetry from its restrictive Victorian technical conventions.

M'Andrew's Hymn

Lord, Thou hast made this world below the shadow of a dream,
An', taught by time, I tak' it so—exceptin' always Steam.
From coupler-flange to spindle-guide I see Thy Hand, O God—
Predestination in the stride o' yon connectin'-rod.
John Calvin might ha' forged the same—enorrmous, certain,
    slow—
Ay, wrought it in the furnace-flame—*my* "Institutio."
I cannot get my sleep to-night; old bones are hard to please;
I 'll stand the middle watch up here—alone wi' God an' these
My engines, after ninety days o' race an' rack an' strain
Through all the seas of all Thy world, slam-bangin' home again.
Slam-bang too much—they knock a wee—the crosshead-gibs are
    loose,
But thirty thousand mile o' sea has gied them fair excuse. . . .
Fine, clear an' dark—a full-draught breeze, wi' Ushant out o'
    sight,
An' Ferguson relievin' Hay. Old girl, ye 'll walk to-night!
His wife 's at Plymouth. . . . Seventy—One—Two—Three since
    he began—
Three turns for Mistress Ferguson . . . and who 's to blame the
    man?
There 's none at any port for me, by drivin' fast or slow,
Since Elsie Campbell went to Thee, Lord, thirty years ago.
(The year the *Sarah Sands* was burned. Oh roads we used to
    tread,
Fra' Maryhill to Pollokshaws—fra' Govan to Parkhead!)
Not but they 're ceevil on the Board. Ye 'll hear Sir Kenneth
    say:
"Good morrn, M'Andrew! Back again? An' how 's your bilge
    to-day?"
Miscallin' technicalities but handin' me my chair
To drink Madeira wi' three Earls—the auld Fleet Engineer
That started as a boiler-whelp—when steam and he were low.
I mind the time we used to serve a broken pipe wi' tow!
Ten pound was all the pressure then— Eh! Eh!—a man wad
    drive;
An' here, our workin' gauges give one hunder sixty-five!

We 're creepin' on wi' each new rig—less weight an' larger power:
There 'll be the loco-boiler next an' thirty knots an' hour!
Thirty an' more. What I ha' seen since ocean-steam began
Leaves me no doot for the machine: but what about the man?
The man that counts, wi' all his runs, one million mile o' sea:
Four time the span from earth to moon. . . . How far, O Lord,
    from Thee?
That wast beside him night an' day. Ye mind my first typhoon?
It scoughed the skipper on his way to jock wi' the saloon.
Three feet were on the stokehold-floor—just slappin' to an' fro—
An' cast me on a furnace-door. I have the marks to show.
Marks! I ha' marks o' more than burns—deep in my soul an'
    black,
An' times like this, when things go smooth, my wickudness comes
    back.
The sins o' four an' forty years, all up an' down the seas,
Clack an' repeat like valves half-fed. . . . Forgie 's our trespasses!
Nights when I 'd come on deck to mark, wi' envy in my gaze
The couples kittlin' in the dark between the funnel-stays;
Years when I raked the Ports wi' pride to fill my cup o' wrong—
Judge not, O Lord, my steps aside at Gay Street in Hong-Kong!
Blot out the wastrel hours of mine in sin when I abode—
Jane Harrigan's an' Number Nine, The Reddick an' Grant Road!
An' waur than all—my crownin' sin—rank blasphemy an' wild.
I was not four and twenty then—Ye wadna judge a child?
I 'd seen the Tropics first that run—new fruit, new smells, new
    air—
How could I tell—blind-fou wi' sun—the Deil was lurkin' there?
By day like playhouse-scenes the shore slid past our sleepy eyes;
By night those soft, lasceevious stars leered from those velvet
    skies,
In port (we used no cargo-steam) I 'd daunder down the streets—
An ijjit grinnin' in a dream—for shells an' parrakeets,
An' walkin'-sticks o' carved bamboo an' blowfish stuffed an'
    dried—
Fillin' my bunk wi' rubbishry the Chief put overside.
Till, off Sambawa Head, Ye mind, I heard a land-breeze ca',
Milk-warm wi' breath o' spice an' bloom: "M'Andrew, come
    awa'!"
Firm, clear an' low—no haste, no hate—the ghostly whisper went,

Just statin' eevidential facts beyon' all argument:
"Your mither's God 's a graspin' deil, the shadow o' yoursel',
"Got out o' books by meenisters clean daft on Heaven an' Hell.
"They mak' him in the Broomielaw, o' Glasgie cold an' dirt,
"A jealous, pridefu' fetich, lad, that 's only strong to hurt,
"Ye 'll not go back to Him again an' kiss His red-hot rod,
"But come wi' Us" (Now, who were *They?)* "an' know the Leevin'
      God,
"That does not kipper souls for sport or break a life in jest,
"But swells the ripenin' cocoanuts an' ripes the woman's breast."
An' there it stopped: cut off: no more; that quiet, certain voice—
For me, six months o' twenty-four, to leave or take at choice.
'T was on me like a thunderclap—it racked me through an'
      through—
Temptation past the show o' speech, unnameable an' new—
The Sin against the Holy Ghost? . . . An' under all, our screw.
That storm blew by but left behind her anchor-shiftin' swell.
Thou knowest all my 'heart an' mind, Thou knowest, Lord, I
      fell.—
Third on the *Mary Gloster* then, and first that night in Hell!
Yet was Thy hand beneath my head, about my feet Thy care—
Fra' Deli clear to Torres Strait, the trial o' despair,
But when we touched the Barrier Reef Thy answer to my prayer!
We dared not run that sea by night but lay an' held our fire,
An' I was drowsin' on the hatch—sick—sick wi' doubt an' tire:
"Better the sight of eyes that see than wanderin' o' desire!"
Ye mind that word? Clear as our gongs—again, an' once again,
When rippin' down through coral-trash ran out our moorin'-
      chain;
An' by Thy Grace I had the Light to see my duty plain.
Light on the engine-room—no more—bright as our carbons burn.
I 've lost it since a thousand times, but never past return!

                              *   *   *

Obsairve. Per annum we 'll have here two thousand souls
      aboard—
Think not I dare to justify myself before the Lord,
But—aaverage fifteen hunder souls safe-borne fra' port to port—
I *am* o' service to my kind. Ye wadna blame the thought?
Maybe they steam from Grace to Wrath—to sin by folly led,—
It isna mine to judge their path—their lives are on my head.

Mine at the last—when all is done it all comes back to me,
The fault that leaves six thousand ton a log upon the sea.
We 'll tak' one stretch—three weeks an' odd by any road ye
    steer—
Fra' Cape Town east to Wellington—ye need an engineer.
Fail there—ye 've time to weld your shaft—ay, eat it, ere ye 're
    spoke;
Or make Kerguelen under sail—three jiggers burned wi' smoke!
An' home again—the Rio run: it 's no child's play to go
Steamin' to bell for fourteen days o' snow an' floe an' blow—
The bergs like kelpies overside that girn an' turn an' shift
Whaur, grindin' like the Mills o' God, goes by the big South
    drift.
(Hail, Snow and Ice that praise the Lord: I 've met them at their
    work,
An' wished we had anither route or they anither kirk.)
Yon 's strain, hard strain, o' head an' hand, for though Thy
    Power brings
All skill to naught, Ye 'll understand a man must think o' things.
Then, at the last, we 'll get to port an' hoist their baggage clear—
The passengers, wi' gloves an' canes—an' this is what I 'll hear:
"Well, thank ye for a pleasant voyage. The tender 's comin' now."
While I go testin' follower-bolts an' watch the skipper bow.
They 've words for every one but me—shake hands wi' half the
    crew,
Except the dour Scots engineer, the man they never knew.
An' yet I like the wark for all we 've dam' few pickin's here—
No pension, an' the most we 'll earn 's four hunder pound a year.
Better myself abroad? Maybe. *I 'd* sooner starve than sail
Wi' such as call a snifter-rod *ross*. . . . French for nightingale.
Commeesion on my stores? Some do; but I cannot afford
To lie like stewards wi' patty-pans. I 'm older than the Board.
A bonus on the coal I save? Ou ay, the Scots are close,
But when I grudge the strength Ye gave I 'll grudge their food
    to *those*.
(There 's bricks that I might recommend—an' clink the fire-bars
    cruel.
No! Welsh—Wangarti at the worst—an' damn all patent fuel!)
Inventions? Ye must stay in port to mak' a patent pay.
My Deeferential Valve-Gear taught me how that business lay,

I blame no chaps wi' clearer head for aught they make or sell.
I found that I could not invent an' look to these as well.
So, wrestled wi' Apollyon—Nah!—fretted like a bairn—
But burned the workin'-plans last run wi' all I hoped to earn.
Ye know how hard an Idol dies, an' what that meant to me—
E'en tak' it for a sacrifice acceptable to Thee. . . .
Below there! Oiler! What 's your wark? Ye find it runnin' hard?
Ye need n't swill the cup wi' oil—this is n't the Cunard!
Ye thought? Ye are not paid to think. Go, sweat that off again!
Tck! Tck! It 's deeficult to sweer nor tak' The Name in vain!
Men, ay an' women, call me stern. Wi' these to oversee
Ye 'll note I 've little time to burn on social repartee.
The bairns see what their elders miss; they 'll hunt me to an' fro,
Till for the sake of—well, a kiss—I tak' 'em down below.
That minds me of our Viscount loon—Sir Kenneth's kin—the chap
Wi' Russia leather tennis-shoon an' spar-decked yachtin'-cap.
I showed him round last week, o'er all—an' at the last says he:
"Mister M'Andrew, don't you think steam spoils romance at sea?"
Damned ijjit! I 'd been doon that morn to see what ailed the
    throws,
Manholin', on my back—the cranks three inches off my nose.
Romance! Those first-class passengers they like it very well,
Printed an' bound in little books; but why don't poets tell?
I'm sick of all their quirks an' turns—the loves an' doves they
    dream—
Lord, send a man like Robbie Burns to sing the Song o' Steam!
To match wi' Scotia's noblest speech yon orchestra sublime
Whaurto—uplifted like the Just—the tail-rods mark the time.
The crank-throws give the double-bass, the feed pump sobs an'
    heaves,
An' now the main eccentrics start their quarrel on the sheaves:
Her time, her own appointed time, the rocking link-head bides,
Till—hear that note?—the rod's return whings glimmerin' through
    the guides.
They 're all awa! True beat, full power, the clangin' chorus goes
Clear to the tunnel where they sit, my purrin' dynamoes
Interdependence absolute, foreseen, ordained, decreed,
To work, Ye 'll note, at any tilt an' every rate o' speed.
Fra skylight-lift to furnace-bars, backed, bolted, braced an' stayed,
An' singin' like the Mornin' Stars for joy that they are made;

While, out o' touch o' vanity, the sweatin' thrust-block says:
"Not unto us the praise, or man—not unto us the praise!"
Now, a' together, hear them lift their lesson—theirs an' mine:
"Law, Orrder, Duty an' Restraint, Obedience, Discipline!"
Mill forge an' try-pit taught them that when roarin' they arose,
An' whiles I wonder if a soul was gien them wi' the blows.
Oh for a man to weld it then, in one trip-hammer strain,
Till even first-class passengers could tell the meanin' plain!
But no one cares except mysel' that serve an' understand
My seven thousand horse-power here. Eh, Lord! They 're grand—
 they 're grand!
Uplift am I? When first in store the new-made beasties stood,
Were Ye cast down that breathed the Word declarin' all things
 good?
Not so! O' that warld-liftin' joy no after-fall could vex,
Ye've left a glimmer still to cheer the Man—the Arrtifex!
That holds, in spite o' knock and scale, o' friction, waste an' slip,
An' by that light—now, mark my word—we 'll build the Perfect
 Ship.
I 'll never last to judge her lines or take her curve—not I.
But I ha' lived an' I ha' worked. 'Be thanks to Thee, Most High!
An' I ha' done what I ha' done—judge Thou if ill or well—
Always Thy Grace preventin' me. . . .
      Losh! Yon 's the "Stand by" bell.
Pilot so soon? His flare it is. The mornin'-watch is set.
Well, God be thanked, as I was sayin', I 'm no Pelagian yet.
Now I 'll tak' on. . . .
  'Morrn, Ferguson. Man, have ye ever thought
What your good leddy costs in coal? . . . I 'll burn 'em down to
 port.

A Song of the English

Fair is our lot—O goodly is our heritage!
(Humble ye, my people, and be fearful in your mirth!)
   For the Lord our God most High
   He hath made the deep as dry,
He hath smote for us a pathway to the ends of all the Earth!

Yea, though we sinned—and our rulers went from righteousness—
Deep in all dishonour though we stained our garments' hem.
   Oh be ye not dismayed,
   Though we stumbled and we strayed,
We were led by evil counsellors—the Lord shall deal with them!

Hold ye the Faith—the Faith our Fathers sealèd us;
Whoring not with visions—overwise and overstale.
   Except ye pay the Lord
   Single heart and single sword,
Of your children in their bondage He shall ask them treble-tale!

Keep ye the Law—be swift in all obedience—
Clear the land of evil, drive the road and bridge the ford.
   Make ye sure to each his own
   That he reap where he hath sown;
By the peace among Our peoples let men know we serve the
     Lord!

*   *   *

Hear now a song—a song of broken interludes—
A song of little cunning; of a singer nothing worth.
   Through the naked words and mean
   May ye see the truth between
As the singer knew and touched it in the ends of all the Earth!

Our Lady of the Snows

(CANADIAN PREFERENTIAL TARIFF, 1897)

A nation spoke to a Nation,
   A Queen sent word to a Throne:
"Daughter am I in my mother's house,
   But mistress in my own.
The gates are mine to open,
   As the gates are mine to close,
And I set my house in order,"
   Said our Lady of the Snows.

"Neither with laughter nor weeping,
   Fear or the child's amaze—
Soberly under the White Man's law
   My white men go their ways.
Not for the Gentiles' clamour—
   Insult or threat of blows—
Bow we the knee to Baal,"
   Said our Lady of the Snows.

"My speech is clean and single,
   I talk of common things—
Words of the wharf and the market-place
   And the ware the merchant brings:
Favour to those I favour,
   But a stumbling-block to any foes.
Many there be that hate us,"
   Said our Lady of the Snows.

"I called my chiefs to council
   In the din of a troubled year;
For the sake of a sign ye would not see,
   And a word ye would not hear.
This is our message and answer;
   This is the path we chose:
For we be also a people,"
   Said our Lady of the Snows.

"Carry the word to my sisters—
  To the Queens of the East and the South.
I have proven faith in the Heritage
  By more than the word of the mouth.
They that are wise may follow
  Ere the world's war-trumpet blows,
But I—I am first in the battle,"
  Said our Lady of the Snows.

A Nation spoke to a Nation,
  A Throne sent word to a Throne:
"Daughter am I in my mother's house,
  But mistress in my own.
The gates are mine to open,
  As the gates are mine to close,
And I abide by my Mother's House,"
  Said our Lady of the Snows.

The Ballad of East and West

Oh, East is East, and West is West, and never the twain shall
  meet,
Till Earth and Sky stand presently at God's great Judgment Seat;
But there is neither East nor West, Border, nor Breed, nor Birth,
When two strong men stand face to face, tho' they come from the
  ends of the earth!

Kamal is out with twenty men to raise the Borderside,
And he has lifted the Colonel's mare that is the Colonel's pride:
He has lifted her out of the stable-door between the dawn and
  the day,
And turned the calkins upon her feet, and ridden her far away.
Then up and spoke the Colonel's son that led a troop of the
  Guides:
"Is there never a man of all my men can say where Kamal
  hides?"
Then up and spoke Mohammed Khan, the son of the Ressaldar:
"If ye know the track of the morning-mist, ye know where his
  pickets are.

"At dusk he harries the Abazai—at dawn he is into Bonair,
"But he must go by Fort Bukloh to his own place to fare,
"So if ye gallop to Fort Bukloh as fast as a bird can fly,
"By the favour of God ye may cut him off ere he win to the
    Tongue of Jagai.
"But if he be past the Tongue of Jagai, right swiftly turn ye
    then,
"For the length and the breadth of that grisly plain is sown with
    Kamal's men.
"There is rock to the left, and rock to the right, and low lean
    thorn between,
"And ye may hear a breech-bolt snick where never a man is seen."
The Colonel's son has taken a horse, and a raw rough dun was
    he,
With the mouth of a bell and the heart of Hell and the head of
    a gallows-tree.
The Colonel's son to the Fort has won, they bid him stay to eat—
Who rides at the tail of a Border thief, he sits not long at his
    meat.
He 's up and away from Fort Bukloh as fast as he can fly,
Till he was aware of his father's mare in the gut of the Tongue
    of Jagai,
Till he was aware of his father's mare with Kamal upon her
    back,
And when he could spy the white of her eye, he made the pistol
    crack.
He has fired once, he has fired twice, but the whistling ball went
    wide.
"Ye shoot like a soldier," Kamal said. "Show now if ye can ride."
It 's up and over the Tongue of Jagai, as blown dust-devils go,
The dun he fled like a stag of ten, but the mare like a barren doe.
The dun he leaned against the bit and slugged his head above,
But the red mare played with the snaffle-bars, as a maiden plays
    with a glove.
There was rock to the left and rock to the right, and low lean
    thorn between,
And thrice he heard a breech-bolt snick tho' never a man was
    seen.
They have ridden the low moon out of the sky, their hoofs drum
    up the dawn,

The dun he went like a wounded bull, but the mare like a new-
roused fawn.
The dun he fell at a water-course—in a woeful heap fell he,
And Kamal has turned the red mare back, and pulled the rider
free.
He has knocked the pistol out of his hand—small room was there
to strive,
" 'T was only by favour of mine," quoth he, "ye rode so long
alive:
"There was not a rock for twenty mile, there was not a clump of
tree,
"But covered a man of my own men with his rifle cocked on his
knee.
"If I had raised my bridle-hand, as I have held it low,
"The little jackals that flee so fast were feasting all in a row:
"If I had bowed my head on my breast, as I have held it high,
"The kite that whistles above us now were gorged till she could
not fly."
Lightly answered the Colonel's son: "Do good to bird and beast,
"But count who come for the broken meats before thou makest a
feast.
"If there should follow a thousand swords to carry my bones
away,
"Belike the price of a jackal's meal were more than a thief could
pay.
"They will feed their horse on the standing crop, their men on
the garnered grain,
"The thatch of the byres will serve their fires when all the cattle
are slain.
"But if thou thinkest the price be fair,—thy brethren wait to
sup,
"The hound is kin to the jackal-spawn,—howl, dog, and call
them up!
"And if thou thinkest the price be high, in steer and gear and
stack,
"Give me my father's mare again, and I'll fight my own way
back!"
Kamal has gripped him by the hand and set him upon his feet.
"No talk shall be of dogs," said he, "when wolf and grey wolf
meet.

"May I eat dirt if thou hast hurt of me in deed or breath;
"What dam of lances brought thee forth to jest at the dawn with
 Death?"
Lightly answered the Colonel's son: "I hold by the blood of my
 clan:
"Take up the mare for my father's gift—by God, she has carried
 a man!"
The red mare ran to the Colonel's son, and nuzzled against his
 breast;
"We be two strong men," said Kamal then, "but she loveth the
 younger best.
"So she shall go with a lifter's dower, my turquoise-studded rein,
"My broidered saddle and saddle-cloth, and silver stirrups twain."
The Colonel's son a pistol drew, and held it muzzle-end,
"Ye have taken the one from a foe," said he; "will ye take the
 mate from a friend?"
"A gift for a gift," said Kamal straight; "a limb for the risk of
 a limb.
"Thy father has sent his son to me, I'll send my son to him!"
With that he whistled his only son, that dropped from a
 mountain-crest—
He trod the ling like a buck in spring, and he looked like a
 lance in rest.
"Now here is thy master," Kamal said, "who leads a troop of the
 Guides,
"And thou must ride at his left side as shield on shoulder rides.
"Till Death or I cut loose the tie, at camp and board and bed,
"Thy life is his—thy fate it is to guard him with thy head.
"So, thou must eat the White Queen's meat, and all her foes are
 thine,
"And thou must harry thy father's hold for the peace of the
 Border-line,
"And thou must make a trooper tough and hack thy way to
 power—
"Belike they will raise thee to Ressaldar when I am hanged in
 Peshawur."
They have looked each other between the eyes, and there they
 found no fault,
They have taken the Oath of the Brother-in-Blood on leavened
 bread and salt:

They have taken the Oath of the Brother-in-Blood on fire and
    fresh-cut sod,
On the hilt and the haft of the Khyber knife, and the Wondrous
    Names of God.
The Colonel's son he rides the mare and Kamal's boy the dun,
And two have come back to Fort Bukloh where there went forth
    but one.
And when they drew to the Quarter-Guard, full twenty swords
    flew clear—
There was not a man but carried his feud with the blood of the
    mountaineer.
"Ha' done! ha' done!" said the Colonel's son. "Put up the steel
    at your sides!
"Last night ye had struck at a Border thief—to-night 't is a man
    of the Guides!"

Oh, East is East, and West is West, and never the twain shall meet,
Till Earth and Sky stand presently at God's great Judgment Seat;
But there is neither East nor West, Border, nor Breed, nor Birth,
When two strong men stand face to face, tho' they come from the
    ends of the earth!

The Islanders

No doubt but ye are the People—your throne is above the King's.
Whoso speaks in your presence must say acceptable things
Bowing the head in worship, bending the knee in fear—
Bringing the word well smoothen—such as a King should hear.

Fenced by your careful fathers, ringed by your leaden seas,
Long did ye wake in quiet and long lie down at ease;
Till ye said of Strife, "What is it?" of the Sword, "It is far from
    our ken";
Till ye made a sport of your shrunken hosts and a toy of your
    armed men.
Ye stopped your ears to the warning—ye would neither look
    nor heed—
Ye set your leisure before their toil and your lusts above their
    need.

Because of your witless learning and your beasts of warren and
    chase,
Ye grudged your sons to their service and your fields for their
    camping-place.
Ye forced them glean in the highways the straw for the bricks
    they brought;
Ye forced them follow in byways the craft that ye never taught.
Ye hindered and hampered and crippled; ye thrust out of sight
    and away
Those that would serve you for honour and those that served
    you for pay.
Then were the judgments loosened; then was your shame revealed,
At the hands of a little people, few but apt in the field.
Yet ye were saved by a remnant (and your land's long-suffering
    star),
When your strong men cheered in their millions while your
    striplings went to the war.
Sons of the sheltered city—unmade, unhandled, unmeet—
Ye pushed them raw to the battle as ye picked them raw from
    the street.
And what did ye look they should compass? Warcraft learned in
    a breath,
Knowledge unto occasion at the first far view of Death?
So! And ye train your horses and the dogs ye feed and prize?
How are the beasts more worthy than the souls you sacrifice?
But ye said, "Their valour shall show them"; but ye said, "The
    end is close."
And ye sent them comfits and pictures to help them harry your
    foes,
And ye vaunted your fathomless power, and ye flaunted your
    iron pride,
Ere—ye fawned on the Younger Nations for the men who could
    shoot and ride!
Then ye returned to your trinkets; then ye contented your souls
With the flannelled fools at the wicket or the muddied oafs at
    the goals.
Given to strong delusion, wholly believing a lie,
Ye saw that the land lay fenceless, and ye let the months go by
Waiting some easy wonder: hoping some saving sign—
Idle—openly idle—in the lee of the forespent Line.

Idle—except for your boasting—and what is your boasting worth
If ye grudge a year of service to the lordliest life on earth?
Ancient, effortless, ordered, cycle on cycle set,
Life so long untroubled, that ye who inherit forget
It was not made with the mountains, it is not one with the deep.
Men, not gods, devised it. Men, not gods, must keep.
Men, not children, servants, or kinsfolk called from afar,
But each man born in the Island broke to the matter of war
Soberly and by custom taken and trained for the same;
Each man born in the Island entered at youth to the game—
As it were almost cricket, not to be mastered in haste,
But after trial and labour, by temperance, living chaste.
As it were almost cricket—as it were even your play,
Weighed and pondered and worshipped, and practised day and
   day.
So ye shall bide sure-guarded when the restless lightnings wake
In the womb of the blotting war-cloud, and the pallid nations
   quake.
So, at the haggard trumpets, instant your soul shall leap
Forthright, accoutred, accepting—alert from the wells of sleep.
So at the threat ye shall summon—so at the need ye shall send
Men, not children or servants, tempered and taught to the end;
Cleansed of servile panic, slow to dread or despise,
Humble because of knowledge, mighty by sacrifice. . . .
But ye say, "It will mar our comfort." Ye say, "It will minish
   our trade."
Do ye wait for the spattered shrapnel ere ye learn how a gun
   is laid?
For the low, red glare to southward when the raided coast-towns
   burn?
(Light ye shall have on that lesson, but little time to learn.)
Will ye pitch some white pavilion, and lustily even the odds,
With nets and hoops and mallets, with rackets and bats and rods?
Will the rabbit war with your foemen—the red deer horn them
   for hire?
Your kept cock-pheasant keep you?—he is master of many a
   shire.
Arid, aloof, incurious, unthinking, unthanking, gelt,
Will ye loose your schools to flout them till their brow-beat
   columns melt?

Will ye pray them or preach them, or print them, or ballot them
    back from your shore?
Will your workmen issue a mandate to bid them strike no more?
Will ye rise and dethrone your rulers? (Because ye were idle
    both?
Pride by Insolence chastened? Indolence purged by Sloth?)
No doubt but ye are the People; who shall make you afraid?
Also your gods are many; no doubt but your gods shall aid.
Idols of greasy altars built for the body's ease;
Proud little brazen Baals and talking fetishes;
Teraphs of sept and party and wise wood-pavement gods—
These shall come down to the battle and snatch you from under
    the rods?
From the gusty, flickering gun-roll with viewless salvoes rent,
And the pitted hail of the bullets that tell not whence they were
    sent.
When ye are ringed as with iron, when ye are scourged as with
    whips,
When the meat is yet in your belly, and the boast is yet on your
    lips;
When ye go forth at morning and the noon beholds you broke,
Ere ye lie down at even, your remnant, under the yoke?

No doubt but ye are the People—absolute, strong, and wise;
Whatever your heart has desired ye have not withheld from your
    eyes.
On your own heads, in your own hands, the sin and the saving
    lies!

The Old Men

This is our lot if we live so long and labour unto the end—
That we outlive the impatient years and the much too patient
    friend:
And because we know we have breath in our mouth and think we
    have thought in our head,
We shall assume that we are alive, whereas we are really dead.

We shall not acknowledge that old stars fade or alien planets
    arise
(That the sere bush buds or the desert blooms or the ancient
    well-head dries),
Or any new compass wherewith new men adventure 'neath new
    skies.

We shall lift up the ropes that constrained our youth, to bind
    on our children's hands;
We shall call to the water below the bridges to return and
    replenish our lands;
We shall harness horses (Death's own pale horses) and scholarly
    plough the sands.

We shall lie down in the eye of the sun for lack of a light on
    our way—
We shall rise up when the day is done and chirrup, "Behold,
    it is day!"
We shall abide till the battle is won ere we amble into the fray.

We shall peck out and discuss and dissect, and evert and extrude
    to our mind,
The flaccid tissues of long-dead issues offensive to God and
    mankind—
(Precisely like vultures over an ox that the Army has left behind).

We shall make walk preposterous ghosts of the glories we once
    created—
(Immodestly smearing from muddled palettes amazing pigments
    mismated)
And our friends will weep when we ask them with boasts if our
    natural force be abated.

The Lamp of our Youth will be utterly out: but we shall subsist
    on the smell of it,
And whatever we do, we shall fold our hands and suck our gums
    and think well of it.
Yes, we shall be perfectly pleased with our work, and that is
    the Perfectest Hell of it!

This is our lot if we live so long and listen to those who love us—
That we are shunned by the people about and shamed by the
  Powers above us.
Wherefore be free of your harness betimes; but being free be
  assured,
That he who hath not endured to the death, from his birth he hath
  never endured!

The White Man's Burden

Take up the White Man's burden—
  Send forth the best ye breed—
Go bind your sons to exile
  To serve your captives' need;
To wait in heavy harness,
  On fluttered folk and wild—
Your new-caught, sullen peoples,
  Half-devil and half-child.

Take up the White Man's burden—
  In patience to abide,
To veil the threat of terror
  And check the show of pride;
By open speech and simple,
  An hundred times made plain,
To seek another's profit,
  And work another's gain.

Take up the White Man's burden—
  The savage wars of peace—
Fill full the mouth of Famine
  And bid the sickness cease;
And when your goal is nearest
  The end for others sought,
Watch Sloth and heathen Folly
  Bring all your hope to nought.

Take up the White Man's burden—
  No tawdry rule of kings,

But toil of serf and sweeper—
　　The tale of common things.
The ports ye shall not enter,
　　The roads ye shall not tread,
Go make them with your living,
　　And mark them with your dead.

Take up the White Man's burden—
　　And reap his old reward:
The blame of those ye better,
　　The hate of those ye guard—
The cry of hosts ye humour
　　(Ah, slowly!) toward the light:—
"Why brought ye us from bondage,
　　"Our loved Egyptian night?"

Take up the White Man's burden—
　　Ye dare not stoop to less—
Nor call too loud on Freedom
　　To cloak your weariness;
By all ye cry or whisper,
　　By all ye leave or do,
The silent, sullen peoples
　　Shall weigh your Gods and you.

Take up the White Man's burden—
　　Have done with childish days—
The lightly proffered laurel,
　　The easy, ungrudged praise.
Comes now, to search your manhood
　　Through all the thankless years,
Cold, edged with dear-bought wisdom,
　　The judgment of your peers!

Hymn Before Action

The earth is full of anger,
　　The seas are dark with wrath,

The Nations in their harness
  Go up against our path:
Ere yet we loose the legions—
  Ere yet we draw the blade,
Jehovah of the Thunders,
  Lord God of Battles, aid!

High lust and froward bearing,
  Proud heart, rebellious brow—
Deaf ear and soul uncaring,
  We seek Thy mercy now!
The sinner that forswore Thee,
  The fool that passed Thee by,
Our times are known before Thee—
  Lord, grant us strength to die!

For those who kneel beside us
  At altars not Thine own,
Who lack the lights that guide us,
  Lord, let their faith atone!
If wrong we did to call them,
  By honour bound they came;
Let not Thy Wrath befall them,
  But deal to us the blame.

From panic, pride, and terror,
  Revenge that knows no rein,
Light haste and lawless error,
  Protect us yet again.
Cloke Thou our undeserving,
  Make firm the shuddering breath,
In silence and unswerving
  To taste Thy lesser death!

Ah, Mary pierced with sorrow,
  Remember, reach and save
The soul that comes to-morrow
  Before the God that gave!
Since each was born of woman,
  For each at utter need—

True comrade and true foeman—
  Madonna, intercede!

E'en now their vanguard gathers,
  E'en now we face the fray—
As Thou didst help our fathers,
  Help Thou our host to-day!
Fulfilled of signs and wonders,
  In life, in death made clear—
Jehovah of the Thunders,
  Lord God of Battles, hear!

Recessional

God of our fathers, known of old,
  Lord of our far-flung battle-line,
Beneath whose awful Hand we hold
  Dominion over palm and pine—
Lord God of Hosts, be with us yet,
Lest we forget—lest we forget!

The tumult and the shouting dies;
  The captains and the kings depart:
Still stands Thine ancient sacrifice,
  An humble and a contrite heart.
Lord God of Hosts, be with us yet,
Lest we forget—lest we forget!

Far-called, our navies melt away;
  On dune and headland sinks the fire:
Lo, all our pomp of yesterday
  Is one with Nineveh and Tyre!
Judge of the Nations, spare us yet,
Lest we forget—lest we forget!

If, drunk with sight of power, we loose
  Wild tongues that have not Thee in awe,
Such boastings as the Gentiles use,
  Or lesser breeds without the Law—

Lord God of Hosts, be with us yet,
Lest we forget—lest we forget!

For heathen heart that puts her trust
   In reeking tube and iron shard,
All valiant dust that builds on dust,
   And guarding, calls not Thee to guard,
For frantic boast and foolish word—
Thy Mercy on Thy People, Lord!

The Conundrum
of the Workshops

When the flush of a new-born sun fell first on Eden's green and
   gold,
Our father Adam sat under the Tree and scratched with a stick
   in the mould;
And the first rude sketch that the world had seen was joy to his
   mighty heart,
Till the Devil whispered behind the leaves, "It 's pretty, but is
   it Art?"

Wherefore he called to his wife, and fled to fashion his work
   anew—
The first of his race who cared a fig for the first, most dread
   review;
And he left his lore to the use of his sons—and that was a
   glorious gain
When the Devil chuckled "Is it Art?" in the ear of the branded
   Cain.

They builded a tower to shiver the sky and wrench the stars
   apart,
Till the Devil grunted behind the bricks: "It 's striking, but is it
   Art?"
The stone was dropped at the quarry-side and the idle derrick
   swung,

While each man talked of the aims of Art, and each in an alien
    tongue.

The fought and they talked in the North and the South; they
    talked and they fought in the West,
Till the waters rose on the pitiful land, and the poor Red Clay
    had rest—
Had rest till the dank blank-canvas dawn when the dove was
    preened to start,
And the Devil bubbled below the keel: "It 's human, but is it
    Art?"

The tale is as old as the Eden Tree—and new as the new-cut
    tooth—
For each man knows ere his lip-thatch grows he is master of Art
    and Truth;
And each man hears as the twilight nears, to the beat of his dying
    heart,
The Devil drum on the darkened pane: "You did it, but was it
    Art?"

We have learned to whittle the Eden Tree to the shape of a
    surplice-peg,
We have learned to bottle our parents twain in the yelk of an
    addled egg,
We know that the tail must wag the dog, for the horse is drawn
    by the cart;
But the Devil whoops, as he whooped of old: "It 's clever, but
    is it Art?"

When the flicker of London sun falls faint on the Club-room's
    green and gold,
The sons of Adam sit them down and scratch with their pens in
    the mould—
They scratch with their pens in the mould of their graves, and
    the ink and the anguish start,
For the Devil mutters behind the leaves: "It 's pretty, but is it
    Art?"

Now, if we could win to the Eden Tree where the Four Great
    Rivers flow,
And the Wreath of Eve is red on the turf as she left it long ago,
And if we could come when the sentry slept and softly scurry
    through,
By the favour of God we might know as much—as our father
    Adam knew.

"Mary, Pity Women!"

You call yourself a man,
    For all you used to swear,
An' leave me, as you can,
    My certain shame to bear?
I 'ear! You do not care—
You done the worst you know.
    I 'ate you, grinnin' there. . . .
Ah, Gawd, I love you so!

Nice while it lasted, an' now it is over—
Tear out your 'eart an' good-bye to your lover!
What 's the use o' grievin', when the mother that bore you
(Mary, pity women!) knew it all before you?

It are n't no false alarm,
    The finish to your fun;
You—you 'ave brung the 'arm,
    An' I 'm the ruined one;
    An' now you 'll off an' run
With some new fool in tow.
    Your 'eart? You 'ave n't none. . . .
Ah, Gawd, I love you so!

When a man is tired there is naught will bind 'im;
All 'e solemn promised 'e will shove be'ind 'im.
What 's the good o' prayin' for The Wrath to strike 'im
(Mary, pity women!), when the rest are like 'im?

What 'ope for me or—it?
   What 's left for us to do?
I 've walked with men a bit,
   But this—but this is you.
   So 'elp me Christ, it 's true!
Where can I 'ide or go?
   You coward through and through! . . .
Ah, Gawd, I love you so!

All the more you give 'em the less are they for givin'—
Love lies dead, an' you can not kiss 'im livin'.
Down the road 'e led you there is no returnin'
(Mary, pity women!), but you 're late in learnin'!

You 'd like to treat me fair?
   You can't, because we 're pore?
We 'd starve? What do I care!
   We might, but *this* is shore!
   I want the name—no more—
The name, an' lines to show,
   An' not to be an 'ore. . . .
Ah, Gawd, I love you so!

What 's the good o' pleadin', when the mother that bore you
(Mary, pity women!) knew it all before you?
Sleep on 'is promises an' wake to your sorrow
(Mary, pity women!), for we sail to-morrow!

The Return

(ALL ARMS)

Peace is declared, an' I return
   To 'Ackneystadt, but not the same;
Things 'ave transpired which made me learn
   The size and meanin' of the game.
I did no more than others did,
   I don't know where the change began;

I started as a average kid,
   I finished as a thinkin' man.

> *If England was what England seems,*
>   *An' not the England of our dreams,*
> *But only putty, brass, an' paint,*
>   *'Ow quick we 'd drop 'er! But she ain't!*

Before my gappin' mouth could speak
   I 'eard it in my comrade's tone;
I saw it on my neighbour's cheek
   Before I felt it flush my own.
An' last it come to me—not pride,
   Nor yet conceit, but on the 'ole
(If such a term may be applied),
   The makin's of a bloomin' soul.

Rivers at night that cluck an' jeer,
   Plains which the moonshine turns to sea,
Mountains which never let you near,
   An' stars to all eternity;
An' the quick-breathin' dark that fills
   The 'ollows of the wilderness,
When the wind worries through the 'ills—
   These may 'ave taught me more or less.

Towns without people, ten times took,
   An' ten times left an' burned at last;
An' starvin' dogs that come to look
   For owners when a column passed;
An' quiet, 'omesick talks between
   Men, met by night, you never knew
Until—'is face—by shellfire seen—
   Once—an' struck off. *They* taught me too.

The day's lay-out—the mornin' sun
   Beneath your 'at-brim as you sight;
The dinner-'ush from noon till one,
   An' the full roar that lasts till night:
An' the pore dead that look so old

An' was so young an hour ago,
An' legs tied down before they're cold—
    These are the things which make you know.

Also Time runnin' into years—
    A thousand Places left be'ind—
An' Men from both two 'emispheres
    Discussin' things of every kind;
So much more near than I 'ad known,
    So much more great than I 'ad guessed—
An' me, like all the rest, alone—
    But reachin' out to all the rest!

So 'ath it come to me—not pride,
    Nor yet conceit, but on the 'ole
(If such a term may be applied),
    The makin's of a bloomin' soul.
But now, discharged, I fall away
    To do with little things again. . . .
Gawd, 'oo knows all I cannot say,
    Look after me in Thamesfontein!

> *If England was what England seems,*
> *An' not the England of our dreams,*
> *But only putty, brass, an' paint,*
> *'Ow quick we 'd chuck 'er!* But she ain't!

The Storm Cone

This is the midnight—let no star
Delude us—dawn is very far.
This is the tempest long foretold—
Slow to make head but sure to hold.

Stand by! The lull 'twixt blast and blast
Signals the storm is near, not past;
And worse than present jeopardy
May our forlorn to-morrow be.

If we have cleared the expectant reef,
Let no man look for his relief.
Only the darkness hides the shape
Of further peril to escape.

It is decreed that we abide
The weight of gale against the tide
And those huge waves the outer main
Sends in to set us back again.

They fall and whelm. We strain to hear
The pulses of her labouring gear,
Till the deep throb beneath us proves,
After each shudder and check, she moves!

She moves, with all save purpose lost,
To make her offing from the coast;
But, till she fetches open sea,
Let no man deem that he is free!

D. H. Lawrence

DAVID HENRY LAWRENCE (1885–1930) was born in the colliery town of Eastwood in Nottinghamshire, the son of miner, his mother a schoolteacher. Although hampered by his poor, working-class background and a father whose reputation for heavy drinking was well known, Lawrence managed to pass through grammar school and a teachers' training college before being employed as a teacher in an elementary school in Croydon, near London. In 1911 his first novel, *The White Peacock,* appeared, and the following year he eloped with Frieda von Richthofen, the wife of a Nottingham professor. After Frieda's divorce she and Lawrence married. Lawrence's poor health kept him out of the 1914–1918 war, and both he and his German-born wife professed complete indifference to it, an attitude which brought them into trouble with the authorities. From 1919 to 1922 the Lawrences lived in Italy; they spent the summers of 1922 and 1924 in New Mexico; and then returned to Italy, where Lawrence's health rapidly declined. He died in Vence, in the South of France, from tuberculosis, having been confined to sanatoriums for the greater part of the two years before his death.

Lawrence is one of the major novelists of the twentieth century, whose glorification of Priapus brought him into difficulties with the puritanically minded early in his literary career. Lawrence believed that sexual satisfaction was part of one's struggle toward self-realization, and that the puritanical middle class inhibited one's development, ideas which he propounded in his novels no less than in his poetry. Stylistically, Lawrence owes much to the Imagists, but his experiments in free verse are perhaps his most significant contribution to the technical development of English poetry.

Snake

A snake came to my water-trough
On a hot, hot day, and I in pyjamas for the heat,
To drink there.

In the deep, strange-scented shade of the great dark carob tree
I came down the steps with my pitcher
And must wait, must stand and wait, for there he was at the
    trough before me.

He reached down from a fissure in the earth-wall in the gloom
And trailed his yellow-brown slackness soft-bellied down, over
    the edge of the stone trough
And rested his throat upon the stone bottom,
And where the water had dripped from the tap, in a small
    clearness,
He sipped with his straight mouth,
Softly drank through his straight gums, into his slack long body,
Silently.

Someone was before me at my water-trough,
And I, like a second comer, waiting.

He lifted his head from his drinking, like cattle do,
And looked at me vaguely, as drinking cattle do,
And flickered his two-forked tongue from his lips, and mused a
    moment,
And stooped and drank a little more,
Being earth-brown, earth-golden from the burning bowels of the
    earth
On the day of Sicilian July, with Etna smoking.

The voice of my education said to me
He must be killed,
For in Sicily the black, black snakes are innocent, the gold are
    venomous.

And voices in me said, If you were a man

You would take a stick and break him now, and finish him
    off.

But I must confess how I liked him,
How glad I was he had come like a guest in quiet, to drink at
    my water-trough
And depart peaceful, pacified, and thankless,
Into the burning bowels of this earth.

Was it cowardice, that I dared not kill him?
Was it perversity, that I longed to talk to him?
Was it humility, to feel so honoured?
I felt so honoured.

And yet those voices:
If you were not afraid, you would kill him!

And truly I was afraid, I was most afraid,
But even so, honoured still more
That he should seek my hospitality
From out the dark door of the secret earth.

He drank enough
And lifted his head, dreamily, as one who has drunken,
And flickered his tongue like a forked night on the air, so black,
Seeming to lick his lips,
And looking around like a god, unseeing, into the air,
And slowly turned his head,
And slowly, very slowly, as if thrice adream,
Proceeded to draw his slow length curving round
And climb again the broken bank of my wall-face.

And as he put his head into that dreadful hole,
And as he slowly drew up, snake-easing his shoulders, and
    entered farther,
A sort of horror, a sort of protest against his withdrawing into
    that horrid black hole,
Deliberately going into the blackness, and slowly drawing himself
    after,
Overcame me now his back was turned.

I looked around, I put down my pitcher,
I picked up a clumsy log
And threw it at the water-trough with a clatter.

I think I did not hit him,
But suddenly that part of him that was left behind convulsed in
    undignified haste,
Writhed like lightning, and was gone
Into the black hole, the earth-lipped fissure in the wall-front,
At which, in the intense still noon, I stared with fascination.

And immediately I regretted it.
I thought how paltry, how vulgar, what a mean act!
I despised myself and the voices of my accursed human education.

And I thought of the albatross,
And I wished he would come back, my snake.

For he seemed to me again like a king,
Like a king in exile, uncrowned in the underworld,
Now due to be crowned again.

And so, I missed my chance with one of the lords
Of life.
And I have something to expiate;
A pettiness.

How Beastly the Bourgeois Is

How beastly the bourgeois is
especially the male of the species—
Presentable, eminently presentable—
shall I make you a present of him?

Isn't he handsome? isn't he healthy? isn't he a fine specimen?
doesn't he look the fresh clean englishman, outside?
Isn't it god's own image? tramping his thirty miles a day
after partridges, or a little rubber ball?
wouldn't you like to be like that, well off, and quite the thing?

Oh, but wait!
Let him meet a new emotion, let him be faced with another
    man's need,
let him come home to a bit of moral difficulty, let life face him
    with a new demand on his understanding
and then watch him go soggy, like a wet meringue.
Watch him turn into a mess, either a fool or a bully.
Just watch the display of him, confronted with a new demand on
    his intelligence,
a new life-demand.

How beastly the bourgeois is
especially the male of the species—

Nicely groomed, like a mushroom
standing there so sleek and erect and eyeable—
and like a fungus, living on the remains of bygone life
sucking his life out of the dead leaves of greater life than his own.

And even so, he's stale, he's been there too long.
Touch him, and you'll find he's all gone inside
just like an old mushroom, all wormy inside, and hollow
under a smooth skin and an upright appearance.

Full of seething, wormy, hollow feelings
rather nasty—
How beastly the bourgeois is!

Standing in their thousands, these appearances, in damp England
what a pity they can't all be kicked over
like sickening toadstools, and left to melt back, swiftly
into the soil of England.

The Elephant Is Slow to Mate

> The elephant, the huge old beast
>   is slow to mate;
> he finds a female, they show no haste,
>   they wait

for the sympathy in their vast shy hearts
    slowly, slowly to rouse
as they loiter along the river-beds
    and drink and browse

and dash in panic through the brake
    of forest with the herd,
and sleep in massive silence, and wake
    together, without a word.

So slowly the great hot elephant hearts
    grow full of desire,
and the great beasts mate in secret at last,
    hiding their fire.

Oldest they are and the wisest of beasts
    so they know at last
how to wait for the loneliest of feasts,
    for the full repast.

They do not snatch, they do not tear;
    their massive blood
moves as the moon-tides, near, more near,
    till they touch in flood.

Bavarian Gentians

Not every man has gentians in his house
in Soft September, at slow, sad Michaelmas.

Bavarian gentians, big and dark, only dark
darkening the day-time, torch-like with the smoking blueness of
        Pluto's gloom,
ribbed and torch-like, with their blaze of darkness spread blue
down flattening into points, flattened under the sweep of white
        day
torch-flower of the blue-smoking darkness, Pluto's dark-blue
        daze,

black lamps from the halls of *Dis,* burning dark blue,
giving off darkness, blue darkness, as Demeter's pale lamps give
    off light,
lead me then, lead the way.

Reach me a gentian, give me a torch!
let me guide myself with the blue, forked torch of this flower
down the darker and darker stairs, where blue is darkened on
    blueness
even where Persephone goes, just now, from the frosted Sep-
    tember
to the sightless realm where darkness is awake upon the dark
and Persephone herself is but a voice
or a darkness invisible enfolded in the deeper dark
of the arms Plutonic, and pierced with the passion of dense
    gloom,
among the splendour of torches of darkness, shedding darkness
    on the lost bride and her groom.

John Masefield

JOHN MASEFIELD (1878-1967), late Poet Laureate, was born in Herefordshire, educated at King's School, Warwick, and later on the Conway, a training ship for the British merchant navy. As a boy he sailed on a windjammer, but soon left the sea, living for a time in New York before returning to London, where he began his literary career. His first volume of poems, *Salt Water Ballads,* appeared in 1902, and was soon followed by several more, a number of long narrative poems, some verse dramas, and several prose romances. In 1930 he succeeded Robert Bridges as Poet Laureate, and in 1935 he received the Order of Merit. He lived on a farm in Oxfordshire during his last years, still writing poetry, and in 1966 published some autobiographical reminiscences of his boyhood.

Masefield properly belongs to the Georgian school, and in his early years he thought of himself as an iconoclastic rebel, combating the poetic artificiality of the Victorians. Although his slangy realism and breezy rhythms sometimes make for admirable directness and simplicity, his poetry is frequently marred by factitious romance and sentimentality. Masefield's main contribution to modern English poetry was his effort to bring the long verse narrative back into public favor, for both *Dauber* (1912) and the pseudo-Chaucerian *Reynard the Fox* (1919), his two most famous poetic narratives, were widely acclaimed, and it is believed that the latter was mainly responsible for his appointment as Poet Laureate.

Cape Horn Gospel   I

"I was in a hooker once," said Karlssen,
"And Bill, as was a seaman, died,
So we lashed him in an old tarpaulin
And tumbled him across the side;
And the fun of it was that all his gear was
Divided up among the crew
Before that blushing human error,
Our crawling little captain, knew.

"On the passage home one morning
(As certain as I prays for grace)
There was old Bill's shadder a-hauling
At the weather mizzen-topsail brace.
He was all grown green with sea-weed,
He was all lashed up and shored;
So I says to him, I says, 'Why, Billy!
What's a-bringing of you back aboard?'

" 'I'm a-weary of them there mermaids,'
Says old Bill's ghost to me;
'It ain't no place for a Christian
Below there—under sea.
For it 's all blown sand and shipwrecks,
And old bones eaten bare,
And them cold fishy females
With long green weeds for hair.

" 'And there ain't no dances shuffled,
And no old yarns is spun,
And there ain't no stars but starfish,
And never any moon or sun.
I heard your keel a-passing
And the running rattle of the brace,'
And he says 'Stand by,' says William,
'For a shift towards a better place.'

"Well, he sogered about decks till sunrise,
When a rooster in the hen-coop crowed,
And as so much smoke he faded
And as so much smoke he goed;
And I've often wondered since, Jan,
How his old ghost stands to fare
Long o' them cold fishy females
With long green weeds for hair."

Cape Horn Gospel   II

Jake was a dirty Dago lad, an' he gave the skipper chin,
An' the skipper up an' took him a crack with an iron belaying-pin
Which stiffened him out a rusty corp, as pretty as you could
    wish,
An' then we shovelled him up in a sack an' dumped him to the
    fish.
        That was jest arter we'd got sail on her.

Josey slipped from the tops'l-yard an' bust his bloody back
(Which comed from playing the giddy goat an' leavin' go the
    jack);
We lashed his chips in clouts of sail an' ballasted him with
    stones,
"The Lord hath taken away," we says, an' we give him to Davy
    Jones.
        An' that was afore we were up with the Line.

Joe were chippin' a rusty plate a-squattin' upon the deck,
An' all the watch he had the sun a-singein' him on the neck,
An' forrard he falls at last, he does, an' he lets his mallet go,
Dead as a nail with calenture, an' that was the end of Joe.
        An' that was just afore we made the Plate.

All o' the rest were sailor-men, an' it come to rain an' squall,
An' then it was halliards, sheets, an' tacks "clue up, an' let go
    all."
We snugged her down an' hove her to, an' the old contrairy cuss
Started a plate, an' settled an' sank, an' that was the end of us.

We slopped around on coops an' planks in the cold an' in the
        dark,
An' Bill were drowned, an' Tom were ate by a swine of a cruel
        shark,
An' a mail-boat reskied Harry an' I (which comed of pious
        prayers),
Which brings me here a-kickin' my heels in the port of Buenos
        Ayres.

I'm bound for home in the *Oronook,* in a suit of looted duds,
A D.B.S. a-earnin' a stake by helpin' peelin' spuds,
An' if ever I fetch to Prince's Stage an' sets my feet ashore,
You bet your hide that there I stay, an' follers the sea no more.

Sea-Fever

I must go down to the seas again, to the lonely sea and the sky,
And all I ask is a tall ship and a star to steer her by,
And the wheel's kick and the wind's song and the white sail's
        shaking,
And a grey mist on the sea's face and a grey dawn breaking.

I must go down to the seas again, for the call of the running tide
Is a wild call and a clear call that may not be denied;
And all I ask is a windy day with the white clouds flying,
And the flung spray and the blown spume, and the sea-gulls
        crying.

I must go down to the seas again, to the vagrant gypsy life,
To the gull's way and the whale's way where the wind 's like a
        whetted knife;
And all I ask is a merry yarn from a laughing fellow-rover,
And quiet sleep and a sweet dream when the long trick 's over.

A Wanderer's Song

A wind 's in the heart of me, a fire 's in my heels,
I am tired of brick and stone and rumbling wagon-wheels;

I hunger for the sea's edge, the limits of the land,
Where the wild old Atlantic is shouting on the sand.

Oh I'll be going, leaving the noises of the street,
To where a lifting foresail-foot is yanking at the sheet;
To a windy, tossing anchorage where yawls and ketches ride,
Oh I'll be going, going, until I meet the tide.

And first I'll hear the sea-wind, the mewing of the gulls,
The clucking, sucking of the sea about the rusty hulls,
The songs at the capstan in the hooker warping out,
And then the heart of me 'll know I'm there or thereabout.

Oh I am tired of brick and stone, the heart of me is sick,
For windy green, unquiet sea, the realm of Moby Dick;
And I'll be going, going, from the roaring of the wheels,
For a wind 's in the heart of me, a fire 's in my heels.

Cargoes

Quinquireme of Nineveh from distant Ophir
Rowing home to haven in sunny Palestine,
With a cargo of ivory,
And apes and peacocks,
Sandalwood, cedarwood, and sweet white wine.

Stately Spanish galleon coming from the Isthmus,
Dipping through the Tropics by the palm-green shores,
With a cargo of diamonds,
Emeralds, amethysts,
Topazes, and cinnamon, and gold moidores.

Dirty British coaster with a salt-caked smoke stack
Butting through the Channel in the mad March days,
With a cargo of Tyne coal,
Road-rail, pig-lead,
Firewood, iron-ware, and cheap tin trays.

From Reynard the Fox

The pure clean air came sweet to his lungs,
Till he thought foul scorn on those crying tongues.
In a three mile more he would reach the haven
In the Wan Dyke croaked on by the raven.
In a three mile more he would make his berth
On the hard cool floor of a Wan Dyke earth,
Too deep for spade, too curved for terrier,
With the pride of the race to make rest the merrier.
In a three mile more he would reach his dream,
So his game heart gulped and he put on steam.

*   *   *

Like a rocket shot to a ship ashore
The lean red bolt of his body tore,
Like a ripple of wind running swift on grass;
Like a shadow on wheat when a cloud blows past,
Like a turn at the buoy in a cutter sailing
When the bright green gleam lips white at the railing,
Like the April snake whipping back to sheath,
Like the gannets' hurtle on fish beneath,
Like a kestrel chasing, like a sickle reaping,
Like all things swooping, like all things sweeping,
Like a hound for stay, like a stag for swift,
With his shadow beside like spinning drift.

*   *   *

Past the gibbet-stock all stuck with nails,
Where they hanged in chains what had hung in jails,
Past Ashmundshowe where Ashmund sleeps,
And none but the tumbling peewit weeps,
Past Curlew Calling, the gaunt grey corner
Where the curlew comes as a summer mourner,
Past Blowbury Beacon, shaking his fleece,
Where all winds hurry and none brings peace;
Then down on the mile-long green decline,
Where the turf's like spring and the air's like wine,
Where the sweeping spurs of the downland spill
Into Wan Brook Valley and Wan Dyke Hill.

*   *   *

On he went with a galloping rally
Past Maesbury Clump for Wan Brook Valley.
The blood in his veins went romping high,
"Get on, on, on, to the earth or die."
The air of the downs went purely past
Till he felt the glory of going fast,
Till the terror of death, though there indeed,
Was lulled for a while by his pride of speed.
He was romping away from hounds and hunt,
He had Wan Dyke Hill and his earth in front,
In a one mile more when his point was made
He would rest in safety from dog or spade;
Nose between paws he would hear the shout
Of the "Gone to earth!" to the hounds without,
The whine of the hounds, and their cat-feet gadding,
Scratching the earth, and their breath pad-padding;
He would hear the horn call hounds away,
And rest in peace till another day.

      *   *   *

In one mile more he would lie at rest,
So for one mile more he would go his best.
He reached the dip at the long droop's end,
And he took what speed he had still to spend.

      *   *   *

So down past Maesbury beech-clump grey
That would not be green till the end of May,
Past Arthur's Table, the white chalk boulder,
Where pasque flowers purple the down's grey shoulder,
Past Quichelm's Keeping, past Harry's Thorn,
To Thirty Acre all thin with corn.

      *   *   *

As he raced the corn towards Wan Dyke Brook
The pack had view of the way he took;
Robin hallooed from the downland's crest,
He capped them on till they did their best.
The quarter-mile to the Wan Brook's brink
Was raced as quick as a man can think.

      *   *   *

And here, as he ran to the huntsman's yelling,
The fox first felt that the pace was telling;

His body and lungs seemed all grown old,
His legs less certain, his heart less bold,
The hound-noise nearer, the hill-slope steeper,
The thud in the blood of his body deeper.
His pride in his speed, his joy in the race,
Were withered away, for what use was pace?
He had run his best, and the hounds ran better,
Then the going worsened, the earth was wetter.
Then his brush drooped down till it sometimes dragged,
And his fur felt sick and his chest was tagged
With taggles of mud, and his pads seemed lead,
It was well for him he'd an earth ahead.

* * *

Down he went to the brook and over,
Out of the corn and into the clover,
Over the slope that the Wan Brook drains,
Past Battle Tump where they earthed the Danes,
Then up the hill that the Wan Dyke rings
Where the Sarsen Stones stand grand like kings.

* * *

Seven Sarsens of granite grim,
As he ran them by they looked at him;
As he leaped the lip of their earthen paling
The hounds were gaining and he was failing.

.   .   .   .

He passed the Sarsens, he left the spur,
He pressed uphill to the blasted fir,
He slipped as he leaped the hedge; he slithered.
"He's mine," thought Robin. "He's done; he's dithered."

* * *

At the second attempt he cleared the fence,
He turned half-right where the gorse was dense,
He was leading the hounds by a furlong clear.
He was past his best, but his earth was near.
He ran up gorse to the spring of the ramp,
The steep green wall of the dead men's camp,
He sidled up it and scampered down
To the deep green ditch of the Dead Men's Town.

* * *

Within, as he reached that soft green turf,
The wind, blowing lonely, moaned like surf,
Desolate ramparts rose up steep
On either side, for the ghosts to keep.
He raced the trench, past the rabbit warren,
Close-grown with moss which the wind made barren;
He passed the spring where the rushes spread,
And there in the stones was his earth ahead.
One last short burst upon failing feet—
There life lay waiting, so sweet, so sweet,
Rest in a darkness, balm for aches.

* * *

The earth was stopped. It was barred with stakes.

Alice Meynell

ALICE MEYNELL (1847–1922) was born at Barnes near London, and received an irregular education in England and on the Continent mostly from her father, a charming and sensitive dilettante. She converted to Roman Catholicism around 1872, and her first volume of poems, *Preludes,* appeared three years later. In 1877 she married Wilfrid Meynell, who became editor of *Merry England* from 1883–1895, acting as his journalistic helpmeet in between the births of eight children, and contributing numerous essays on all kinds of literary subjects to both *Merry England* and other periodicals as well. She was an intelligent woman of considerable charm, who could maintain a warm friendship with such different personalities as Coventry Patmore and George Meredith, and also sympathize with the misfortunes of Francis Thompson, the young Catholic poet she and her husband rescued from starvation and drug addiction.

As a poet Alice Meynell has probably been underrated. Her early verse is inclined to be mournful and a little sugary, but that which she wrote later has more intellectual depth and subtlety, some of it betraying the influence of the poets of the seventeenth century.

The Visiting Sea

As the inhastening tide doth roll,
Home from the deep, along the whole
  Wide shining strand, and floods the caves,
  —Your love comes filling with happy waves
The open sea-shore of my soul.

But inland from the seaward spaces,
None knows, not even you, the places
  Brimmed, at your coming, out of sight,
  —The little solitudes of delight
This tide constrains in dim embraces.

You see the happy shore, wave-rimmed,
But know not of the quiet dimmed
  Rivers your coming floods and fills,
  The little pools 'mid happier hills,
My silent rivulets, over-brimmed.

What! I have secrets from you? Yes.
But, visiting Sea, your love doth press
  And reach in further than you know,
  And fills all these; and, when you go,
There's loneliness in loneliness.

The Young Neophyte

Who knows what days I answer for to-day?
  Giving the bud I give the flower. I bow
  This yet unfaded and a faded brow;
Bending these knees and feeble knees, I pray.
Thoughts yet unripe in me I bend one way,
  Give one repose to pain I know not now,
  One check to joy that comes, I guess not how.
I dedicate my fields when Spring is grey.

O rash! (I smile) to pledge my hidden wheat.
I fold to-day at altars far apart
Hands trembling with what toils? In their retreat
I seal my love to-be, my folded art.
I light the tapers at my head and feet,
And lay the crucifix on this silent heart.

To the Body

Thou inmost, ultimate
Council of judgement, palace of decrees,
Where the high senses hold their spiritual state,
Sued by earth's embassies,
And sign, approve, accept, conceive, create;

Create—thy senses close
With the world's pleas. The random odours reach
Their sweetness in the place of thy repose,
Upon thy tongue the peach,
And in thy nostrils breathes the breathing rose.

To thee, secluded one,
The dark vibrations of the sightless skies,
The lovely inexplicit colours, run;
The light gropes for those eyes.
O thou august! thou dost command the sun.

Music, all dumb, hath trod
Into thine ear her one effectual way;
And fire and cold approach to gain thy nod,
Where thou call'st up the day,
Where thou awaitest the appeal of God.

Summer in England, 1914

On London fell a clearer light;
Caressing pencils of the sun

Defined the distances, the white
   Houses transfigured one by one,
The "long, unlovely street" impearled.
Oh, what a sky has walked the world!

Most happy year! And out of town
   The hay was prosperous, and the wheat;
The silken harvest climbed the down:
   Moon after moon was heavenly-sweet,
Stroking the bread within the sheaves,
Looking 'twixt apples and their leaves.

And while this rose made round her cup,
   The armies died convulsed. And when
This chaste young silver sun went up
   Softly, a thousand shattered men,
One wet corruption, heaped the plain,
After a league-long throb of pain.

Flower following tender flower; and birds,
   And berries; and benignant skies
Made thrive the serried flocks and herds.—
   Yonder are men shot through the eyes.
      Love, hide thy face
From man's unpardonable race.

Who said "No man hath greater love than this,
   To die to serve his friend"?
So these have loved us all unto the end.
   Chide thou no more, O thou unsacrificed!
The soldier dying dies upon a kiss,
   The very kiss of Christ.

The Threshing-Machine

No "fan is in his hand" for these
Young villagers beneath the trees,
   Watching the wheels. But I recall

The rhythm of rods that rise and fall,
Purging the harvest, over-seas.

No fan, no flail, no threshing-floor!
And all their symbols evermore
    Forgone in England now—the sign,
    The visible pledge, the threat divine,
The chaff dispersed, the wheat in store.

The unbreathing engine marks no tune,
Steady at sunrise, steady at noon,
    Inhuman, perfect, saving time,
    And saving measure, and saving rhyme—
And did our Ruskin speak too soon?

"No noble strength on earth" he sees
"Save Hercules' arm". His grave decrees
    Curse wheel and steam. As the wheels ran
    I saw the other strength of man,
I knew the brain of Hercules.

Harold Monro

HAROLD MONRO (1879–1932) was born in Brussels and lived there until the age of seven, when his family returned to England, settling at Wells in Somerset. He was educated at Radley and Caius College, Cambridge, and in later years spent much of his time in Ireland, Italy, and Switzerland. It was in Florence where he met the novelist Maurice Hewlett, who encouraged him to seek a career in the writing and promotion of poetry, and in 1913 he founded the Poetry Bookshop, which was responsible for the publication of the *Georgian Poetry* volumes. He edited *Poetry and Drama* for a time, and from 1919 to 1925 he produced *The Chapbook,* a journal which favored the poetry not only of the Georgians but the Imagists as well. Monro's catholic taste was further demonstrated by his wide choice of poems in his influential anthology *Twentieth Century Poetry* (1929).

Monro's own poetry reflects his association with the Georgians, but it also looks forward to Eliot. In the September, 1913, issue of *Poetry and Drama* he quoted with approval Marinetti's Futuristic manifesto, in which he advocated audacity and revolt, and the beauty of speed, adding that the poet should "forget God, Heaven, Hell" and "sentimental contemplation of the past," remembering above all *"to live,* in the future of the earth." Thus although much of Monro's verse is unmistakably Georgian, he tried to avoid the genteel insipidity of some of the poets of that school, and not surprisingly he was able to appreciate the poetry of Eliot and the Sitwells. Latterly his poetry took on a somber, almost nightmarish quality which gave it a distinctly individual note.

Week-End

I

The train! The twelve o'clock for paradise.
   Hurry, or it will try to creep away.
Out in the country every one is wise:
   We can be only wise on Saturday.
There you are waiting, little friendly house:
   Those are your chimney-stacks with you between,
Surrounded by old trees and strolling cows,
   Staring through all your windows at the green.
Your homely floor is creaking for our tread;
   The smiling tea-pot with contented spout
Thinks of the boiling water, and the bread
   Longs for the butter. All their hands are out
     To greet us, and the gentle blankets seem
     Purring and crooning: "Lie in us, and dream."

II

The key will stammer, and the door reply,
   The hall wake, yawn, and smile; the torpid stair
Will grumble at our feet, the table cry:
   "Fetch my belongings for me; I am bare."
A clatter! Something in the attic falls.
   A ghost has lifted up his robes and fled.
The loitering shadows move along the walls;
   Then silence very slowly lifts his head.
The starling with impatient screech has flown
   The chimney, and is watching from the tree.
They thought us gone for ever: mouse alone
   Stops in the middle of the floor to see.
     Now all you idle things, resume your toil.
     Hearth, put your flames on. Sulky kettle, boil.

III

Contented evening; comfortable joys;
  The snoozing fire, and all the fields are still:
Tranquil delight, no purpose, and no noise—
  Unless the slow wind flowing round the hill.
"Murry" (the kettle) dozes; little mouse
  Is rambling prudently about the floor.
There's lovely conversation in this house:
  Words become princes that were slaves before.
What a sweet atmosphere for you and me
  The people that have been here left behind. . . .
Oh, but I fear it may turn out to be
  Built of a dream, erected in the mind:
      So if we speak too loud, we may awaken
      To find it vanished, and ourselves mistaken.

IV

Lift up the curtain carefully. All the trees
  Stand in the dark like drowsy sentinels.
  The oak is talkative to-night; he tells
The little bushes crowding at his knees
That formidable, hard, voluminous
  History of growth from acorn into age.
They titter like school-children; they arouse
  Their comrades, who exclaim: "He is very sage."
Look how the moon is staring through that cloud,
  Laying and lifting idle streaks of light.
O hark! was that the monstrous wind, so loud
And sudden, prowling always through the night?
      Let down the shaking curtain. They are queer,
      Those foreigners. They and we live so near.

V

Come, come to bed. The shadows move about,
  And some one seems to overhear our talk.
The fire is low; the candles flicker out;
  The ghosts of former tenants want to walk.
Already they are shuffling through the gloom.
  I felt an old man touch my shoulder-blade;
Once he was married here; they love this room,
  He and his woman and the child they made.
Dead, dead, they are, yet some familiar sound,
  Creeping along the brink of happy life,
Revives their memory from under ground—
  The farmer and his troublesome old wife.
     Let us be going: as we climb the stairs,
     They'll sit down in our warm half-empty chairs.

VI

Morning! Wake up! Awaken! All the boughs
  Are rippling on the air across the green.
The youngest birds are singing to the house.
  Blood of the world!—and is the country clean?
Disturb the precinct. Cool it with a shout.
  Sing as you trundle down to light the fire.
Turn the encumbering shadows tumbling out,
  And fill the chambers with a new desire.
Life is no good, unless the morning brings
  White happiness and quick delight of day.
These half-inanimate domestic things
  Must all be useful, or must go away.
     Coffee, be fragrant. Porridge in my plate,
     Increase the vigour to fulfil my fate.

VII

The fresh air moves like water round a boat.
　The white clouds wander. Let us wander too.
The whining, wavering plover flap and float.
　That crow is flying after that cuckoo.
Look! Look! . . . They're gone. What are the great trees calling?
　Just come a little farther, by that edge
Of green, to where the stormy ploughland, falling　˳
　Wave upon wave, is lapping to the hedge.
Oh, what a lovely bank! Give me your hand.
　Lie down and press your heart against the ground.
Let us both listen till we understand,
　Each through the other, every natural sound. . . .
　　　I can't hear anything to-day, can you,
　　　But, far and near: "Cuckoo! Cuckoo! Cuckoo!"?

VIII

The everlasting grass—how bright, how cool!
　The day has gone too suddenly, too soon.
There's something white and shiny in that pool—
　Throw in a stone, and you will hit the moon.
Listen, the church-bell ringing! Do not say
　We must go back to-morrow to our work.
We'll tell them we are dead: we died to-day.
　We're lazy. We're too happy. We will shirk.
We're cows. We're kettles. We'll be anything
　Except the manikins of time and fear.
We'll start away to-morrow wandering,
　And nobody will notice in a year. . . .
　　　Now the great sun is slipping under ground.
　　　Grip firmly!—How the earth is whirling round!

IX

Be staid; be careful; and be not too free.
Temptation to enjoy your liberty
May rise against you, break into a crime,
And smash the habit of employing Time.
It serves no purpose that the careful clock
    Mark the appointment, the officious train
Hurry to keep it, if the minutes mock
    Loud in your ear: "Late. Late. Late. Late again."
Week-end is very well on Saturday:
    On Monday it's a different affair—
A little episode, a trivial stay
    In some oblivious spot somehow, somewhere.
        On Sunday night we hardly laugh or speak:
        Week-end begins to merge itself in Week.

X

Pack up the house, and close the creaking door.
    The fields are dull this morning in the rain.
It's difficult to leave that homely floor.
    Wave a light hand; we will return again.
(What was that bird?) Good-bye, ecstatic tree,
    Floating, bursting, and breathing on the air.
The lonely farm is wondering that we
    Can leave. How every window seems to stare!
That bag is heavy. Share it for a bit.
    You like that gentle swashing of the ground
As we tread? . . .
            It is over. Now we sit
Reading the morning paper in the sound
    Of the debilitating heavy train.
        London again, again. London again.

Milk for the Cat

When the tea is brought at five o'clock,
And all the neat curtains are drawn with care,
The little black cat with bright green eyes
Is suddenly purring there.

At first she pretends, having nothing to do,
She has come in merely to blink by the grate,
But, though tea may be late or the milk may be sour,
She is never late.

And presently her agate eyes
Take a soft large milky haze,
And her independent casual glance
Becomes a stiff, hard gaze.

Then she stamps her claws or lifts her ears,
Or twists her tail and begins to stir,
Till suddenly all her lithe body becomes
One breathing, trembling purr.

The children eat and wriggle and laugh;
The two old ladies stroke their silk:
But the cat is grown small and thin with desire,
Transformed to a creeping lust for milk.

The white saucer like some full moon descends
At last from the clouds of the table above;
She sighs and dreams and thrills and glows,
Transfigured with love.

She nestles over the shining rim,
Buries her chin in the creamy sea;
Her tail hangs loose; each drowsy paw
Is doubled under each bending knee.

A long, dim ecstasy holds her life;
Her world is an infinite shapeless white,

Till her tongue has curled the last holy drop,
Then she sinks back into the night,

Draws and dips her body to heap
Her sleepy nerves in the great arm-chair,
Lies defeated and buried deep
Three or four hours unconscious there.

Bitter Sanctuary

I

She lives in the porter's room; the plush is nicotined.
Clients have left their photos there to perish.
She watches through green shutters those who press
To reach unconsciousness.

She licks her varnished thin magenta lips,
She picks her foretooth with a finger nail,
She pokes her head out to greet new clients, or
To leave them (to what torture) waiting at the door.

II

Heat has locked the heavy earth,
Given strength to every sound,
He, where his life still holds him to the ground,
In anaesthesia, groaning for re-birth,
Leans at the door.
From out the house there comes the dullest flutter;
A lackey; and thin giggling from behind that shutter.

III

His lost eyes lean to find and read the number.
Follows his knuckled rap, and hesitating curse.
He cannot wake himself; he may not slumber;

While on the long white wall across the road
Drives the thin outline of a dwindling hearse.

IV

Now the door opens wide.

    He: "Is there room inside?"
    She: "Are you past the bounds of pain?"
    He: "May my body lie in vain
              Among the dreams I cannot keep!"
    She: "Let him drink the cup of sleep."

V

Thin arms and ghostly hands; faint sky-blue eyes;
Long drooping lashes, lids like full-blown moons,
Clinging to any brink of floating skies:
What hope is there? What fear?—Unless to wake and see
Lingering flesh, or cold eternity.

O yet some face, half living, brings
Far gaze to him and croons:
    She: "You're white. You are alone.
              Can you not approach my sphere?"
    He: "I'm changing into stone."
    She: "Would I were! Would *I* were!"
Then the white attendants fill the cup.

VI

In the morning through the world,
Watch the flunkeys bring the coffee;
Watch the shepherds on the downs,
Lords and ladies at their toilet,
Farmers, merchants, frothing towns.

But look how he, unfortunate, now fumbles
Through unknown chambers, unheedful stumbles.
Can he evade the overshadowing night?
Are there not somewhere chinks of braided light?

VII

How do they leave who once are in those rooms?
Some may be found, they say, deeply asleep
In ruined tombs.
Some in white beds, with faces round them. Some
Wander the world, and never find a home.

Henry Newbolt

SIR HENRY JOHN NEWBOLT (1862–1938) was born at Bilston, Staffordshire, and educated at Clifton and Corpus Christi College, Oxford. After graduation he practiced law for twelve years, but began to devote more and more time to literature, writing poetry, drama, literary criticism, and indeed about anything which captured his attention. From 1900–1904 he was editor of the *Monthly Review*, and during the war served in the Admiralty and the Foreign Office. From this time especially, his involvement in public affairs increased; he sat on numerous committees and commissions, and in 1923 at the request of the Imperial Defense Committee undertook to complete vols. IV and V of the official *History of the Great War: Naval Operations*. He was knighted in 1915, and was awarded honorary degrees by several universities, including Oxford and Cambridge.

Newbolt's verses about ships and the sea were an immediate popular success, and today his reputation as a poet is mainly on their account, most people tending to regard him as a sort of nautical Rudyard Kipling. However, Newbolt wrote poetry on a variety of subjects, some of his later verse, especially, betraying an almost Keatsian lyricism. He was a staunch Christian and a believer in the traditions of the past as a living inspiration for the present. Stylistically Newbolt was a traditionalist, some of his more thoughtful verse showing the influence of Hardy, a writer whom he especially admired.

Drake's Drum

Drake he's in his hammock an' a thousand mile away,
  (Capten, art tha sleepin' there below?),
Slung atween the round shot in Nombre Dios Bay,
  An' dreamin' arl the time o' Plymouth Hoe.
Yarnder lumes the Island, yarnder lie the ships,
  Wi' sailor-lads a-dancin' heel-an'-toe,
An' the shore-lights flashin', and the night-tide dashin',
  He sees et arl so plainly as he saw et long ago.

Drake he was a Devon man, an' ruled the Devon seas,
  (Capten, art tha sleepin' there below?),
Rovin' tho' his death fell, he went wi' heart at ease,
  An' dreamin' arl the time o' Plymouth Hoe.
"Take my drum to England, hang et by the shore,
  Strike et when your powder's runnin' low;
If the Dons sight Devon, I'll quit the port o' Heaven,
  An' drum them up the Channel as we drummed them long
    ago."

Drake he's in his hammock till the great Armadas come,
  (Capten, art tha sleepin' there below?),
Slung atween the round shot, listenin' for the drum,
  An' dreamin' arl the time o' Plymouth Hoe.
Call him on the deep sea, call him up the Sound,
  Call him when ye sail to meet the foe;
Where the old trade's plyin' an' the old flag flyin'
  They shall find him ware an' wakin', as they found him long
    ago!

The Death of Admiral Blake

(AUGUST 17TH, 1657)

Laden with spoil of the South, fulfilled with the glory of
    achievement,
  And freshly crowned with never-dying fame,

Sweeping by shores where the names are the names of the
    victories of England,
  Across the Bay the squadron homeward came.

Proudly they came, but their pride was the pomp of a funeral
    at midnight,
  When dreader yet the lonely morrow looms;
Few are the words that are spoken, and faces are gaunt beneath
    the torchlight
  That does but darken more the nodding plumes.

Low on the field of his fame, past hope lay the Admiral
    triumphant,
  And fain to rest him after all his pain;
Yet for the love that he bore to his own land, ever unforgotten,
  He prayed to see the western hills again.

Fainter than stars in a sky long gray with the coming of the
    daybreak,
  Or sounds of night that fade when night is done,
So in the death-dawn faded the splendour and loud renown of
    warfare,
  And life of all its longings kept but one.

"Oh! to be there for an hour when the shade draws in beside
    the hedgerows,
  And falling apples wake the drowsy noon:
Oh! for the hour when the elms grow sombre and human in the
    twilight,
  And gardens dream beneath the rising moon.

"Only to look once more on the land of the memories of
    childhood,
  Forgetting weary winds and barren foam:
Only to bid farewell to the combe and the orchard and the
    moorland,
  And sleep at last among the fields of home!"

So he was silently praying, till now, when his strength was
    ebbing faster,

The Lizard lay before them faintly blue;
Now on the gleaming horizon the white cliffs laughed along the
    coast-line,
    And now the forelands took the shapes they knew.

There lay the Sound and the Island with green leaves down
    beside the water,
    The town, the Hoe, the masts with sunset fired—
Dreams! ay, dreams of the dead! for the great heart faltered on
    the threshold,
    And darkness took the land his soul desired.

Clifton Chapel

This is the Chapel: here, my son,
    Your father thought the thoughts of youth,
And heard the words that one by one
    The touch of Life has turned to truth.
Here in a day that is not far
    You too may speak with noble ghosts,
Of manhood and the vows of war
    You made before the Lord of Hosts.

To set the Cause above renown,
    To love the game beyond the prize,
To honour while you strike him down
    The foe that comes with fearless eyes:
To count the life of battle good,
    And dear the land that gave you birth,
And dearer yet the brotherhood
    That binds the brave of all the earth.—

My son, the oath is yours: the end
    Is His, Who built the world of strife,
Who gave His children Pain for friend,
    And Death for surest hope of life.

Today and here the fight's begun
    Of the great fellowship you're free;

Henceforth the School and you are one,
    And what You are, the race shall be.

God send you fortune: yet be sure,
    Among the lights that gleam and pass,
You'll live to follow none more pure
    Than that which glows on yonder brass:
"Qui procul hinc," the legend's writ,—
    The frontier-grave is far away—
"Qui ante diem periit:
    Sed miles, sed pro patria."

Wilfred Owen

WILFRED OWEN (1893–1918), the son of a railway clerk, was
educated at Birkenhead Institute and University College, Reading (then part of London University). At the outbreak of the
war he joined the Artists' Rifles and saw much action before
suffering a nervous breakdown which necessitated his return
to England. While convalescing at Craiglockhart War Hospital
near Edinburgh he met Siegfried Sassoon; the two men became
friends and Sassoon encouraged Owen to publish his yet unpublished poems. In 1918 Owen had recovered sufficiently to
return to the front, where he received the Military Cross. He
was killed one week before the armistice was signed.

Owen is generally acknowledged to be the greatest poet of
the 1914–1918 war. Although some of his early verse was
published in Edith Sitwell's *Wheels,* it has little in common with
that of the Sitwellian group. On the contrary, it is frequently
realistic and especially bitter in its denunciation of the horror
of modern war, betraying an acutely perceptive awareness of the
pity and suffering which war involved.

Music

I have been urged by earnest violins
And drunk their mellow sorrows to the slake
Of all my sorrows and my thirsting sins.
My heart has beaten for a brave drum's sake.
Huge chords have wrought me mighty: I have hurled
Thuds of God's thunder. And with old winds pondered
Over the curse of this chaotic world,—
With low lost winds that maundered as they wandered.

I have been gay with trivial fifes that laugh;
And songs more sweet than possible things are sweet;
And gongs, and oboes. Yet I guessed not half
Life's symphony till I had made hearts beat,
And touched Love's body into trembling cries,
And blown my love's lips into laughs and sighs.

Insensibility

I

Happy are men who yet before they are killed
Can let their veins run cold.
Whom no compassion fleers
Or makes their feet
Sore on the alleys cobbled with their brothers.
The front line withers,
But they are troops who fade, not flowers
For poets' tearful fooling:
Men, gaps for filling:
Losses, who might have fought
Longer; but no one bothers.

II

And some cease feeling
Even themselves or for themselves.
Dullness best solves
The tease and doubt of shelling,
And Chance's strange arithmetic
Comes simpler than the reckoning of their shilling.
They keep no check on armies' decimation.

III

Happy are these who lose imagination:
They have enough to carry with ammunition.
Their spirit drags no pack,
Their old wounds, save with cold, can not more ache.
Having seen all things red,
Their eyes are rid
Of the hurt of the colour of blood for ever.
And terror's first constriction over,
Their hearts remain small-drawn.
Their senses in some scorching cautery of battle
Now long since ironed,
Can laugh among the dying, unconcerned.

IV

Happy the soldier home, with not a notion
How somewhere, every dawn, some men attack,
And many sighs are drained.
Happy the lad whose mind was never trained:
His days are worth forgetting more than not.
He sings along the march
Which we march taciturn, because of dusk,
The long, forlorn, relentless trend
From larger day to huger night.

V

We wise, who with a thought besmirch
Blood over all our soul,
How should we see our task
But through his blunt and lashless eyes?
Alive, he is not vital overmuch;
Dying, not mortal overmuch;
Nor sad, nor proud,
Nor curious at all.
He cannot tell
Old men's placidity from his.

VI

But cursed are dullards whom no cannon stuns,
That they should be as stones;
Wretched are they, and mean
With paucity that never was simplicity.
By choice they made themselves immune
To pity and whatever mourns in man
Before the last sea and the hapless stars;
Whatever mourns when many leave these shores;
Whatever shares
The eternal reciprocity of tears.

Strange Meeting

It seemed that out of battle I escaped
Down some profound dull tunnel, long since scooped
Through granites which titanic wars had groined.
Yet also there encumbered sleepers groaned,
Too fast in thought or death to be bestirred.
Then, as I probed them, one sprang up, and stared

With piteous recognition in fixed eyes,
Lifting distressful hands as if to bless.
And by his smile, I knew that sullen hall,
By his dead smile I knew we stood in Hell.
With a thousand pains that vision's face was grained;
Yet no blood reached there from the upper ground,
And no guns thumped, or down the flues made moan.
"Strange friend," I said, "here is no cause to mourn."
"None," said that other, "save the undone years,
The hopelessness. Whatever hope is yours,
Was my life also; I went hunting wild
After the wildest beauty in the world,
Which lies not calm in eyes, or braided hair,
But mocks the steady running of the hour,
And if it grieves, grieves richlier than here.
For of my glee might many men have laughed,
And of my weeping something had been left,
Which must die now. I mean the truth untold,
The pity of war, the pity war distilled.
Now men will go content with what we spoiled,
Or, discontent, boil bloody, and be spilled.
They will be swift with swiftness of the tigress.
None will break ranks, though nations trek from progress.
Courage was mine, and I had mystery,
Wisdom was mine, and I had mastery:
To miss the march of this retreating world
Into vain citadels that are not walled.
Then, when much blood had clogged their chariot-wheels,
I would go up and wash them from sweet wells,
Even with truths that lie too deep for taint.
I would have poured my spirit without stint
But not through wounds; not on the cess of war.
Foreheads of men have bled where no wounds were.
I am the enemy you killed, my friend.
I knew you in this dark: for so you frowned
Yesterday through me as you jabbed and killed.
I parried; but my hands were loath and cold.
Let us sleep now. . . ."

Apologia Pro Poemate Meo

I, too, saw God through mud,—
 The mud that cracked on cheeks when wretches smiled.
 War brought more glory to their eyes than blood,
 And gave their laughs more glee than shakes a child.

Merry it was to laugh there—
 Where death becomes absurd and life absurder.
 For power was on us as we slashed bones bare
 Not to feel sickness or remorse of murder.

I, too, have dropped off fear—
 Behind the barrage, dead as my platoon,
 And sailed my spirit surging light and clear
 Past the entanglement where hopes lay strewn;

And witnessed exultation—
 Faces that used to curse me, scowl for scowl,
 Shine and lift up with passion of oblation,
 Seraphic for an hour; though they were foul.

I have made fellowships—
 Untold of happy lovers in old song.
 For love is not the binding of fair lips
 With the soft silk of eyes that look and long,

By Joy, whose ribbon slips,—
 But wound with war's hard wire whose stakes are strong;
 Bound with the bandage of the arm that drips;
 Knit in the webbing of the rifle-thong.

I have perceived much beauty
 In the hoarse oaths that kept our courage straight;
 Heard music in the silentness of duty;
 Found peace where shell-storms spouted reddest spate.

Nevertheless, except you share

With them in hell the sorrowful dark of hell,
Whose world is but the trembling of a flare,
And heaven but as the highway for a shell,

You shall not hear their mirth:
    You shall not come to think them well content
By any jest of mine. These men are worth
Your tears. You are not worth their merriment.

Greater Love

Red lips are not so red
    As the stained stones kissed by the English dead.
Kindness of wooed and wooer
Seems shame to their love pure.
O Love, your eyes lose lure
    When I behold eyes blinded in my stead!

Your slender attitude
    Trembles not exquisite like limbs knife-skewed,
Rolling and rolling there
Where God seems not to care;
Till the fierce love they bear
    Cramps them in death's extreme decrepitude.

Your voice sings not so soft,—
    Though even as wind murmuring through raftered loft,—
Your dear voice is not dear,
Gentle, and evening clear,
As theirs whom none now hear,
    Now earth has stopped their piteous mouths that coughed.

Heart, you were never hot
    Nor large, nor full like hearts made great with shot;
And though your hand be pale,
Paler are all which trail
Your cross through flame and hail:
    Weep, you may weep, for you may touch them not.

Anthem for Doomed Youth

What passing-bells for these who die as cattle?
Only the monstrous anger of the guns.
Only the stuttering rifles' rapid rattle
Can patter out their hasty orisons.
No mockeries now for them, no prayers nor bells,
Nor any voice of mourning save the choirs,—
The shrill, demented choirs of wailing shells;
And bugles calling for them from sad shires.

What candles may be held to speed them all?
Not in the hands of boys, but in their eyes
Shall shine the holy glimmers of good-byes.
The pallor of girls' brows shall be their pall;
Their flowers the tenderness of patient minds,
And each slow dusk a drawing-down of blinds.

Dulce et Decorum Est

Bent double, like old beggars under sacks,
Knock-kneed, coughing like hags, we cursed through sludge,
Till on the haunting flares we turned our backs
And towards our distant rest began to trudge.
Men marched asleep. Many had lost their boots
But limped on, blood-shod. All went lame; all blind;
Drunk with fatigue; deaf even to the hoots
Of tired, outstripped Five-Nines that dropped behind.

Gas! *Gas!* Quick, boys!—An ecstasy of fumbling,
Fitting the clumsy helmets just in time;
But someone still was yelling out and stumbling
And flound'ring like a man in fire or lime . . .
Dim, through the misty panes and thick green light,
As under a green sea, I saw him drowning.

In all my dreams, before my helpless sight,
He plunges at me, guttering, choking, drowning.

If in some smothering dreams you too could pace
Behind the wagon that we flung him in,
And watch the white eyes writhing in his face,
His hanging face, like a devil's sick of sin;
If you could hear, at every jolt, the blood
Come gargling from the froth-corrupted lungs,
Obscene as cancer, bitter as the cud
Of vile, incurable sores on innocent tongues,—
My friend, you would not tell with such high zest
To children ardent for some desperate glory,
The old Lie: Dulce et decorum est
Pro patria mori.

Futility

Move him into the sun—
Gently its touch awoke him once,
At home, whispering of fields unsown.
Always it woke him, even in France,
Until this morning and this snow.
If anything might rouse him now
The kind old sun will know.

Think how it wakes the seeds,—
Woke, once, the clays of a cold star.
Are limbs, so dear-achieved, are sides,
Full-nerved—still warm—too hard to stir?
Was it for this the clay grew tall?
—O what made fatuous sunbeams toil
To break earth's sleep at all?

The Dead-Beat

He dropped,—more sullenly than wearily,
Lay stupid like a cod, heavy like meat,
And none of us could kick him to his feet;

Just blinked at my revolver, blearily;
—Didn't appear to know a war was on,
Or see the blasted trench at which he stared.
"I'll do 'em in," he whined. "If this hand's spared,
I'll murder them, I will."
                                    A low voice said,
"It's Blighty, p'raps, he sees; his pluck's all gone,
Dreaming of all the valiant, that aren't dead:
Bold uncles, smiling ministerially;
Maybe his brave young wife, getting her fun
In some new home, improved materially.
It's not these stiffs have crazed him; nor the Hun."

We sent him down at last, out of the way.
Unwounded;—stout lad, too, before that strafe.
Malingering? Stretcher-bearers winked, "Not half!"
Next day I heard the Doc's well-whiskied laugh:
"That scum you sent last night soon died. Hooray!"

Isaac Rosenberg

Isaac Rosenberg (1890–1918) was born in Bristol of lower-class parents, the family moving to London seven years later, where Isaac attended an elementary school in the East End until he was fourteen. At this age he was apprenticed to an engraver, took evening classes at Birkbeck College, and in 1911 was able to enter the Slade School of Art. In 1914 he went to South Africa, in the hope of curing a weakness in his lungs, but returned to England the following year, entered the army, and was killed in action in April, 1918.

Though Rosenberg hoped to make his way as a painter, he also enjoyed writing poetry, but with neither was he able to achieve financial success. As a poet he recognized the pity of war, but the horror especially, viewing the conflict with classical stoicism, at times almost with detachment. Though his early verse betrays the influence of Keats, that which he wrote later demonstrates an admiration for Donne.

Dawn

O tender first cold flush of rose,
O budded dawn, wake dreamily;
Your dim lips as your lids unclose
Murmur your own sad threnody.
O as the soft and frail lights break
Upon your eyelids, and your eyes
Wider and wider grow and wake,
The old pale glory dies.

And then as sleep lies down to sleep
And all her dreams lie somewhere dead,
(While naked day digs goldly deep
For light to lie uncoverèd),
Your own ghost fades with dream-ghosts there,
Our lorn eyes see, mid glimmering lips,
Pass through the haunted dream-moved air,
Slowly, their laden ships.

God

In his malodorous brain what slugs and mire,
Lanthorned in his oblique eyes, guttering burned!
His body lodged a rat where men nursed souls.
The world flashed grape-green eyes of a foiled cat
To him. On fragments of an old shrunk power,
On shy and maimed, on women wrung awry,
He lay, a bullying hulk, to crush them more.
But when one, fearless, turned and clawed like bronze,
Cringing was easy to blunt these stern paws,
And he would weigh the heavier on those after.

Who rests in God's mean flattery now? Your wealth
Is but his cunning to make death more hard.
Your iron sinews take more pain in breaking.
And he has made the market for your beauty
Too poor to buy, although you die to sell.

Only that he has never heard of sleep;
And when the cats come out the rats are sly.
Here we are safe till he slinks in at dawn.

But he has gnawed a fibre from strange roots,
And in the morning some pale wonder ceases.
Things are not strange and strange things are forgetful.
Ah! if the day were arid, somehow lost
Out of us, but it is as hair of us,
And only in the hush no wind stirs it.
And in the light vague trouble lifts and breathes,
And restlessness still shadows the lost ways.
The fingers shut on voices that pass through,
Where blind farewells are taken easily. . . .

Ah! this miasma of a rotting God!

Break of Day in the Trenches

The darkness crumbles away—
It is the same old druid Time as ever.
Only a live thing leaps my hand—
A queer sardonic rat—
As I pull the parapet's poppy
To stick behind my ear.
Droll rat, they would shoot you if they knew
Your cosmopolitan sympathies.
Now you have touched this English hand
You will do the same to a German—
Soon, no doubt, if it be your pleasure
To cross the sleeping green between.
It seems you inwardly grin as you pass
Strong eyes, fine limbs, haughty athletes
Less chanced than you for life,
Bonds to the whims of murder,
Sprawled in the bowels of the earth,

The torn fields of France.
What do you see in our eyes
At the shrieking iron and flame
Hurled through still heavens?
What quaver—what heart aghast?
Poppies whose roots are in man's veins
Drop, and are ever dropping;
But mine in my ear is safe,
Just a little white with the dust.

Louse Hunting

Nudes—stark and glistening,
Yelling in lurid glee. Grinning faces
And raging limbs
Whirl over the floor one fire.
For a shirt verminously busy
Yon soldier tore from his throat, with oaths
Godhead might shrink at, but not the lice.
And soon the shirt was aflare
Over the candle he'd lit while we lay.

Then we all sprang up and stript
To hunt the verminous brood.
Soon like a demon's pantomime
The place was raging.
See the silhouettes agape,
See the gibbering shadows
Mixed with the battled arms on the wall.
See gargantuan hooked fingers
Pluck in supreme flesh
To smutch supreme littleness.
See the merry limbs in hot Highland fling
Because some wizard vermin
Charmed from the quiet this revel
When our ears were half lulled
By the dark music
Blown from Sleep's trumpet.

Returning, We Hear the Larks

Sombre the night is.
And though we have our lives, we know
What sinister threat lurks there.

Dragging these anguished limbs, we only know
This poison-blasted track opens on our camp—
On a little safe sleep.

But hark! joy—joy—strange joy.
Lo! heights of night ringing with unseen larks.
Music showering on our upturned list'ning faces.

Death could drop from the dark
As easily as song—
But song only dropped,
Like a blind man's dreams on the sand
By dangerous tides,
Like a girl's dark hair for she dreams no ruin lies there,
Or her kisses where a serpent hides.

Dead Man's Dump

The plunging limbers over the shattered track
Racketed with their rusty freight,
Stuck out like many crowns of thorns,
And the rusty stakes like sceptres old
To stay the flood of brutish men
Upon our brothers dear.

The wheels lurched over sprawled dead
But pained them not, though their bones crunched,
Their shut mouths made no moan.
They lie there huddled, friend and foeman,
Man born of man, and born of woman,

And shells go crying over them
From night till night and now.

Earth has waited for them,
All the time of their growth
Fretting for their decay:
Now she has them at last!
In the strength of their strength
Suspended—stopped and held.

What fierce imaginings their dark souls lit?
Earth! have they gone into you!
Somewhere they must have gone,
And flung on your hard back
Is their soul's sack
Emptied of God-ancestralled essences.
Who hurled them out? Who hurled?

None saw their spirits' shadow shake the grass,
Or stood aside for the half used life to pass
Out of those doomed nostrils and the doomed mouth,
When the swift iron burning bee
Drained the wild honey of their youth.

What of us who, flung on the shrieking pyre,
Walk, our usual thoughts untouched,
Our lucky limbs as on ichor fed,
Immortal seeming ever?
Perhaps when the flames beat loud on us,
A fear may choke in our veins
And the startled blood may stop.

The air is loud with death,
The dark air spurts with fire,
The explosions ceaseless are.
Timelessly now, some minutes past,
These dead strode time with vigorous life,
Till the shrapnel called "An end!"
But not to all. In bleeding pangs

Some borne on stretchers dreamed of home,
Dear things, war-blotted from their hearts.

Maniac Earth! howling and flying, your bowel
Seared by the jagged fire, the iron love,
The impetuous storm of savage love.
Dark Earth! dark Heavens! swinging in chemic smoke,
What dead are born when you kiss each soundless soul
With lightning and thunder from your mined heart,
Which man's self dug, and his blind fingers loosed?

A man's brains splattered on
A stretcher-bearer's face;
His shook shoulders slipped their load,
But when they bent to look again
The drowning soul was sunk too deep
For human tenderness.

They left this dead with the older dead,
Stretched at the cross roads.

Burnt black by strange decay
Their sinister faces lie,
The lid over each eye,
The grass and coloured clay
More motion have than they,
Joined to the great sunk silences.

Here is one not long dead;
His dark hearing caught our far wheels,
And the choked soul stretched weak hands
To reach the living word the far wheels said,
The blood-dazed intelligence beating for light,
Crying through the suspense of the far torturing wheels
Swift for the end to break
Or the wheels to break,
Cried as the tide of the world broke over his sight.

Will they come? Will they ever come?
Even as the mixed hoofs of the mules,

The quivering-bellied mules,
And the rushing wheels all mixed
With his tortured upturned sight.
So we crashed round the bend,
We heard his weak scream,
We heard his very last sound,
And our wheels grazed his dead face.

Siegfried Sassoon

SIEGFRIED SASSOON (1886-1967) was born in Kent and educated at Marlborough and Clare College, Cambridge. Although bitterly opposed to war and at heart a pacifist, Sassoon served with distinction during the 1914-1918 war and was awarded the Military Cross. During the war he was sent to Craiglockhart Hospital, suffering from shellshock, where he met Wilfred Owen, who immediately responded to him and looked to him for advice concerning his own poetry. After the war Sassoon engaged in literary journalism, and from 1918 onward published volumes of lyrics and satires and eventually, in 1947, his *Collected Poems*.

Sassoon has described himself as essentially a poet of the pre-Eliot era, and is chiefly remembered for his early satires in which he strove to shock people out of their complacent wartime belief that the three cardinal virtues were glory, duty, and sacrifice. His earliest poetry, however, is somewhat vapid and romantic, while his more recent meditative lyricism, expressed in traditional forms and conventional language, is elegant but on the whole innocuous.

The Death-Bed

He drowsed and was aware of silence heaped
Round him, unshaken as the steadfast walls;
Aqueous like floating rays of amber light,
Soaring and quivering in the wings of sleep,—
Silence and safety; and his mortal shore
Lipped by the inward, moonless waves of death.

Someone was holding water to his mouth.
He swallowed, unresisting; moaned and dropped
Through crimson gloom to darkness and forgot
The opiate throb and ache that was his wound.
Water—calm, sliding green above the weir;
Water—a sky-lit alley for his boat,
Bird-voiced, and bordered with reflected flowers
And shaken hues of summer: drifting down,
He dipped contented oars, and sighed, and slept.

Night, with a gust of wind, was in the ward,
Blowing the curtain to a glimmering curve.
Night. He was blind; he could not see the stars
Glinting among the wraiths of wandering cloud;
Queer blots of colour, purple, scarlet, green,
Flickered and faded in his drowning eyes.

Rain; he could hear it rustling through the dark
Fragrance and passionless music woven as one;
Warm rain on drooping roses; pattering showers
That soak the woods; not the harsh rain that sweeps
Behind the thunder, but a trickling peace
Gently and slowly washing life away.
            .   .   .   .
He stirred, shifting his body; then the pain
Leaped like a prowling beast, and gripped and tore
His groping dreams with grinding claws and fangs.
But some one was beside him; soon he lay
Shuddering because that evil thing had passed.
And Death, who'd stepped toward him, paused and stared.

Light many lamps and gather round his bed.
Lend him your eyes, warm blood, and will to live.
Speak to him; rouse him; you may save him yet.
He's young; he hated war; how should he die
When cruel old campaigners win safe through?

But Death replied: "I choose him." So he went,
And there was silence in the summer night;
Silence and safety; and the veils of sleep.
Then, far away, the thudding of the guns.

Counter-Attack

We'd gained our first objective hours before
While dawn broke like a face with blinking eyes,
Pallid, unshaved and thirsty, blind with smoke.
Things seemed all right at first. We held their line,
With bombers posted, Lewis guns well placed,
And clink of shovels deepening the shallow trench.
The place was rotten with dead; green clumsy legs
High-booted, sprawled and grovelled along the saps;
And trunks, face downwards, in the sucking mud,
Wallowed like trodden sand-bags loosely filled;
And naked sodden buttocks, mats of hair,
Bulged, clotted heads slept in the plastering slime.

And then the rain began,—the jolly old rain!
A yawning soldier knelt against the bank,
Staring across the morning blear with fog;
He wondered when the Allemands would get busy;
And then, of course, they started with five-nines
Traversing, sure as fate, and never a dud.
Mute in the clamour of shells he watched them burst,
Spouting dark earth and wire with gusts from hell,
While posturing giants dissolved in drifts of smoke.
He crouched and flinched, dizzy with galloping fear,
Sick for escape,—loathing the strangled horror
And butchered, frantic gestures of the dead.

An officer came blundering down the trench:
"Stand to and man the fire-step!" On he went . . .
Gasping and bawling, "Fire-step. . . . Counter-Attack!"
Then the haze lifted. Bombing on the right
Down the old sap: machine-guns on the left;
And stumbling figures looming out in front.
"O Christ, they're coming at us!" Bullets spat,
And he remembered his rifle . . . rapid fire . . .
And started blazing wildly. . . . Then a bang
Crumpled and spun him sideways, knocked him out
To grunt and wriggle: none heeded him; he choked
And fought the flapping veils of smothering gloom,
Lost in a blurred confusion of yells and groans. . . .
Down, and down, and down, he sank and drowned,
Bleeding to death. The counter-attack had failed.

Dreamers

Soldiers are citizens of death's grey land,
  Drawing no dividend from time's to-morrows.
In the great hour of destiny they stand,
  Each with his feuds, and jealousies, and sorrows.
Soldiers are sworn to action; they must win
  Some flaming, fatal climax with their lives.
Soldiers are dreamers; when the guns begin
  They think of firelit homes, clean beds, and wives.

I see them in foul dug-outs, gnawed by rats,
  And in the ruined trenches, lashed with rain,
Dreaming of things they did with balls and bats,
  And mocked by hopeless longing to regain
Bank-holidays, and picture shows, and spats,
  And going to the office in the train.

Attack

At dawn the ridge emerges massed and dun
In the wild purple of the glowering sun,

Smouldering through spouts of drifting smoke that shroud
The menacing scarred slope; and, one by one,
Tanks creep and topple forward to the wire.
The barrage roars and lifts. Then, clumsily bowed
With bombs and guns and shovels and battle-gear,
Men jostle and climb to meet the bristling fire.
Lines of grey, muttering faces, masked with fear,
They leave their trenches, going over the top,
While time ticks blank and busy on their wrists,
And hope with furtive eyes and grappling fists,
Flounders in mud. O Jesus, make it stop!

Aftermath

Have you forgotten yet?
For the world's events have rumbled on since those gagged days,
Like traffic checked awhile at the crossing of city ways:
And the haunted gap in your mind has filled with thoughts
    that flow
Like clouds in the lit heavens of life; and you're a man reprieved
    to go,
Taking your peaceful share of Time, with joy to spare.
But the past is just the same—and War's a bloody game . . .
Have you forgotten yet? . . .
Look down, and swear by the slain of the War that you'll never
    forget.

Do you remember the dark months you held the sector at
    Mametz—
The nights you watched and wired and dug and piled sandbags
    on parapets?
Do you remember the rats; and the stench
Of corpses rotting in front of the front-line trench—
And dawn coming, dirty-white, and chill with a hopeless rain?
Do you ever stop and ask, "Is it all going to happen again?"

Do you remember that hour of din before the attack—
And the anger, the blind compassion that seized and shook you
    then

As you peered at the doomed and haggard faces of your men?
Do you remember the stretcher-cases lurching back
With dying eyes and lolling heads—those ashen-grey
Masks of the lads who once were keen and kind and gay?

Have you forgotten yet? . . .
Look up, and swear by the green of the spring that you'll never
    forget.

"They"

The Bishop tells us: "When the boys come back
They will not be the same; for they'll have fought
In a just cause: they lead the last attack
On Anti-Christ; their comrades' blood has bought
New right to breed an honourable race,
They have challenged Death and dared him face to face."

"We're none of us the same!" the boys reply.
"For George lost both his legs; and Bill's stone blind;
Poor Jim's shot through the lungs and like to die;
And Bert's gone syphilitic: you'll not find
A chap who's served that hasn't found *some* change!"
And the Bishop said: "The ways of God are strange!"

Storm on Fifth Avenue

A sallow waiter brings me six huge oysters. . . .
Gloom shutters up the sunset with a plague
Of unpropitious twilight jagged asunder
By flashlight demonstrations. *Gee, what a peach
Of a climate!* (Pardon slang: these sultry storms
Afflict me with neurosis: rumbling thunder
Shakes my belief in academic forms.)

An oyster-coloured atmospheric rumpus
Beats up to blot the sunken daylight's gildings.
Against the looming cloud-bank, ivory-pale,

Stand twenty-storied blocks of office buildings.
Snatched upward on a gust, lost news-sheets sail
Forlorn in lone arena of mid-air;
Flapping like melancholy kites, they scare
My gaze, a note of wildness in the scene.

Out on the pattering side-walk, people hurry
For shelter, while the tempest swoops to scurry
Across to Brooklyn. Bellying figures clutch
At wide-brimmed hats and bend to meet the weather
Alarmed for fresh-worn silks and flurried feather.

Then hissing deluge splashes down to beat
The darkly glistening flatness of the street.
Only the cars nose on through rain-lashed twilight:
Only the Sherman statue, angel-guided,
Maintains its mock-heroic martial gesture.

* * *

A sallow waiter brings me beans and pork . . .
Outside there's fury in the firmament.
Ice-cream, of course, will follow; and I'm content.
O Babylon! O Carthage! O New York!

Falling Asleep

Voices moving about in the quiet house:
Thud of feet and a muffled shutting of doors:
Everyone yawning. Only the clocks are alert.

Out in the night there's autumn-smelling gloom
Crowded with whispering trees; across the park
A hollow cry of hounds like lonely bells:
And I know that the clouds are moving across the moon;
The low, red, rising moon. Now herons call
And wrangle by their pool; and hooting owls
Sail from the wood above pale stooks of oats.

Waiting for sleep, I drift from thoughts like these;
And where to-day was dream-like, build my dreams.

Music . . . there was a bright white room below,
And someone singing a song about a soldier,
One hour, two hours ago: and soon the song
Will be *"last night";* but now the beauty swings
Across my brain, ghost of remembered chords
Which still can make such radiance in my dream
That I can watch the marching of my soldiers,
And count their faces; faces; sunlit faces.

Falling asleep . . . the herons, and the hounds. . . .
September in the darkness; and the world
I've known; all fading past me into peace.

Owen Seaman

OWEN SEAMAN (1861-1936) was educated at Shrewsbury and
Clare College, Cambridge, where he distinguished himself by
taking a First in the Classical Tripos and being Captain of
Clare Boats. He became a schoolmaster at Rossal, and later
Professor of Literature at Durham College of Science at
Newcastle-upon-Tyne. For a time he practiced law, but in
1897 he joined the staff of *Punch* magazine and so began his
long career with that journal, culminating in his editorship
from 1906 to 1932.

Seaman's talent was for parody and satire, in both prose
and verse, his most successful being his verse parodies of his
Decadent contemporaries included in *The Battle of the Bays*
(1896). During the 1914-1918 war he wrote a number of verses
of a somewhat mindless, patriotic kind, reflecting his optimism
and devotion to his native land rather than the stirrings of
poetic genius.

A Ballad of a Bun

(AFTER J.D.)

"I am sister to the mountains now,
  And sister to the sun and moon."

"Heed not bellettrist jargon."
                                JOHN DAVIDSON.

From Whitsuntide to Whitsuntide—
  That is to say, all through the year—
Her patient pen was occupied
  With songs and tales of pleasant cheer.

But still her talent went to waste
  Like flotsam on an open sea;
She never hit the public taste,
  Or knew the knack of Bellettrie.

Across the sounding City's fogs
  There hurtled round her weary head
The thunder of the rolling logs;
  "The Critics' Carnival!" she said.

Immortal prigs took heaven by storm,
  Prigs scattered largesses of praise;
The work of both was rather warm;
  "This is," she said, "the thing that pays!"

Sharp envy turned her wine to blood—
  I mean it turned her blood to wine;
And this resolve came like a flood—
  "The cake of knowledge must be mine!

"I am in Eve's predicament—
  I sha'n't be happy till I've sinned;
Away!" She lightly rose, and sent
  Her scruples sailing down the wind.

She did not tear her open breast,
　Nor leave behind a track of gore,
But carried flannel next her chest,
　And wore the boots she always wore.

Across the sounding City's din
　She wandered, looking indiscreet,
And ultimately landed in
　The neighbourhood of Regent Street.

She ran against a resolute
　Policeman standing like a wall;
She kissed his feet and asked the route
　To where they held the Carnival.

Her strange behaviour caused remark;
　They said, "Her reason has been lost;"
Beside her eyes the gas was dark,
　But that was owing to the frost.

A Decadent was dribbling by;
　"Lady," he said, "you seem undone;
You need a panacea; try
　This sample of the Bodley bun.

"It is fulfilled of precious spice,
　Whereof I give the recipe;—
Take common dripping, stew in vice,
　And serve with vertu; taste and see!

"And lo! I brand you on the brow
　As kin to Nature's lowest germ;
You are sister to the microbe now,
　And second-cousin to the worm."

He gave her of his golden store,
　Such hunger hovered in her look;
She took the bun, and asked for more,
　And went away and wrote a book.

To put the matter shortly, she
   Became the topic of the town;
In all the lists of Bellettrie
   Her name was regularly down.

"We recognise," the critics wrote,
   "Maupassant's verve and Heine's wit;"
Some even made a verbal note
   Of Shakespeare being out of it.

The seasons went and came again;
   At length the languid Public cried:
"It is a sorry sort of Lane
   That hardly ever turns aside.

"We want a little change of air;
   On that," they said, "we must insist;
We cannot any longer bear
   The seedy sex-impressionist."

Across the sounding City's din
   This rumour smote her on the ear:
"The publishers are going in
   For songs and tales of pleasant cheer!"

"Alack!" she said, "I lost the art,
   And left my womanhood foredone,
When first I trafficked in the mart
   All for a mess of Bodley bun.

"I cannot cut my kin at will,
   Or jilt the protoplastic germ;
I am sister to the microbe still,
   And second-cousin to the worm!"

The Rhyme of the Kipperling

(AFTER R. K.)

[N.B.—No nautical terms or statements guaranteed.]

Away by the haunts of the Yang-tse-boo,
  Where the Yuletide runs cold gin,
And the rollicking sign of the *Lord Knows Who*
  Sees mariners drink like sin;
Where the *Jolly Roger* tips his quart
  To the luck of the *Union Jack;*
And some are screwed on the foreign port,
  And some on the starboard tack;—
Ever they tell the tale anew
  Of the chase for the kipperling swag;
How the smack *Tommy This* and the smack *Tommy That*
They broached each other like a whiskey-vat,
  And the *Fuzzy-Wuz* took the bag.

Now this is the law of the herring fleet that harries the northern
  main
Tattooed in scars on the chests of the tars with a brand like
  the brand of Cain:
That none may woo the sea-born shrew save such as pay their
  way
With a kipperling netted at noon of night and cured ere the
  crack of day.

It was the woman Sal o' the Dune, and the men were three to
  one,
Bill the Skipper and Ned the Nipper and Sam that was Son of
  a Gun;
Bill was a Skipper and Ned was a Nipper and Sam was the Son
  of a Gun,
And the woman was Sal o' the Dune, as I said, and the men
  were three to one.

There was never a light in the sky that night of the soft
  midsummer gales,

But the great man-bloaters snorted low, and the young 'uns
  sang like whales;
And out laughed Sal (like a dog-toothed wheel was the laugh
  that Sal laughed she):
"Now who's for a bride on the shady side of up'ards of forty-
  three?"

And Neddy he swore by butt and bend, and Billy by bend and
  bitt,
And nautical names that no man frames but your amateur
  nautical wit;
And Sam said, "Shiver my topping-lifts and scuttle my foc's'le
  yarn,
And may I be curst, if I'm not in first with a kipperling slued
  astarn!"

Now the smack *Tommy This* and the smack *Tommy That* and
  the *Fuzzy-Wuz* smack, all three,
Their captains bold, they were Bill and Ned and Sam
  respectivelee.

And it's writ in the rules that the primary schools of kippers
  should get off cheap
For a two mile reach off Foulness beach when the July tide's at
  neap;

And the lawless lubbers that lust for loot and filch the yearling
  stock
They get smart raps from the coastguard chaps with their
  blunderbuss fixed half-cock.

Now Bill the Skipper and Ned the Nipper could tell green
  cheese from blue,
And Bill knew a trick and Ned knew a trick, but Sam knew a
  trick worth two.

So Bill he sneaks a corporal's breeks and a belt of pipeclayed
  hide,
And splices them on to the jibsail-boom like a troopship on the
  tide.

And likewise Ned to his masthead he runs a rag of the Queen's,
With a rusty sword and a moke on board to bray like the Horse
    Marines.

But Sam sniffs gore and he keeps off-shore and he waits for
    things to stir,
Then he tracks for the deep with a long fog-horn rigged up
    like a bowchasér.

Now scarce had Ned dropped line and lead when he spots the
    pipeclayed hide,
And the corporal's breeks on the jibsail-boom like a troopship
    on the tide;
And Bill likewise, when he ups and spies the slip of a rag of
    the Queen's,
And the rusty sword, and he sniffs aboard the moke of the
    Horse Marines.

So they each luffed sail, and they each turned tail, and they
    whipped their wheels like mad,
When the one he said "By the Lord, it's Ned!" and the other,
    "It's Bill, by Gad!"

Then about and about, and nozzle to snout, they rammed
    through breach and brace,
And the splinters flew as they mostly do when a Government
    test takes place.

Then up stole Sam with his little ram and the nautical talk
    flowed free,
And in good bold type might have covered the two front sheets
    of the *P. M. G.*

But the fog-horn bluff was safe enough, where all was weed and
    weft,
And the conger-eels were a-making meals, and the pick of the
    tackle left
Was a binnacle-lid and a leak in the bilge and the chip of a
    cracked sheerstrake

And the corporal's belt and the moke's cool pelt and a portrait
    of Francis Drake.

So Sam he hauls the dead men's trawls and he booms for the
    harbour-bar,
And the splitten fry are salted dry by the blink of the morning
    star.

And Sal o' the Dune was wed next moon by the man that paid
    his way
With a kipperling netted at noon of night and cured ere the
    crack of day;
For such is the law of the herring fleet that bloats on the
    northern main,
Tattooed in scars on the chests of the tars with a brand like the
    brand of Cain.

And still in the haunts of the Yang-tse-boo
Ever they tell the tale anew
    Of the chase for the kipperling swag;
How the smack *Tommy This* and the smack *Tommy That*
They broached each other like a whiskey-vat,
    And the *Fuzzy-Wuz* took the bag.

To a Boy-Poet
of the Decadence

[Showing curious reversal of epigram—"La nature l'a fait sanglier; la
civilisation l'a réduit à l'état de cochon."]

But my good little man, you have made a mistake
    If you really are pleased to suppose
That the Thames is alight with the lyrics you make;
    We could all do the same if we chose.

From Solomon down, we may read, as we run,
    Of the ways of a man and a maid;
There is nothing that's new to us under the sun,
    And certainly not in the shade.

The erotic affairs that you fiddle aloud
   Are as vulgar as coin of the mint;
And you merely distinguish yourself from the crowd
   By the fact that you put 'em in print.

You're a 'prentice, my boy, in the primitive stage,
   And you itch, like a boy, to confess:
When you know a bit more of the arts of the age
   You will probably talk a bit less.

For your dull little vices we don't care a fig,
   It is *this* that we deeply deplore;
You were cast for a common or usual pig,
   But you play the invincible bore.

Pro Patria

England, in this great fight to which you go
   Because, where Honour calls you, go you must,
Be glad, whatever comes, at least to know
   You have your quarrel just.

Peace was your care; before the nations' bar
   Her cause you pleaded and her ends you sought;
But not for her sake, being what you are,
   Could you be bribed and bought.

Others may spurn the pledge of land to land,
   May with the brute sword stain a gallant past;
But by the seal to which *you* set your hand,
   Thank God, you still stand fast!

Forth, then, to front that peril of the deep
   With smiling lips and in your eyes the light,
Steadfast and confident, of those who keep
   Their storied scutcheon bright.

And we, whose burden is to watch and wait—
   High-hearted ever, strong in faith and prayer,

We ask what offering we may consecrate,
   What humble service share.

To steel our souls against the lust of ease;
   To find our welfare in the common good;
To hold together, merging all degrees
   In one wide brotherhood;—

To teach that he who saves himself is lost;
   To bear in silence though our hearts may bleed;
To spend ourselves, and never count the cost,
   For others' greater need;—

To go our quiet ways, subdued and sane;
   To hush all vulgar clamour of the street;
With level calm to face alike the strain
   Of triumph or defeat;—

This be our part, for so we serve you best,
   So best confirm their prowess and their pride,
Your warrior sons, to whom in this high test
   Our fortunes we confide.

Thomas of the Light Heart

Facing the guns, he jokes as well
   As any Judge upon the Bench;
Between the crash of shell and shell
   His laughter rings along the trench;
He seems immensely tickled by a
Projectile which he calls a "Black Maria."

He whistles down the day-long road,
   And, when the chilly shadows fall
And heavier hangs the weary load,
   Is he down-hearted? Not at all.
'Tis then he takes a light and airy
View of the tedious route to Tipperary.

His songs are not exactly hymns;
   He never learned them in the choir;
And yet they brace his dragging limbs
   Although they miss the sacred fire;
Although his choice and cherished gems
Do not include "The Watch upon the Thames."

He takes to fighting as a game;
   He does no talking, through his hat,
Of holy missions; all the same
   He has his faith—be sure of that;
He'll not disgrace his sporting breed,
Nor play what isn't cricket. There's his creed.

To the Enemy, on His Achievement

Now wanes the third moon since your conquering host
   Was to have laid our weakling army low,
And walked through France at will. For that loud boast
     What have you got to show?

A bomb that chipped a tower of Notre Dame,
   Leaving its mark like trippers' knives that scar
The haunts of beauty—that's the best *réclame*
     You have achieved so far.

Paris, that through her humbled Triumph-Arch
   Was doomed to see you tread your fathers' tracks—
Paris, your goal, now lies a six days' march
     Behind your homing backs.

Pressed to the borders where you lately passed
   Bulging with insolence and fat with pride,
You stake your all upon a desperate cast
     To stem the gathering tide.

Eastward the Russian draws you to his fold,
   Content, on his own ground, to bide his day,

Out of whose toils not many feet of old
    Found the returning way.

And still along the seas our watchers keep
    Their grip upon your throat with bands of steel,
While that Armada, which should rake the deep,
    Skulks in its hole at Kiel.

So stands your record—stay, I cry you grace—
    I wronged you. There is Belgium, where your sword
Has bled to death a free and gallant race
    Whose life you held in ward;

Where on your trail the smoking land lies bare
    Of hearth and homestead, and the dead babe clings
About its murdered mother's breast—ah, there,
    Yes, you have done great things!

Edith Sitwell

EDITH SITWELL (1887-1964), perhaps the most distinguished of the family trio comprising Osbert, Sacheverell, and Edith herself, was born of aristocratic parents at Scarborough in Yorkshire, and educated privately. Though a poet of distinction, she also made her name as a literary critic of sound judgment if excessive sensibility, her study of Alexander Pope in particular being well received. In 1954 she was made Dame Commander, Order of the British Empire, the first poet to be so honored, and she also received honorary degrees from several British universities including Oxford. In 1958 she became a convert to Roman Catholicism.

In the Introduction to her *Canticle of the Rose* Edith Sitwell wrote:

> At the time I began to write, a change in the direction, imagery, and rhythm in poetry had become necessary, owing to the rhythmical flaccidity, the verbal deadness, the dead and expected patterns, of some of the poetry immediately preceding us.

Thus her early poetry was a conscious attempt to break with the traditions of the immediate past. Her employment of bizarre and exotic images, jigging modern dance rhythms, and violent *transpositions des sens* are perhaps best understood as a counterblast against the vapidities of the Georgian tradition. Later, however, believing poetry to be the "deification of reality," Edith Sitwell's verse took on a more serious tone, the poetry she wrote during the Second World War, especially, revealing a thoughtfulness and humility which many thought her incapable of achieving.

337

Green Geese

The trees were hissing like green geese . . .
The words they tried to say were these:

"When the great Queen Claude was dead
They buried her deep in the potting-shed."

The moon smelt sweet as nutmeg-root
On the ripe peach-trees' leaves and fruit,

And her sandal-wood body leans upright,
To the gardener's fright, through the summer night.

* * *

The bee-wing'd warm afternoon light roves
Gilding her hair (wooden nutmegs and cloves),

And the gardener plants his seedsman's samples
Where no wild unicorn herd tramples—

In clouds like potting-sheds he pots
The budding planets in leaves cool as grots,

For the great Queen Claude when the light's gilded gaud
Sings Miserere, Gloria, Laud.

But when he passes the potting-shed,
Fawning upon him comes the dead—

Each cupboard's wooden skeleton
Is a towel-horse when the clock strikes one,

And light is high—yet with ghosts it winces
All night 'mid wrinkled tarnished quinces,

When the dark air seems soft down
Of the wandering owl brown.

They know the clock-faced sun and moon
Must wrinkle like the quinces soon

(That once in dark blue grass dew-dabbled
Lay) . . . those ghost-like turkeys gabbled

To the scullion baking the Castle bread—
"The Spirit, too, must be fed, be fed;

Without our flesh we cannot see—
Oh, give us back Stupidity!" . . .

But death had twisted their thin speech,
It could not fit the mind's small niche—

Upon the warm blue grass outside,
They realised that they had died.

Only the light from their wooden curls roves
Like the sweet smell of nutmegs and cloves

Buried deep in the potting-shed,
Sighed those green geese, "Now the Queen is dead."

Two Kitchen Songs

I

The harsh bray and hollow
Of the pot and the pan
Seems Midas defying
The great god Apollo!
The leaves' great golden crowns
Hang on the trees;
The maids in their long gowns
Hunt me through these.
Grand'am, Grand'am,
From the pan I am
Flying . . . country gentlemen

Took flying Psyche for a hen
And aimed at her; then turned a gun
On harmless chicken-me—for fun.
The beggars' dogs howl all together,
Their tails turn to a ragged feather;
Pools, like mirrors hung in garrets,
Show each face as red as a parrot's,
Whistling hair that raises ire
In cocks and hens in the kitchen fire!
Every flame shrieks cockle-doo-doo
(With their cockscombs flaring high too);
The witch's rag-rug takes its flight
Beneath the willows' watery light:
The wells of water seem a-plume—
The old witch sweeps them with her broom—
All are chasing chicken-me. . . .
But Psyche—where, oh where, is she?

II

Grey as a guinea-fowl is the rain
Squawking down from the boughs again.
    "Anne, Anne,
      Go fill the pail,"
Said the old witch who sat on the rail.
"Though there is a hole in the bucket,
Anne, Anne,
It will fill my pocket;
The water-drops when they cross my doors
Will turn to guineas and gold moidores. . . ."
The well-water hops across the floors;
Whimpering, "Anne" it cries, implores,
And the guinea-fowl-plumaged rain,
Squawking down from the boughs again,
Cried, "Anne, Anne, go fill the bucket,
There is a hole in the witch's pocket—
And the water-drops like gold moidores,
Obedient girl, will surely be yours.
So, Anne, Anne,

Go fill the pail
Of the old witch who sits on the rail!"

Solo for Ear-Trumpet

The carriage brushes through the bright
Leaves (violent jets from life to light);
Strong polished speed is plunging, heaves
Between the showers of bright hot leaves
The window-glasses glaze our faces
And jar them to the very basis—
But they could never put a polish
Upon my manners or abolish
My most distinct disinclination
For calling on a rich relation!
In her house—(bulwark built between
The life man lives and visions seen)—
The sunlight hiccups white as chalk,
Grown drunk with emptiness of talk,
And silence hisses like a snake—
Invertebrate and rattling ache. . . .
Then suddenly Eternity
Drowns all the houses like a sea
And down the street the Trump of Doom
Blares madly—shakes the drawing-room
Where raw-edged shadows sting forlorn
As dank dark nettles. Down the horn
Of her ear-trumpet I convey
The news that "It is Judgment Day!"
"Speak louder: I don't catch, my dear."
I roared: *"It is the Trump we hear!"*
"The *What?*" *"THE TRUMP!"* "I shall complain!
. . . the boy-scouts practising again."

Eventail

Lovely Semiramis
Closes her slanting eyes:

Dead is she long ago,
From her fan sliding slow
Parrot-bright fire's feathers
Gilded as June weathers,
Plumes like the greenest grass
Twinkle down; as they pass
Through the green glooms in Hell,
Fruits with a tuneful smell—
Grapes like an emerald rain
Where the full moon has lain,
Greengages bright as grass,
Melons as cold as glass
Piled on each gilded booth
Feel their cheeks growing smooth;
Apes in plumed head-dresses
Whence the bright heat hisses,
Nubian faces sly,
Pursing mouth, slanting eye,
Feel the Arabian
Winds floating from that fan:
See how each gilded face
Paler grows, nods apace:
"Oh, the fan's blowing
Cold winds . . . It is snowing!"

Fox Trot

Old
   Sir
      Faulk,
Tall as a stork,
Before the honeyed fruits of dawn were ripe, would walk,
And stalk with a gun
The reynard-coloured sun,
Among the pheasant-feathered corn the unicorn has torn, forlorn the
Smock-faced sheep

Sit
  And
    Sleep;
Periwigged as William and Mary, weep . . .
"Sally, Mary, Mattie, what's the matter, why cry?"
The huntsman and the reynard-coloured sun and I sigh;
"Oh, the nursery-maid Meg
With a leg like a peg
Chased the feathered dreams like hens, and when they laid
    an egg
In the sheepskin
Meadows
Where
The serene King James would steer
Horse and hounds, then he
From the shade of a tree
Picked it up as spoil to boil for nursery tea," said the mourners.
    In the
Corn, towers strain,
Feathered tall as a crane,
And whistling down the feathered rain, old Noah goes again—
An old dull mome
With a head like a pome,
Seeing the world as a bare egg,
Laid by the feathered air; Meg
Would beg three of these
For the nursery teas
Of Japhet, Shem, and Ham; she gave it
Underneath the trees,
Where the boiling
Water
  Hissed,
Like the goose-king's feathered daughter—kissed
Pot and pan and copper kettle
Put upon their proper mettle,
Lest the Flood—the Flood—the Flood begin again through these!

Charles Sorley

CHARLES SORLEY (1895–1915) was born in Aberdeen, Scotland, where his father was Professor of Moral Philosophy at the university. After being tutored by his parents he went to Marlborough, where he won a scholarship to University College, Oxford, but the outbreak of war prevented his going up. After spending some months with a family in Germany and attending briefly the University of Jena, Sorley returned to England where he joined the Suffolk Regiment. He served in France and was killed during the Battle of Loos.

The corpus of Sorley's work is small, but in it there is sufficient evidence to suggest that had he lived, he might have become an important modern poet. His attitude to the war is balanced. He was sensitive enough to react against the brutality, but was equally mindful that though the public-school code in which he grew up appeared to sanction such brutality, it nonetheless had its good points, inculcating a spirit of courage and self-discipline. Though almost forgotten, in recent years Sorley is experiencing a minor revival.

To Poets

We are the homeless, even as you,
Who hope and never can begin.
Our hearts are wounded through and through
Like yours, but our hearts bleed within.
We too make music, but our tones
'Scape not the barrier of our bones.

We have no comeliness like you.
We toil, unlovely, and we spin.
We start, return: we wind, undo:
We hope, we err, we strive, we sin,
We love: your love's not greater, but
The lips of our love's might stay shut.

We have the evil spirits too
That shake our soul with battle-din.
But we have an eviller spirit than you,
We have a dumb spirit within:
The exceeding bitter agony
But not the exceeding bitter cry.

German Rain

The heat came down and sapped away my powers.
The laden heat came down and drowsed my brain,
Till through the weight of overcoming hours
    I felt the rain.

Then suddenly I saw what more to see
I never thought: old things renewed, retrieved.
The rain that fell in England fell on me,
    And I believed.

All the Hills and Vales Along

All the hills and vales along
Earth is bursting into song,
And the singers are the chaps
Who are going to die perhaps.
    O sing, marching men,
      Till the valleys ring again.
        Give your gladness to earth's keeping,
        So be glad, when you are sleeping.

Cast away regret and rue,
Think what you are marching to.
Little live, great pass.
Jesus Christ and Barabbas
Were found the same day.
This died, that went his way.
        So sing with joyful breath.
        For why, you are going to death.
        Teeming earth will surely store
        All the gladness that you pour.

Earth that never doubts nor fears,
Earth that knows of death, not tears,
Earth that bore with joyful ease
Hemlock for Socrates,
Earth that blossomed and was glad
'Neath the cross that Christ had,
Shall rejoice and blossom too
When the bullet reaches you.
        Wherefore, men marching
        On the road to death, sing!
        Pour your gladness on earth's head,
        So be merry, so be dead.

From the hills and valleys earth
Shouts back the sound of mirth,
Tramp of feet and lilt of song

Ringing all the road along.
All the music of their going,
Ringing swinging glad song-throwing,
Earth will echo still, when foot
Lies numb and voice mute.
            On, marching men, on
            To the gates of death with song.
            Sow your gladness for earth's reaping,
            So you may be glad, though sleeping.
            Strew your gladness on earth's bed,
            So be merry, so be dead.

To Germany

You are blind like us. Your hurt no man designed,
And no man claimed the conquest of your land.
But gropers both, through fields of thought confined,
We stumble and we do not understand.
You only saw your future bigly planned,
And we the tapering paths of our own mind,
And in each other's dearest ways we stand,
And hiss and hate. And the blind fight the blind.
When it is peace, then we may view again
With new-won eyes each other's truer form,
And wonder. Grown more loving-kind and warm
We'll grasp firm hands and laugh at the old pain,
When it is peace. But until peace, the storm,
The darkness and the thunder and the rain.

J. C. Squire

SIR JOHN SQUIRE, "J. C. SQUIRE" (1884–1958) was born at
Plymouth and educated at Blundell's and St. John's College,
Cambridge, before becoming a literary journalist. For a long
time he was literary editor of *The New Statesman,* and from
1919 to 1934 was editor of *The London Mercury.* After Edward
Marsh ceased editing *Georgian Poetry* in 1922, Squire became
the acknowledged leader of the Georgian movement, his followers being referred to ironically as "the Squirearchy."

Squire was a versatile poet of considerable range, though
lacking in depth and vision. He was in his early years influenced
by Baudelaire and the French Parnassians, but in the poetry he
wrote during the twenties he is typically Georgian. Oddly
enough, his best work is probably parodic, especially the verses
included in *Tricks of the Trade* (1917), where he ridicules
brilliantly some of his contemporaries, W. H. Davies, Belloc,
Chesterton, John Masefield, and Henry Newbolt in particular.

349

To a Bull-Dog

(*W.H.S., CAPT. [ACTING MAJOR] R.F.A.; KILLED APRIL 12, 1917*)

We shan't see Willy any more, Mamie,
　He won't be coming any more:
He came back once and again and again,
　But he won't get leave any more.

We looked from the window and there was his cab,
　And we ran downstairs like a streak,
And he said "Hullo, you bad dog," and you crouched to the floor,
　Paralysed to hear him speak,

And then let fly at his face and his chest
　Till I had to hold you down,
While he took off his cap and his gloves and his coat,
　And his bag and his thonged Sam Browne.

We went upstairs to the studio,
　The three of us, just as of old,
And you lay down and I sat and talked to him
　As round the room he strolled.

Here in the room where, years ago
　Before the old life stopped,
He worked all day with his slippers and his pipe,
　He would pick up the threads he'd dropped,

Fondling all the drawings he had left behind,
　Glad to find them all still the same,
And opening the cupboards to look at his belongings
　. . . Every time he came.

But now I know what a dog doesn't know,
　Though you'll thrust your head on my knee,
And try to draw me from the absent-mindedness
　That you find so dull in me.

And all your life you will never know
    What I wouldn't tell you even if I could,
That the last time we waved him away
    Willy went for good.

But sometimes as you lie on the hearthrug
    Sleeping in the warmth of the stove,
Even through your muddled old canine brain
    Shapes from the past may rove.

You'll scarcely remember, even in a dream,
    How we brought home a silly little pup,
With a big square head and little crooked legs
    That could scarcely bear him up,

But your tail will tap at the memory
    Of a man whose friend you were,
Who was always kind though he called you a naughty dog
    When he found you on his chair;

Who'd make you face a reproving finger
    And solemnly lecture you
Till your head hung downwards and you looked very sheepish!
    And you'll dream of your triumphs too.

Of summer evening chases in the garden
    When you dodged us all about with a bone:
We were three boys, and you were the cleverest,
    But now we're two alone.

When summer comes again,
    And the long sunsets fade,
We shall have to go on playing the feeble game for two
    That since the war we've played.

And though you run expectant as you always do
    To the uniforms we meet,
You'll never find Willy among all the soldiers
    In even the longest street,

Nor in any crowd; yet, strange and bitter thought,
    Even now were the old words said,
If I tried the old trick and said 'Where's Willy?'
    You would quiver and lift your head,

And your brown eyes would look to ask if I were serious,
    And wait for the word to spring.
Sleep undisturbed: I shan't say *that* again,
    You innocent old thing.

I must sit, not speaking, on the sofa,
    While you lie asleep on the floor;
For he's suffered a thing that dogs couldn't dream of,
    And he won't be coming here any more.

The Discovery

There was an Indian, who had known no change,
    Who strayed content along a sunlit beach
Gathering shells. He heard a sudden strange
    Commingled noise; looked up; and gasped for speech.
For in the bay, where nothing was before,
    Moved on the sea, by magic, huge canoes,
With bellying cloths on poles, and not one oar,
    And fluttering coloured signs and clambering crews.

And he, in fear, this naked man alone,
    His fallen hands forgetting all their shells,
His lips gone pale, knelt low behind a stone,
    And stared, and saw, and did not understand,
Columbus' doom-burdened caravels
    Slant to the shore, and all their seamen land.

Crepuscular

No creature stirs in the wide fields.
The rifted western heaven yields
The dying sun's illumination.

This is the hour of tribulation
When, with clear sight of eve engendered,
Day's homage to delusion rendered,
   Mute at her window sits the soul.

Clouds and skies and lakes and seas,
Valleys and hills and grass and trees,
Sun, moon, and stars, all stand to her
Limbs of one lordless challenger,
Who, without deigning taunt or frown,
Throws a perennial gauntlet down:
   "Come conquer me and take thy toll."

No cowardice or fear she knows,
But, as once more she girds, there grows
An unresignèd hopelessness
From memory of former stress.
Head bent, she muses whilst he waits:
How with such weapons dint his plates?
How quell this vast and sleepless giant
Calmly, immortally defiant,
   How fell him, bind him, and control
   With a silver cord and a golden bowl?

Ballade of the Poetic Life

The fat men go about the streets,
  The politicians play their game,
The prudent bishops sound retreats
  And think the martyrs much to blame;
  Honour and love are halt and lame
And Greed and Power are deified,
  The wild are harnessed by the tame;
For this the poets lived and died.

Shelley's a trademark used on sheets:
  Aloft the sky in words of flame
We read "What porridge had John Keats?
  Why, Brown's! A hundred years the same!"

Arcadia's an umbrella frame,
Milton's a toothpaste; from the tide
Sappho's been dredged to rouge my Dame—
For this the poets lived and died.

And yet, to launch ideal fleets
Lost regions in the stars to claim,
To face all ruins and defeats,
To sing a beaten world to shame,
To hold each bright impossible aim
Deep in the heart; to starve in pride
For fame, and never know their fame—
For this the poets lived and died.

Envoi

Princess, inscribe beneath my name
"He never begged, he never sighed,
He took his medicine as it came"—
For this the poets lived—and died.

The Lily of Malud

The lily of Malud is born in secret mud.
It is breathed like a word in a little dark ravine
Where no bird was ever heard and no beast was ever seen,
And the leaves are never stirred by the panther's velvet sheen.

It blooms once a year in summer moonlight,
In a valley of dark fear full of pale moonlight:
It blooms once a year, and dies in a night,
And its petals disappear with the dawn's first light;
And when that night has come, black small-breasted maids,
With ecstatic terror dumb, steal fawn-like through the shades
To watch, hour by hour, the unfolding of the flower.

When the world is full of night, and the moon reigns alone
And drowns in silver light the known and the unknown,
When each hut is a mound, half blue-silver and half black,

And casts upon the ground the hard shadow of its back,
When the winds are out of hearing and the tree-tops never shake,
When the grass in the clearing is silent but awake
'Neath a moon-paven sky: all the village is asleep
And the babes that nightly cry dream deep:
From the doors the maidens creep,
Tiptoe over dreaming curs, soft, so soft, that not one stirs,
And stand curved and a-quiver, like bathers by a river,
Looking at the forest wall, groups of slender naked girls,
Whose black bodies shine like pearls where the moonbeams fall.

They have waked, they knew not why, at a summons from the
night,
They have stolen fearfully from the dark to the light,
Stepping over sleeping men, who have moved and slept again:
And they know not why they go to the forest, but they know,
As their moth-feet pass to the shore of the grass
And the forest's dreadful brink, that their tender spirits shrink:
They would flee, but cannot turn, for their eyelids burn
With frenzy, and each maid, ere she leaves the moonlit space,
If she sees another's face is thrilled and afraid.

Now like little phantom fawns they thread the outer lawns
Where the boles of giant trees stand about in twos and threes,
Till the forest grows more dense and the darkness more intense,
And they only sometimes see in a lone moon-ray
A dead and spongy trunk in the earth half-sunk,
Or the roots of a tree with fungus grey,
Or a drift of muddy leaves, or a banded snake that heaves.

And the towering unseen roof grows more intricate, and soon
It is featureless and proof to the lost forgotten moon.
But they could not look above as with blind-drawn feet they move
Onwards on the scarce-felt path, with quick and desperate breath,
For their circling fingers dread to caress some slimy head,
Or to touch the icy shape of a hunched and hairy ape,
And at every step they fear in their very midst to hear
A lion's rending roar or a tiger's snore, . . .
And when things swish or fall, they shiver but dare not call.

O what is it leads the way that they do not stray?
What unimagined arm keeps their bodies from harm?
What presence concealed lifts their little feet that yield
Over dry ground and wet till their straining eyes are met
With a thinning of the darkness?
And the foremost faintly cries in awed surprise:
And they one by one emerge from the gloom to the verge
Of a small sunken vale full of moonlight pale,
And they hang along the bank, clinging to the branches dank,
A shadowy festoon out of sight of the moon;
And they see in front of them, rising from the mud,
A single straight stem and a single pallid bud
In that little lake of light from the moon's calm height.

A stem, a ghostly bud, on the moon-swept mud
That shimmers like a pond; and over there beyond
The guardian forest high, menacing and strange,
Invades the empty sky with its wild black range.

And they watch hour by hour that small lonely flower
In that deep forest place that hunter never found.

It shines without sound, as a star in space.

And the silence all around that solitary place
Is like silence in a dream; till a sudden flashing gleam
Down their dark faces flies; and their lips fall apart
And their glimmering great eyes with excitement dart
And their fingers, clutching the branches they were touching,
Shake and arouse hissing leaves on the boughs.
And they whisper aswoon: Did it move in the moon?

O it moved as it grew!
It is moving, opening, with calm and gradual will,
And their bodies where they cling are shadowed and still,
And with marvel they mark that the mud now is dark,
For the unfolding flower, like a goddess in her power,
Challenges the moon with a light of her own,
That lovelily grows as the petals unclose,

Wider, more wide, with an awful inward pride,
Till the heart of it breaks, and stilled is their breath,
For the radiance it makes is as wonderful as death.

The morning's crimson stain tinges their ashen brows
As they part the last boughs and slowly step again
On to the village grass, and chill and languid pass
Into the huts to sleep.
                    Brief slumber, yet so deep
That, when they wake to day, darkness and splendour seem
Broken and far away, a faint miraculous dream;
And when those maidens rise they are as they ever were
Save only for a rare shade of trouble in their eyes.
And the surly thick-lipped men, as they sit about their huts
Making drums out of guts, grunting gruffly now and then,
Carving sticks of ivory, stretching shields of wrinkled skin,
Smoothing sinister and thin squatting gods of ebony,
Chip and grunt and do not see.
                  But each mother, silently,
Longer than her wont stays shut in the dimness of her hut,
For she feels a brooding cloud of memory in the air,
A lingering thing there that makes her sit bowed
With hollow shining eyes, as the night-fire dies,
And stare softly at the ember, and try to remember
Something sorrowful and far, something sweet and vaguely seen
Like an early evening star when the sky is pale green:
A quiet silver tower that climbed in an hour,
Or a ghost like a flower, or a flower like a queen:
Something holy in the past that came and did not last.

But she knows not what it was.

How They Do It

(SIR HENRY NEWBOLT)

It was eight bells in the forenoon and hammocks running sleek
   (It's a fair sea flowing from the West),

When the little Commodore came a-sailing up the Creek
  (Heave Ho! I think you'll know the rest).
Thunder in the halyards and horses leaping high,
Blake and Drake and Nelson are listenin' where they lie,
Four and twenty blackbirds a-bakin' in a pie,
  And the *Pegasus* came waltzing from the West.

Now the little Commodore sat steady on his keel
  (It's a fair sea flowing from the West),
A heart as stout as concrete reinforced with steel
  (Heave Ho! I think you'll know the rest).
Swinging are the scuppers, hark, the rudder snores,
Plugging at the Frenchmen, downing 'em by scores,
Porto Rico, Vera Cruz, and also the Azores,
  And the *Pegasus* came waltzing from the West.

So three cheers more for the little Commodore
  (It's a fair sea flowing from the West),
I tell you so again as I've told you so before
  (Heigh Ho! I think you know the rest).
Aged is the Motherland, old but she is young
  (Easy with the tackle there—don't release the bung),
And I sang a song like all the songs that I have ever sung
  When the *Pegasus* came sailing from the West.

Robert Louis Stevenson

ROBERT LOUIS STEVENSON (1850–1894) was born in Edinburgh, Scotland, the son of an engineer to the Board of Northern Lighthouses. Stevenson studied at Edinburgh University with a view to becoming an engineer himself, but abandoned this to become a lawyer, later still giving up the law for literature. Suffering from diseased lungs, he traveled constantly in an effort to find health, recording his experiences in a series of essays, short stories, and fragments of autobiography as well as in such conventional travel narratives as *Travels with a Donkey in the Cévennes,* published in 1879. In that year he also went to America, crossing the continent to California, where he met Mrs. Fanny Osbourne whom he later married. In 1888 Stevenson went out to the Pacific and settled in Samoa. There he partially recovered his health, and before his death was living happily among the natives as a benevolent, feudal overlord, taking an active interest in their welfare.

Stevenson is perhaps best remembered as a prose writer, the author of such prose romances as *Dr. Jekyll and Mr. Hyde* (1886) and *Treasure Island* (1883), but he also collaborated with W. E. Henley on several dramas. His verse includes some composed especially for children, while that intended for adults reveals the influence of both the Decadent and the Counter-Decadent traditions, sometimes revealing an interesting tension between the two.

The Land of Nod

From breakfast on through all the day
At home among my friends I stay,
But every night I go abroad
Afar into the land of Nod.

All by myself I have to go,
With none to tell me what to do—
All alone beside the streams
And up the mountain-sides of dreams.

The strangest things are there for me,
Both things to eat and things to see,
And many frightening sights abroad
Till morning in the land of Nod.

Try as I like to find the way,
I never can get back by day,
Nor can remember plain and clear
The curious music that I hear.

My Kingdom

Down by a shining water well
I found a very little dell,
    No higher than my head.
The heather and the gorse about
In summer bloom were coming out,
    Some yellow and some red.

I called the little pool a sea;
The little hills were big to me;
    For I am very small.
I made a boat, I made a town,
I searched the caverns up and down,
    And named them one and all.

And all about was mine, I said,
The little sparrows overhead,
 The little minnows too.
This was the world and I was king;
For me the bees came by to sing,
 For me the swallows flew.

I played there were no deeper seas,
Nor any wider plains than these,
 Nor other kings than me.
At last I heard my mother call
Out from the house at evenfall,
 To call me home to tea.

And I must rise and leave my dell,
And leave my dimpled water well,
 And leave my heather blooms.
Alas! and as my home I neared,
How very big my nurse appeared,
 How great and cool the rooms!

The Canoe Speaks

On the great streams the ships may go
About men's business to and fro.
But I, the egg-shell pinnace, sleep
On crystal waters ankle-deep:
I, whose diminutive design,
Of sweeter cedar, pithier pine,
Is fashioned on so frail a mould,
A hand may launch, a hand withhold:
I, rather, with the leaping trout
Wind, among lilies, in and out;
I, the unnamed, inviolate,
Green, rustic rivers, navigate;
My dipping paddle scarcely shakes
The berry in the bramble-brakes;
Still forth on my green way I wend
Beside the cottage garden-end;

And by the nested angler fare,
And take the lovers unaware.
By willow wood and water-wheel
Speedily fleets my touching keel;
By all retired and shady spots
Where prosper dim forget-me-nots;
By meadows where at afternoon
The growing maidens troop in June
To loose their girdles on the grass.
Ah! speedier than before the glass
The backward toilet goes; and swift
As swallows quiver, robe and shift
And the rough country stockings lie
Around each young divinity.
When, following the recondite brook,
Sudden upon this scene I look,
And light with unfamiliar face
On chaste Diana's bathing-place,
Loud ring the hills about and all
The shallows are abandoned. . . .

Et Tu in Arcadia Vixisti

(TO R. A. M. S.)

In ancient tales, O friend, thy spirit dwelt;
There, from of old, thy childhood passed; and there
High expectation, high delights and deeds,
Thy fluttering heart with hope and terror moved.
And thou hast heard of yore the Blatant Beast,
And Roland's horn, and that war-scattering shout
Of all-unarmed Achilles, aegis-crowned.
And perilous lands thou sawest, sounding shores
And seas and forests drear, island and dale
And mountain dark. For thou with Tristram rod'st
Or Bedevere, in farthest Lyonesse.
Thou hadst a booth in Samarcand, whereat
Side-looking Magians trafficked; thence, by night,
An Afreet snatched thee, and with wings upbore

Beyond the Aral mount; or, hoping gain,
Thou, with a jar of money, didst embark,
For Balsorah, by sea. But chiefly thou
In that clear air took'st life; in Arcady
The haunted, land of song; and by the wells
Where most the gods frequent. There Chiron old,
In the Pelethronian antre, taught thee lore;
The plants, he taught, and by the shining stars
In forests dim to steer. There hast thou seen
Immortal Pan dance secret in a glade,
And, dancing, roll his eyes; these, where they fell,
Shed glee, and through the congregated oaks
A flying horror winged; while all the earth
To the god's pregnant footing thrilled within.
Or whiles, beside the sobbing stream, he breathed,
In his clutched pipe, unformed and wizard strains,
Divine yet brutal; which the forest heard,
And thou, with awe; and far upon the plain
The unthinking ploughman started and gave ear.

Now things there are that, upon him who sees,
A strong vocation lay; and strains there are
That whoso hears shall hear for evermore.
For evermore thou hear'st immortal Pan
And those melodious godheads, ever young
And ever quiring, on the mountains old.

What was this earth, child of the gods, to thee?
Forth from thy dreamland thou, a dreamer, cam'st,
And in thine ears the olden music rang,
And in thy mind the doings of the dead,
And those heroic ages long forgot.
To a so fallen earth, alas! too late,
Alas! in evil days, thy steps return,
To list at noon for nightingales, to grow
A dweller on the beach till Argo come
That came long since, a lingerer by the pool
Where that desirèd angel bathes no more.
As when the Indian to Dakota comes,
Or farthest Idaho, and where he dwelt,

He with his clan, a humming city finds;
Thereon awhile, amazed, he stares, and then
To right and leftward, like a questing dog,
Seeks first the ancestral altars, then the hearth
Long cold with rains, and where old terror lodged,
And where the dead. So thee undying Hope,
With all her pack, hunts screaming through the years:
Here, there, thou fleeest: but nor here nor there
The pleasant gods abide, the glory dwells.

That, that was not Apollo, not the god.
This was not Venus, though she Venus seemed
A moment. And though fair yon river move,
She, all the way, from disenchanted fount
To seas unhallowed runs; the gods forsook
Long since her trembling rushes; from her plains
Disconsolate, long since adventure fled;
And now although the inviting river flows,
And every poplared cape, and every bend
Or willowy islet, win upon thy soul
And to thy hopeful shallop whisper speed;
Yet hope not thou at all: hope is no more;
And O, long since the golden groves are dead,
The faery cities vanished from the land!

To W. E. Henley

The year runs through her phases; rain and sun,
Springtime and summer pass; winter succeeds;
But one pale season rules the house of death.
Cold falls the imprisoned daylight; fell disease
By each lean pallet squats, and pain and sleep
Toss gaping on the pillows.

                              But O thou!
Uprise and take thy pipe. Bid music flow,
Strains by good thoughts attended, like the spring
The swallows follow over land and sea.
Pain sleeps at once; at once, with open eyes,

Dozing despair awakes. The shepherd sees
His flock come bleating home; the seaman hears
Once more the cordage rattle. Airs of home!
Youth, love and roses blossom; the gaunt ward
Dislimns and disappears, and, opening out,
Shows brooks and forests, and the blue beyond
Of mountains.

               Small the pipe; but O! do thou,
Peak-faced and suffering piper, blow therein
The dirge of heroes dead; and to these sick,
These dying, sound the triumph over death.
Behold! each greatly breathes; each tastes a joy
Unknown before, in dying; for each knows
A hero dies with him—though unfulfilled,
Yet conquering truly—and not dies in vain.

So is pain cheered, death comforted; the house
Of sorrow smiles to listen. Once again—
O thou, Orpheus and Heracles, the bard
And the deliverer touch the stops again!

The Celestial Surgeon

If I have faltered more or less
In my great task of happiness;
If I have moved among my race
And shown no glorious morning face;
If beams from happy human eyes
Have moved me not; if morning skies,
Books, and my food, and summer rain
Knocked on my sullen heart in vain:—
Lord, thy most pointed pleasure take
And stab my spirit broad awake;
Or, Lord, if too obdurate I,
Choose thou, before that spirit die,
A piercing pain, a killing sin,
And to my dead heart run them in!

Our Lady of the Snows

Out of the sun, out of the blast,
Out of the world, alone I passed
Across the moor and through the wood
To where the monastery stood.
There neither lute nor breathing fife,
Nor rumour of the world of life,
Nor confidences low and dear,
Shall strike the meditative ear.
Aloof, unhelpful, and unkind,
The prisoners of the iron mind,
Where nothing speaks except the bell
The unfraternal brothers dwell.
Poor passionate men, still clothed afresh
With agonising folds of flesh;
Whom the clear eyes solicit still
To some bold output of the will,
While fairy Fancy far before
And musing Memory-Hold-the-door
Now to heroic death invite
And now uncurtain fresh delight:
O, little boots it thus to dwell
On the remote unneighboured hill!
O to be up and doing, O
Unfearing and unshamed to go
In all the uproar and the press
About my human business!
My undissuaded heart I hear
Whisper courage in my ear.
With voiceless calls, the ancient earth
Summons me to a daily birth.
Thou, O my love, ye, O my friends—
The gist of life, the end of ends—
To laugh, to love, to live, to die,
Ye call me by the ear and eye!

Forth from the casemate, on the plain
Where honour has the world to gain,

Pour forth and bravely do your part,
O knights of the unshielded heart!
Forth and forever forward!—out
From prudent turret and redoubt,
And in the mellay charge amain,
To fall but yet to rise again!
Captive? ah, still, to honour bright,
A captive soldier of the right!
Or free and fighting, good with ill?
Unconquering but unconquered still!

And ye, O brethren, what if God,
When from Heav'n's top he spies abroad,
And sees on this tormented stage
The noble war of mankind rage:
What if his vivifying eye,
O monks, should pass your corner by?
For still the Lord is Lord of might;
In deeds, in deeds, he takes delight;
The plough, the spear, the laden barks,
The field, the founded city, marks;
He marks the smiler of the streets,
The singer upon garden seats;
He sees the climber in the rocks;
To him, the shepherd folds his flocks.

For those he loves that underprop
With daily virtues Heaven's top.
And bears the falling sky with ease,
Unfrowning caryatides.
Those he approves that ply the trade,
That rock the child, that wed the maid,
That with weak virtues, weaker hands,
Sow gladness on the peopled lands,
And still with laughter, song, and shout,
Spin the great wheel of earth about.

But ye!—O ye who linger still
Here in your fortress on the hill,
With placid face, with tranquil breath,

The unsought volunteers of death,
Our cheerful General on high
With careless looks may pass you by.

MY BODY which my dungeon is,
And yet my parks and palaces:—
    Which is so great that there I go
All the day long to and fro,
And when the night begins to fall
Throw down my bed and sleep, while all
The building hums with wakefulness—
Even as a child of savages
When evening takes her on her way,
(She having roamed a summer's day
Along the mountain-sides and scalp)
Sleeps in an antre of that alp:—
    Which is so broad and high that there,
As in the topless fields of air,
My fancy soars like to a kite
And faints in the blue infinite:—
    Which is so strong, my strongest throes
And the rough world's besieging blows
Not break it, and so weak withal,
Death ebbs and flows in its loose wall
As the green sea in fishers' nets,
And tops its topmost parapets:—
    Which is so wholly mine that I
Can wield its whole artillery,
And mine so little, that my soul
Dwells in perpetual control,
And I but think and speak and do
As my dead fathers move me to:—
    If this born body of my bones
The beggared soul so barely owns,
What money passed from hand to hand,
What creeping custom of the land,
What deed of author or assign,
Can make a house a thing of mine?

I WILL make you brooches and toys for your delight
Of bird-song at morning and star-shine at night.
I will make a palace fit for you and me
Of green days in forests and blue days at sea.

I will make my kitchen, and you shall keep your room,
Where white flows the river and bright blows the broom,
And you shall wash your linen and keep your body white
In rainfall at morning and dewfall at night.

And this shall be for music when no one else is near,
The fine song for singing, the rare song to hear!
That only I remember, that only you admire,
Of the broad road that stretches and the roadside fire.

To My Old Familiars

Do you remember—can we e'er forget?—
How, in the coiled perplexities of youth,
In our wild climate, in our scowling town,
We gloomed and shivered, sorrowed, sobbed and feared?
The belching winter wind, the missile rain,
The rare and welcome silence of the snows,
The laggard morn, the haggard day, the night,
The grimy spell of the nocturnal town,
Do you remember?—Ah, could one forget!

As when the fevered sick that all night long
Listed the wind intone, and hear at last
The ever-welcome voice of chanticleer
Sing in the bitter hour before the dawn,—
With sudden ardour, these desire the day:
So sang in the gloom of youth the bird of hope;
So we, exulting, hearkened and desired.
For lo! as in the palace porch of life
We huddled with chimeras, from within—
How sweet to hear!—the music swelled and fell,
And through the breach of the revolving doors
What dreams of splendour blinded us and fled!

I have since then contended and rejoiced;
Amid the glories of the house of life
Profoundly entered, and the shrine beheld:
Yet when the lamp from my expiring eyes
Shall dwindle and recede, the voice of love
Fall insignificant on my closing ears,
What sound shall come but the old cry of the wind
In our inclement city? what return
But the image of the emptiness of youth,
Filled with the sound of footsteps and that voice
Of discontent and rapture and despair?
So, as in darkness, from the magic lamp,
The momentary pictures gleam and fade
And perish, and the night resurges—these
Shall I remember, and then all forget.

To S. C.

I heard the pulse of the besieging sea
Throb far away all night. I heard the wind
Fly crying and convulse tumultuous palms.
I rose and strolled. The isle was all bright sand,
And flailing fans and shadows of the palm;
The heaven all moon and wind and the blind vault
The keenest planet slain, for Venus slept.

   The king, my neighbour, with his host of wives
Slept in the precinct of the palisade;
Where single, in the wind, under the moon,
Among the slumbering cabins, blazed a fire,
Sole street-lamp and the only sentinel.

   To other lands and nights my fancy turned—
To London first, and chiefly to your house,
The many-pillared and the well-beloved.
There yearning fancy lighted; there again
In the upper room I lay, and heard far off
The unsleeping city murmur like a shell;
The muffled tramp of the Museum guard
Once more went by me; I beheld again
Lamps vainly brighten the dispeopled street;

Again I longed for the returning morn,
The awaking traffic, the bestirring birds,
The consentaneous trill of tiny song
That weaves round monumental cornices
A passing charm of beauty. Most of all,
For your light foot I wearied, and your knock
That was the glad réveillé of my day.

Lo, now, when to your task in the great house
At morning through the portico you pass,
One moment glance, where by the pillared wall
Far-voyaging island gods, begrimed with smoke,
Sit now unworshipped, the rude monument
Of faiths forgot and races undivined:
Sit now disconsolate, remembering well
The priest, the victim, and the songful crowd,
The blaze of the blue noon, and that huge voice
Incessant, of the breakers on the shore.
As far as these from their ancestral shrine,
So far, so foreign, your divided friends
Wander, estranged in body, not in mind.

Arthur Symons

ARTHUR SYMONS (1865–1945) was born into a strict noncon-
formist family at Milford Haven in Wales, the son of an itinerant
Wesleyan preacher. Symons soon found that he had little in
common with his parents, broke away from them and moved to
London, determined to make a name for himself as a man of
letters. It was not long before he had edited numerous volumes
of poetry, prose, and drama and written in all three genres himself. Most notably, however, Symons became a distinguished
critic of literature, as well as the other arts. His most significant
work is *The Symbolist Movement in Literature* (1899), a collection of essays on contemporary French literature.

In 1908, Symons had a mental breakdown while vacationing
in Italy, which necessitated his confinement in a mental institu-
tion. By 1910 he had recovered his faculties sufficiently to resume
writing, but though he published a vast amount of material,
none of it was as impressive as the work he had completed before 1908. Actually Symons' mental condition never did return
to normal, and he spent the remaining years of his life in a
dream world of the past until his death in 1945.

Symons' verse underwent a series of changes. His first volume,
Days and Nights (1889), was typically Victorian, but *Silhouettes*
(1892) and *London Nights* (1895) were typically Decadent. The
bulk of what he published afterward belongs to no discernible
tradition but is noted for its confessional quality, which at times
becomes embarrassing. Symons was a great admirer of the
French poet Verlaine, and much of the verse he wrote during the
nineties reflects his adulation of him.

The Opium-Smoker

I am engulfed, and drown deliciously.
Soft music like a perfume, and sweet light
Golden with audible odours exquisite,
Swathe me with cerements for eternity.
Time is no more. I pause and yet I flee.
A million ages wrap me round with night.
I drain a million ages of delight.
I hold the future in my memory.

Also I have this garret which I rent,
This bed of straw, and this that was a chair,
This worn-out body like a tattered tent,
This crust, of which the rats have eaten part,
This pipe of opium; rage, remorse, despair;
This soul at pawn and this delirious heart.

Maquillage

The charm of rouge on fragile cheeks,
Pearl-powder, and, about the eyes,
The dark and lustrous eastern dyes;
A voice of violets that speaks
Of perfumed hours of day, and doubtful night
Of alcoves curtained close against the light.

Gracile and creamy white and rose,
Complexioned like the flower of dawn,
Her fleeting colours are as those
That, from an April sky withdrawn,
Fade in a fragrant mist of tears away
When weeping noon leads on the altered day.

At the Cavour

Wine, the red coals, the flaring gas,
Bring out a brighter tone in cheeks

That learn at home before the glass
The flush that eloquently speaks.

The blue-grey smoke of cigarettes
Curls from the lessening ends that glow;
The men are thinking of the bets,
The women of the debts, they owe.

Then their eyes meet, and in their eyes
The accustomed smile comes up to call,
A look half miserably wise,
Half heedlessly ironical.

Javanese Dancers

Twitched strings, the clang of metal, beaten drums,
Dull, shrill, continuous, disquieting;
And now the stealthy dancer comes
Undulantly with cat-like steps that cling;

Smiling between her painted lids a smile,
Motionless, unintelligible, she twines
Her fingers into mazy lines,
The scarves across her fingers twine the while.

One, two, three, four glide forth, and, to and fro,
Delicately and imperceptibly,
Now swaying gently in a row,
Now interthreading slow and rhythmically,

Still, with fixed eyes, monotonously still,
Mysteriously, with smiles inanimate,
With lingering feet that undulate,
With sinuous fingers, spectral hands that thrill

In measure while the gnats of music whirr,
The little amber-coloured dancers move,
Like painted idols seen to stir
By the idolators in a magic grove.

Prologue: In the Stalls

My life is like a music-hall,
Where in the impotence of rage,
Chained by enchantment to my stall,
I see myself upon the stage
Dance to amuse a music-hall.

'Tis I that smoke this cigarette,
Lounge here, and laugh for vacancy,
And watch the dancers turn; and yet
It is my very self I see
Across the cloudy cigarette.

My very self that turns and trips,
Painted, pathetically gay,
An empty song upon the lips
In make-believe of holiday:
I, I, this thing that turns and trips!

The light flares in the music-hall,
The light, the sound, that weary us;
Hour follows hour, I count them all,
Lagging, and loud, and riotous:
My life is like a music-hall.

To a Dancer

Intoxicatingly
Her eyes across the footlights gleam,
(The wine of love, the wine of dream)
Her eyes, that gleam for me!

The eyes of all that see
Draw to her glances, stealing fire
From her desire that leaps to my desire;
Her eyes that gleam for me!

Subtly, deliciously,
A quickening fire within me, beat
The rhythms of her poising feet;
Her feet that poise to me!

Her body's melody,
In silent waves of wandering sound,
Thrills to the sense of all around,
Yet thrills alone for me!

And O, intoxicatingly,
When, at the magic moment's close,
She dies into the rapture of repose,
Her eyes that gleam for me!

Air de Ballet

TO CLÉO DE MÉRODE

Why is it, child, you choose to wear
That artful 1830 air
Of artlessness made artifice?
To lure all lips to long to kiss
The saint-like halo of your hair?

"I am the spirit of a fan.
Ah, once, what wanton breezes ran
Across my silk and ivory!
As a fan's breath is life to me,
I have no heart for any man.

"As a fan fluttered by a wrist,
Bright lips that now are dust have kissed,
I waken, out of other hours,
The phantoms of forgotten flowers
That hold me to a phantom tryst.

"If these calm eyes, if that pure cheek,
If this soft haloed hair, could speak
The false, fantastic, final truth,
In some remote, remembered youth
I loved Gavarni for a week."

La Mélinite: Moulin-Rouge

Olivier Metra's Waltz of Roses
Sheds in a rhythmic shower
The very petals of the flower;
And all is roses,
The rouge of petals in a shower.

Down the long hall the dance returning
Rounds the full circle, rounds
The perfect rose of lights and sounds,
The rose returning
Into the circle of its rounds.

Alone, apart, one dancer watches
Her mirrored, morbid grace;
Before the mirror, face to face,
Alone she watches
Her morbid, vague, ambiguous grace.

Before the mirror's dance of shadows
She dances in a dream,
And she and they together seem
A dance of shadows,
Alike the shadows of a dream.

The orange-rosy lamps are trembling
Between the robes that turn;
In ruddy flowers of flame that burn
The lights are trembling:
The shadows and the dancers turn.

Art Poétique

Music first and foremost of all!
Choose your measure of odd not even,
Let it melt in the air of heaven,
Pose not, poise not, but rise and fall.

Choose your words, but think not whether
Each to other of old belong:
What so dear as the dim grey song
Where clear and vague are joined together?

'Tis veils of beauty for beautiful eyes,
'Tis the trembling light of the naked noon,
'Tis a medley of blue and gold, the moon
And stars in the cool of autumn skies.

Let every shape of its shade be born;
Colour, away! come to me, shade!
Only of shade can the marriage be made
Of dream with dream and of flute with horn.

Shun the Point, lest death with it come,
Unholy laughter and cruel wit
(For the eyes of the angels weep at it)
And all the garbage of scullery-scum.

Take Eloquence, and wring the neck of him!
You had better, by force, from time to time,
Put a little sense in the head of Rhyme:
If you watch him not, you will be at the beck of him.

O, who shall tell us the wrongs of Rhyme?
What witless savage or what deaf boy
Has made for us this twopenny toy
Whose bells ring hollow and out of time?

Music always and music still!
Let your verse be the wandering thing

That flutters in flight from a soul on the wing
Towards other skies at a new whim's will.

Let your verse be the luck of the lure
Afloat on the winds that at morning hint
Of the odours of thyme and the savour of mint . . .
And all the rest is literature.

Cortège

A silver-vested monkey trips
And pirouettes before the face
Of one who twists a kerchief's lace
Between her well-gloved finger-tips.

A little negro, a red elf,
Carries her drooping train, and holds
At arm's-length all the heavy folds,
Watching each fold displace itself.

The monkey never lets his eyes
Wander from the fair woman's breast,
White wonder that to be possessed
Would call a god out of the skies.

Sometimes the little negro seems
To lift his sumptuous burden up
Higher than need be, in the hope
Of seeing what all night he dreams.

She goes by corridor and stair,
Still to the insolent appeals
Of her familiar animals
Indifferent or unaware.

Amends to Nature

I have loved colours, and not flowers;
Their motion, not the swallows' wings;
And wasted more than half my hours
Without the comradeship of things.

How is it, now, that I can see,
With love and wonder and delight,
The children of the hedge and tree,
The little lords of day and night?

How is it that I see the roads,
No longer with usurping eyes,
A twilight meeting-place for toads,
A mid-day mart for butterflies?

I feel, in every midge that hums,
Life, fugitive and infinite,
And suddenly the world becomes
A part of me and I of it.

Edward Thomas

EDWARD THOMAS (1878–1917) is perhaps the most distinguished of the so-called Georgian poets, though actually none of his poems was published in the Georgian anthologies. He was educated at St. Paul's School and Lincoln College, Oxford, before becoming a journalist. He began writing poetry in 1912, receiving encouragement from Robert Frost, a poet he occasionally resembles. His early married life was mainly a struggle against poverty. To earn money he was obliged to devote most of his time to the composition of biographical and critical articles for various literary reviews. He enlisted as a private in the 1914–1918 war, and was eventually commissioned before being killed at Arras in 1917.

Though the subject matter of Thomas's poetry makes his inclusion in the Georgian movement inevitable, both his scrupulously honest, wryly reflective sensibility and his rejection of the sweetness and elegance of much Georgian verse sets him apart from many of his more pallid contemporaries.

Tears

It seems I have no tears left. They should have fallen—
Their ghosts, if tears have ghosts, did fall—that day
When twenty hounds streamed by me, not yet combed out
But still all equals in their rage of gladness
Upon the scent, made one, like a great dragon
In Blooming Meadow that bends towards the sun
And once bore hops: and on that other day
When I stepped out from the double-shadowed Tower
Into an April morning, stirring and sweet
And warm. Strange solitude was there and silence.
A mightier charm than any in the Tower
Possessed the courtyard. They were changing guard,
Soldiers in line, young English countrymen,
Fair-haired and ruddy, in white tunics. Drums
And fifes were playing "The British Grenadiers."
The men, the music piercing that solitude
And silence, told me truths I had not dreamed,
And have forgotten since their beauty passed.

The Owl

Downhill I came, hungry, and yet not starved;
Cold, yet had heat within me that was proof
Against the North wind; tired, yet so that rest
Had seemed the sweetest thing under a roof.

Then at the inn I had food, fire, and rest,
Knowing how hungry, cold, and tired was I.
All of the night was quite barred out except
An owl's cry, a most melancholy cry

Shaken out long and clear upon the hill,
No merry note, nor cause of merriment,
But one telling me plain what I escaped
And others could not, that night, as in I went.

And salted was my food, and my repose,
Salted and sobered, too, by the bird's voice
Speaking for all who lay under the stars,
Soldiers and poor, unable to rejoice.

Swedes

They have taken the gable from the roof of clay
On the long swede pile. They have let in the sun
To the white and gold and purple of curled fronds
Unsunned. It is a sight more tender-gorgeous
At the wood-corner where Winter moans and drips
Than when, in the Valley of the Tombs of Kings,
A boy crawls down into a Pharaoh's tomb
And, first of Christian men, beholds the mummy,
God and monkey, chariot and throne and vase,
Blue pottery, alabaster, and gold.

But dreamless long-dead Amen-hotep lies,
This is the dream of Winter, sweet as Spring.

The Path

Running along a bank, a parapet
That saves from the precipitous wood below
The level road, there is a path. It serves
Children for looking down the long smooth steep,
Between the legs of beech and yew, to where
A fallen tree checks the sight: while men and women
Content themselves with the road, and what they see
Over the bank, and what the children tell.
The path, winding like silver, trickles on,
Bordered and ever invaded by thinnest moss
That tries to cover roots and crumbling chalk
With gold, olive, and emerald, but in vain.
The children wear it. They have flattened the bank
On top, and silvered it between the moss
With the current of their feet, year after year.

But the road is houseless, and leads not to school.
To see a child is rare there, and the eye
Has but the road, the wood that overhangs
And underyawns it, and the path that looks
As if it led on to some legendary
Or fancied place where men have wished to go
And stay; till, sudden, it ends where the wood ends.

Adlestrop

Yes. I remember Adlestrop—
The name, because one afternoon
Of heat the express-train drew up there
Unwontedly. It was late June.

The steam hissed. Someone cleared his throat.
No one left and no one came
On the bare platform. What I saw
Was Adlestrop—only the name

And willows, willow-herb, and grass,
And meadowsweet, and haycocks dry,
No whit less still and lonely fair
Than the high cloudlets in the sky.

And for that minute a blackbird sang
Close by, and round him, mistier,
Farther and farther, all the birds
Of Oxfordshire and Gloucestershire.

Tall Nettles

Tall nettles cover up, as they have done
These many springs, the rusty harrow, the plough
Long worn out, and the roller made of stone:
Only the elm butt tops the nettles now.

This corner of the farmyard I like most:
As well as any bloom upon a flower

I like the dust on the nettles, never lost
Except to prove the sweetness of a shower.

Rain

Rain, midnight rain, nothing but the wild rain
On this bleak hut, and solitude, and me
Remembering again that I shall die
And neither hear the rain nor give it thanks
For washing me cleaner than I have been
Since I was born into this solitude.
Blessed are the dead that the rain rains upon:
But here I pray that none whom I once loved
Is dying tonight or lying still awake
Solitary, listening to the rain,
Either in pain or thus in sympathy
Helpless among the living and the dead,
Like a cold water among broken reeds,
Myriads of broken reeds all still and stiff,
Like me who have no love which this wild rain
Has not dissolved except the love of death,
If love it be for what is perfect and
Cannot, the tempest tells me, disappoint.

Lights Out

I have come to the borders of sleep,
The unfathomable deep
Forest where all must lose
Their way, however straight,
Or winding, soon or late;
They cannot choose.

Many a road and track
That, since the dawn's first crack,
Up to the forest brink,
Deceived the travellers,

Suddenly now blurs,
And in they sink.

Here love ends,
Despair, ambition ends;
All pleasure and all trouble,
Although most sweet or bitter,
Here ends in sleep that is sweeter
Than tasks most noble.

There is not any book
Or face of dearest look
That I would not turn from now
To go into the unknown
I must enter, and leave, alone,
I know not how.

The tall forest towers;
Its cloudy foliage lowers
Ahead, shelf above shelf;
Its silence I hear and obey
That I may lose my way
And myself.

February Afternoon

Men heard this roar of parleying starlings, saw,
   A thousand years ago even as now,
   Black rooks with white gulls following the plough
So that the first are last until a caw
Commands that last are first again,—a law
   Which was of old when one, like me, dreamed how
   A thousand years might dust lie on his brow
Yet thus would birds do between hedge and shaw.

Time swims before me, making as a day
   A thousand years, while the broad ploughland oak
   Roars mill-like and men strike and bear the stroke
Of war as ever, audacious or resigned,

And God still sits aloft in the array
That we have wrought him, stone-deaf and stone-blind.

The New House

Now first, as I shut the door,
  I was alone
In the new house; and the wind
  Began to moan.

Old at once was the house,
  And I was old;
My ears were teased with the dread
  Of what was foretold,

Nights of storm, days of mist, without end;
  Sad days when the sun
Shone in vain: old griefs and griefs
  Not yet begun.

All was foretold me; naught
  Could I foresee;
But I learned how the wind would sound
  After these things should be.

Out in the Dark

Out in the dark over the snow
The fallow fawns invisible go
With the fallow doe;
And the winds blow
Fast as the stars are slow.

Stealthily the dark haunts round
And, when the lamp goes, without sound
At a swifter bound
Than the swiftest hound,
Arrives, and all else is drowned;

And star and I and wind and deer,
Are in the dark together,—near,
Yet far,—and fear
Drums on my ear
In that sage company drear.

How weak and little is the light,
All the universe of sight,
Love and delight,
Before the might,
If you love it not, of night.

Francis Thompson

FRANCIS THOMPSON (1859–1907), son of a homeopathic surgeon, was born at Preston, Lancashire. Both his parents were Catholic converts, and they expected their son to enter the priesthood. Eventually it became clear that Thompson's poor health and dreamy disposition hardly suited him for this career, so he tried to become a surgeon instead. He studied medicine in Manchester, but after having failed his examinations three times gave up hope of a medical career, moving to London in 1885. For three years Thompson managed to keep alive by doing casual work of the most menial kind, all the time writing whenever he could afford paper and ink. In 1888 he was "discovered" by Wilfrid and Alice Meynell, to whom he had submitted copy for inclusion in the journal *Merry England*. The Meynells not only encouraged his writing but also kept parental eyes on him until his death, striving to break him of the opium habit which he had acquired, and encouraging him to retire at periodic intervals to the country for the sake of his health. He died in 1907 of tuberculosis.

Thompson's poetry has perhaps been overrated by those who share his religious beliefs, some of his verses being little more than halting excursions into mawkish sentimentality, unimproved by their lapses into childish archness. At his best, however, as in "The Hound of Heaven," he has a magical way with words which in this poem at least only occasionally degenerates into over-elaborate rhetoric. As a whole his work reflects the influence of the Elizabethan poets in general and Crashaw and the Metaphysicals in particular.

Daisy

Where the thistle lifts a purple crown
    Six foot out of the turf,
And the harebell shakes on the windy hill—
    O the breath of the distant surf!—

The hills look over on the South,
    And southward dreams the sea;
And, with the sea-breeze hand in hand,
    Came innocence and she.

Where 'mid the gorse the raspberry
    Red for the gatherer springs,
Two children did we stray and talk
    Wise, idle, childish things.

She listened with big-lipped surprise,
    Breast-deep 'mid flower and spine:
Her skin was like a grape, whose veins
    Run snow instead of wine.

She knew not those sweet words she spake,
    Nor knew her own sweet way;
But there's never a bird so sweet a song
    Thronged in whose throat that day!

Oh, there were flowers in Storrington
    On the turf and on the spray;
But the sweetest flower on Sussex hills
    Was the Daisy-flower that day!

Her beauty smoothed earth's furrowed face!
    She gave me tokens three:—
A look, a word of her winsome mouth,
    And a wild raspberry.

A berry red, a guileless look,
    A still word,—strings of sand!

And yet they made my wild, wild heart
    Fly down to her little hand.

For, standing artless as the air,
    And candid as the skies,
She took the berries with her hand,
    And the love with her sweet eyes.

The fairest things have fleetest end:
    Their scent survives their close,
But the rose's scent is bitterness
    To him that loved the rose!

She looked a little wistfully,
    Then went her sunshine way:—
The sea's eye had a mist on it,
    And the leaves fell from the day.

She went her unremembering way,
    She went, and left in me
The pang of all the partings gone,
    And partings yet to be.

She left me marvelling why my soul
    Was sad that she was glad;
At all the sadness in the sweet,
    The sweetness in the sad.

Still, still I seemed to see her, still
    Look up with soft replies,
And take the berries with her hand,
    And the love with her lovely eyes.

Nothing begins, and nothing ends,
    That is not paid with moan;
For we are born in other's pain,
    And perish in our own.

The Hound of Heaven

I fled Him, down the nights and down the days;
    I fled Him down the arches of the years;
I fled Him, down the labyrinthine ways
      Of my own mind; and in the mist of tears
I hid from Him, and under running laughter.
           Up vistaed hopes I sped;
           And shot, precipitated,
Adown Titanic glooms of chasmèd fears,
   From those strong Feet that followed, followed after.
          But with unhurrying chase,
          And unperturbèd pace,
    Deliberate speed, majestic instancy,
         They beat—and a Voice beat
         More instant than the Feet—
   "All things betray thee, who betrayest Me."

         I pleaded, outlaw-wise,
By many a hearted casement, curtained red,
   Trellised with intertwining charities;
(For, though I knew His love Who followèd,
         Yet was I sore adread
Lest, having Him, I must have naught beside);
But, if one little casement parted wide,
   The gust of His approach would clash it to
Fear wist not to evade, as Love wist to pursue.
Across the margent of the world I fled,
    And troubled the gold gateways of the stars,
    Smiting for shelter on their clangèd bars;
       Fretted to dulcet jars
And silvern chatter the pale ports o' the moon.
I said to dawn, Be sudden; to eve, Be soon;
    With thy young skiey blossoms heap me over
       From this tremendous Lover!
Float thy vague veil about me, lest He see!
   I tempted all His servitors, but to find
My own betrayal in their constancy,
In faith to Him their fickleness to me,

Their traitorous trueness, and their loyal deceit.
To all swift things for swiftness did I sue;
    Clung to the whistling mane of every wind.
        But whether they swept, smoothly fleet,
      The long savannahs of the blue;
          Or whether, Thunder-driven,
        They clanged his chariot 'thwart a heaven
Plashy with flying lightnings round the spurn o' their feet:—
    Fear wist not to evade as Love wist to pursue.
          Still with unhurrying chase,
          And unperturbèd pace,
      Deliberate speed, majestic instancy,
         Came on the following Feet,
         And a Voice above their beat—
    "Naught shelters thee, who wilt not shelter Me."

I sought no more that after which I strayed
         In face of man or maid;
But still within the little children's eyes
        Seems something, something that replies;
They at least are for me, surely for me!
I turned me to them very wistfully;
But, just as their young eyes grew sudden fair
        With dawning answers there,
Their angel plucked them from me by the hair.
"Come then, ye other children, Nature's—share
With me" (said I) "your delicate fellowship;
         Let me greet you lip to lip,
         Let me twine with you caresses,
           Wantoning
        With our Lady-Mother's vagrant tresses,
           Banqueting
        With her in her wind-walled palace,
        Underneath her azured daïs,
        Quaffing, as your taintless way is,
          From a chalice
Lucent-weeping out of the dayspring."
          So it was done:
I in their delicate fellowship was one—
Drew the bolt of Nature's secrecies.

I knew all the swift importings
On the wilful face of skies;
I knew how the clouds arise
Spumèd of the wild sea-snortings;
    All that's born or dies
Rose and drooped with—made them shapers
Of mine own moods, or wailful or divine—
    With them joyed and was bereaven.
    I was heavy with the even,
    When she lit her glimmering tapers
    Round the day's dead sanctities.
    I laughed in the morning's eyes.
I triumphed and I saddened with all weather,
    Heaven and I wept together,
And its sweet tears were salt with mortal mine;
Against the red throb of its sunset-heart
    I laid my own to beat,
    And share commingling heat;
But not by that, by that, was eased my human smart.
In vain my tears were wet on Heaven's grey cheek.
For ah! we know not what each other says,
    These things and I; in sound *I* speak—
Their sound is but their stir, they speak by silences.
Nature, poor stepdame, cannot slake my drouth;
    Let her, if she would owe me,
Drop yon blue bosom-veil of sky, and show me
    The breasts o' her tenderness:
Never did any milk of hers once bless
    My thirsting mouth.
    Nigh and nigh draws the chase,
    With unperturbèd pace,
Deliberate speed, majestic instancy;
    And past those noisèd Feet
    A voice comes yet more fleet—
    "Lo! naught contents thee, who content'st not
Me."

Naked I wait Thy love's uplifted stroke!
My harness piece by piece Thou hast hewn from me,
    And smitten me to my knee;

I am defenceless utterly.
　　　　I slept, methinks, and woke,
And, slowly gazing, find me stripped in sleep.
In the rash lustihead of my young powers,
　　　　I shook the pillaring hours
And pulled my life upon me; grimed with smears,
I stand amid the dust o' the mounded years—
My mangled youth lies dead beneath the heap
My days have crackled and gone up in smoke,
Have puffed and burst as sun-starts on a stream.
　　　　Yea, faileth now even dream
The dreamer, and the lute the lutanist;
Even the linked fantasies, in whose blossomy twist
I swung the earth a trinket at my wrist,
Are yielding; cords of all too weak account
For earth with heavy griefs so overplussed.
　　　　Ah! is Thy love indeed
A weed, albeit an amaranthine weed,
Suffering no flowers except its own to mount?
　　　　Ah! must—
　　　　Designer infinite!—
Ah! must Thou char the wood ere Thou canst limn with it?
My freshness spent its wavering shower i' the dust;
And now my heart is as a broken fount,
Wherein tear-drippings stagnate, spilt down ever
　　　　From the dank thoughts that shiver
Upon the sighful branches of my mind.
　　　　Such is; what is to be?
The pulp so bitter, how shall taste the rind?
I dimly guess what Time in mists confounds;
Yet ever and anon a trumpet sounds
From the hid battlements of Eternity;
Those shaken mists a space unsettle, then
Round the half-glimpsèd turrets slowly wash again.
　　　　But not ere him who summoneth
　　　　I first have seen, enwound
With glooming robes purpureal, cypress-crowned;
His name I know, and what his trumpet saith.
Whether man's heart or life it be which yields
　　　　Thee harvest, must Thy harvest fields

Be dunged with rotten death?

Now of that long pursuit
Comes on at hand the bruit;
That Voice is round me like a bursting sea:
"And is thy earth so marred,
Shattered in shard on shard?
Lo, all things fly thee, for thou fliest Me!
Strange, piteous, futile thing,
Wherefore should any set thee love apart?
Seeing none but I makes much of naught" (He said),
"And human love needs human meriting:
How hast thou merited—
Of all man's clotted clay the dingiest clot?
Alack, thou knowest not
How little worthy of any love thou art!
Whom wilt thou find to love ignoble thee
Save Me, save only Me?
All which I took from thee I did but take,
Not for thy harms,
But just that thou might'st seek it in My arms
All which thy child's mistake
Fancies as lost, I have stored for thee at home:
Rise, clasp My hand, and come!"

Halts by me that footfall:
Is my gloom, after all,
Shade of His hand, outstretched caressingly?
"Ah, fondest, blindest, weakest,
I am He Whom thou seekest!
Thou dravest love from thee, who dravest Me."

William Watson

SIR WILLIAM WATSON (1858–1935) was born in Yorkshire of middle-class parents and educated at Southport before entering commerce. He began writing poetry before he was twenty, but it was not until the publication of *Wordsworth's Grave and Other Poems* (1890) that he became well known. Admired by Gladstone, he was in 1913 a serious contender for the vacant position of Poet Laureate, but was passed over in favor of Bridges. In 1917 he was knighted, and later made a successful lecture tour of the United States. He continued writing almost until his death, but remained untouched by the various revolutionary poetical movements which were going on about him.

Watson believed that modern life and poetry were virtually incompatible, but this did not prevent him from writing verse on various historical and political issues of his day, sometimes, as in his outspoken defense of the Armenians, even at the risk of incurring official displeasure. He was sincere, frequently dogmatic, distressed to observe what he believed was the decline of English poetry, passionate in his allegiances, and somewhat puritanical. His best verse has a sonorous Victorian grandeur, but too frequently it degenerates into high-sounding but uninspired rhetoric.

Wordsworth's Grave

I

The old rude church, with bare, bald tower, is here;
  Beneath its shadow high-born Rotha flows;
Rotha, remembering well who slumbers near,
  And with cool murmur lulling his repose.

Rotha, remembering well who slumbers near.
  His hills, his lakes, his streams are with him yet.
Surely the heart that read her own heart clear
  Nature forgets not soon; 'tis we forget.

We that with vagrant soul his fixity
  Have slighted; faithless, done his deep faith wrong;
Left him for poorer loves, and bowed the knee
  To misbegotten strange new gods of song.

Yet, led by hollow ghost or beckoning elf
  Far from her homestead to the desert bourn,
The vagrant soul returning to herself
  Wearily wise, must needs to him return.

To him and to the powers that with him dwell—
  Inflowings that divulged not whence they came;
And that secluded Spirit unknowable,
  The mystery we make darker with a name;

The Somewhat which we name but cannot know,
  Ev'n as we name a star and only see
His quenchless flashings forth, which ever show
  And ever hide him, and which are not he.

II

Poet who sleepest by this wandering wave!
  When thou wast born, what birth-gift hadst thou then?

To thee what wealth was that the Immortals gave,
  The wealth thou gavest in thy turn to men?

Not Milton's keen, translunar music thine;
  Not Shakespeare's cloudless, boundless human view;
Not Shelley's flush of rose on peaks divine;
  Nor yet the wizard twilight Coleridge knew.

What hadst thou that could make so large amends
  For all thou hadst not and thy peers possessed,
Motion and fire, swift means to radiant ends?—
  Thou hadst, for weary feet, the gift of rest.

From Shelley's dazzling glow or thunderous haze,
  From Byron's tempest-anger, tempest-mirth,
Men turned to thee and found—not blast and blaze,
  Tumult of tottering heavens, but peace on earth.

Nor peace that grows by Lethe, scentless flower,
  There in white languors to decline and cease;
But peace whose names are also rapture, power,
  Clear sight, and love: for these are parts of peace.

III

I hear it vouched the Muse is with us still—
  If less divinely frenzied than of yore,
In lieu of feeling she has wondrous skill
  To simulate emotion felt no more.

Not such the authentic Presence pure, that made
  This valley vocal in the great days gone!—
In *his* great days, while yet the spring-time played
  About him, and the mighty morning shone.

No word-mosaic artificer, he sang
  A lofty song of lowly weal and dole.
Right from the heart, right to the heart it sprang,
  Or from the soul leapt instant to the soul.

He felt the charm of childhood, grace of youth,
   Grandeur of age, insisting to be sung.
The impassioned argument was simple truth
   Half-wondering at its own melodious tongue.

Impassioned? ay, to the song's ecstatic core!
   But far removed were clangor, storm, and feud;
For plenteous health was his, exceeding store
   Of joy, and an impassioned quietude.

IV

A hundred years ere he to manhood came,
   Song from celestial heights had wandered down,
Put off her robe of sunlight, dew, and flame,
   And donned a modish dress to charm the Town.

Thenceforth she but festooned the porch of things;
   Apt at life's lore, incurious what life meant.
Dextrous of hand, she struck her lute's few strings;
   Ignobly perfect, barrenly content.

Unflushed with ardor and unblanched with awe,
   Her lips in profitless derision curled,
She saw with dull emotion—if she saw—
   The vision of the glory of the world.

The human masque she watched, with dreamless eyes
   In whose clear shallows lurked no trembling shade:
The stars, unkenned by her, might set and rise,
   Unmarked by her, the daisies bloom and fade.

The age grew sated with her sterile wit.
   Herself waxed weary on her loveless throne.
Men felt life's tide, the sweep and surge of it,
   And craved a living voice, a natural tone.

For none the less, though song was but half true,
   The world lay common, one abounding theme.

Man joyed and wept, and fate was ever new,
  And love was sweet, life real, death no dream.

In sad, stern verse the rugged scholar-sage
  Bemoaned his toil unvalued, youth uncheered.
His numbers wore the vesture of the age,
  But, 'neath it beating, the great heart was heard.

From dewy pastures, uplands sweet with thyme,
  A virgin breeze freshened the jaded day.
It wafted Collins' lonely vesper-chime,
  It breathed abroad the frugal note of Gray.

It fluttered here and there, nor swept in vain
  The dusty haunts where futile echoes dwell—
Then, in a cadence soft as summer rain,
  And sad from Auburn voiceless, drooped and fell.

It drooped and fell, and one 'neath northern skies,
  With southern heart, who tilled his father's field,
Found Poesy a-dying, bade her rise
  And touch quick Nature's hem and go forth healed.

On life's broad plain the plowman's conquering share
  Upturned the fallow lands of truth anew,
And o'er the formal garden's trim parterre
  The peasant's team a ruthless furrow drew.

Bright was his going forth, but clouds ere long
  Whelmed him; in gloom his radiance set, and those
Twin morning stars of the new century's song,
  Those morning stars that sang together, rose.

In elfish speech the *Dreamer* told his tale
  Of marvelous oceans swept by fateful wings.—
The *Seër* strayed not from earth's human pale,
  But the mysterious face of common things

He mirrored as the moon in Rydal Mere
  Is mirrored, when the breathless night hangs blue:

Strangely remote she seems and wondrous near,
  And by some nameless difference born anew.

V

Peace—peace—and rest! Ah, how the lyre is loath,
  Or powerless now, to give what all men seek!
Either it deadens with ignoble sloth
  Or deafens with shrill tumult, loudly weak.

Where is the singer whose large notes and clear
  Can heal, and arm, and plenish, and sustain?
Lo, one with empty music floods the ear,
  And one, the heart refreshing, tires the brain.

And idly tuneful, the loquacious throng
  Flutter and twitter, prodigal of time,
And little masters make a toy of song
  Till grave men weary of the sound of rime.

And some go prankt in faded antique dress,
  Abhorring to be hale and glad and free;
And some parade a conscious naturalness—
  The scholar's, not the child's, simplicity.

Enough;—and wisest who from words forbear.
  The gentle river rails not as it glides;
And suave and charitable, the winsome air
  Chides not at all, or only him who chides.

VI

Nature! we storm thine ear with choric notes.
  Thou answerest through the calm great nights and days,
"Laud me who will: not tuneless are your throats;
  Yet if ye paused I should not miss the praise."

We falter, half-rebuked, and sing again.
  We chant thy desertness and haggard gloom,

Or with thy splendid wrath inflate the strain,
  Or touch it with thy color and perfume.

One, his melodious blood aflame for thee,
  Wooed with fierce lust, his hot heart world-defiled.
One, with the upward eye of infancy,
  Looked in thy face, and felt himself thy child.

Thee he approached without distrust or dread—
  Beheld thee throned, an awful queen, above—
Climbed to thy lap and merely laid his head
  Against thy warm wild heart of mother-love.

He heard that vast heart beating—thou didst press
  Thy child so close, and lov'dst him unaware.
Thy beauty gladdened him; yet he scarce less
  Had loved thee, had he never found thee fair!

For thou wast not as legendary lands
  To which with curious eyes and ears we roam.
Nor wast thou as a fane 'mid solemn sands,
  Where palmers halt at evening. Thou wast home.

And here, at home, still bides he; but he sleeps;
  Not to be wakened even at thy word;
Though we, vague dreamers, dream he somewhere keeps
  An ear still open to thy voice still heard—

Thy voice, as heretofore, about him blown,
  Forever blown about his silence now;
Thy voice, though deeper, yet so like his own
  That almost, when he sang, we deemed 'twas thou!

VII

Behind Helm Crag and Silver Howe the sheen
  Of the retreating day is less and less.
Soon will the lordlier summits, here unseen,
  Gather the night about their nakedness.

The half-heard bleat of sheep comes from the hill.
　　Faint sounds of childish play are in the air.
The river murmurs past. All else is still.
　　The very graves seem stiller than they were.

Afar though nation be on nation hurled,
　　And life with toil and ancient pain depressed,
Here one may scarce believe the whole wide world
　　Is not at peace, and all man's heart at rest.

Rest! 'twas the gift *he* gave; and peace! the shade
　　He spread, for spirits fevered with the sun.
To him his bounties are come back—here laid
　　In rest, in peace, his labor nobly done.

Shelley's Centenary

Within a narrow span of time,
Three princes of the realm of rime,
At height of youth or manhood's prime
　　　From earth took wing,
To join the fellowship sublime
　　　Who, dead, yet sing.

He, first, his earliest wreath who wove
Of laurel grown in Latmian grove,
Conquered by pain and hapless love
　　　Found calmer home,
Roofed by the heaven that glows above
　　　Eternal Rome.

A fierier soul, its own fierce prey
And cumbered with more mortal clay,
At Missolonghi flamed away,
　　　And left the air
Reverberating to this day
　　　Its loud despair.

Alike remote from Byron's scorn
And Keats's magic as of morn
Bursting forever newly-born
    On forests old,
To wake a hoary world forlorn
    With touch of gold,

Shelley, the cloud-begot, who grew
Nourished on starbeams, air, and dew,
Into that Essence whence he drew
    His life and lyre
Was fittingly resolved anew
    Through wave and fire.

And it was strangely, wildly meet,
That he, who brooked not Time's slow feet,
With passage thus abrupt and fleet
    Should hurry hence,
Eager the Great Perhaps to greet
    With Why? and Whence?

Impatient of the world's fixed way,
He ne'er could suffer God's delay,
But all the future in a day
    Would build divine,
And the whole past in ruins lay,
    An emptied shrine.

Vain vision! but the glow, the fire,
The passion of benign desire,
These peradventure lift him higher
    Than many a soul
That mounts a million paces nigher
    Its meaner goal.

And power is his, if naught besides,
In that thin ether where he rides,
Above the roar of human tides
    To ascend afar,

Lost in a storm of light that hides
    His dizzy car.

Below, the unhasting world toils on,
And here and there are victories won,
Some dragon slain, some justice done,
    While, 'mid the skies,
A meteor rushing on the sun,
    He flares and dies.

But, as he cleaves yon ether clear,
Notes from the unattempted sphere
He scatters to the far-off ear
    Of Earth's dim throng,
Nay, from the zenith he flings sheer
    His torrent of song.

In other shapes than he forecast,
Fate molds the Morrow. His fierce blast—
His wild assault upon the Past—
    These things are vain.
Brief is Revolt, but born to last
    Was the arrowy strain,

That seems the wandering voices blent
Of every virgin element;
A sound from azure spaces sent—
    An airy call
From the Uranian firmament
    O'erdoming all.

And in this world of worldlings, where
Souls rush in apathy, and ne'er
A great emotion shakes the air,
    And life flags tame,
And rare is noble impulse, rare
    The impassioned aim,

'Tis no mean fortune to have heard
A singer who, if errors blurred

His sight, had yet a spirit stirred
    By vast desire,
And ardor fledging the swift word
    With plumes of fire.

A creature of impetuous breath,
Our torpor deadlier than death
He knew not; whatsoe'er he saith
    Flashes with life;
He spurreth men, he quickeneth
    To splendid strife.

And in his gusts of song he brings
Wild odors shaken from strange wings,
And carries secret whisperings
    From far lips blown,
While all the rapturous heart of things
    Throbs through his own—

His own that from the burning pyre
One who had loved his wind-swept lyre
Out of the sharp teeth of the fire.
    Unmolten drew,
Beside the sea that in her ire
    Smote him and slew.

After the Titans

England, in good Victoria's latter reign,
    Two potent councillors by turns have led,
    Little alike in build of heart or head,
Yet owning this resemblance,—that the twain
Are visibly of Britain's ancient strain,
    Sprung of the lineage of her stalwart dead,
    Strong souls and massive, such as England bred
In the brave day that cometh not again.

To these succeeds another, newer race,
    Men light and slight, on narrower scale designed,

Offspring and image of the change we trace
   In art, arms, action, manners, morals, mind,—
The burly oak departing, in its place
   The lissom willow, swaying to the wind.

Ode on the Day of
the Coronation of King Edward VII

I

Sire, we have looked on many and mighty things
In these eight hundred summers of renown
Since the Gold Dragon of the Wessex Kings
On Hastings field went down;
And slowly in the ambience of this crown
Have many crowns been gathered, till, to-day,
How many peoples crown thee, who shall say?
Time, and the ocean, and some fostering star,
In high cabal have made us what we are,
Who stretch one hand to Huron's bearded pines,
And one on Kashmir's snowy shoulder lay,
And round the streaming of whose raiment shines
The iris of the Australasian spray.
For waters have connived at our designs,
And winds have plotted with us—and behold,
Kingdom in kingdom, sway in oversway,
Dominion fold in fold:
Like to that immemorial regal stone
Thy namesake from the northland reft away,
Symbol of sovereignty and spoil of fray,
And closed in England's throne.
So wide of girth this little cirque of gold,
So great are we, and old.
Proud from the ages are we come, O King;
Proudly, as fits a nation that hath now
So many dawns and sunsets on her brow,
This duteous heart we bring.

II

The kings thy far forerunners; he that came
And smote us into greatness; he whose fame,
In dark armipotence and ivied pride,
Towers above Conway's tide,
And where Carnarvon ponders on the sea;
He, that adventurous name,
Who left at Agincourt the knightly head
Of France and all its charging plumes o'erthrown,
But hath in Shakespeare's conquest merged his own;
And she, a queen, yet fashioned king-like, she
Before whose prows, before whose tempests, fled
Spain on the ruining night precipitately;
And that worn face, in camps and councils bred,
The guest who brought us law and liberty
Raised well-nigh from the dead;
Yea, she herself, in whose immediate stead
Thou standest, in the shadow of her soul;
All these, O King, from their seclusion dread,
And guarded palace of eternity,
Mix in thy pageant with phantasmal tread,
Hear the long waves of acclamation roll,
And with yet mightier silence marshal thee
To the awful throne thou hast inherited.

III

Lo, at the Earth's high feast, ere Autumn bring
His afterthoughts on greatness to her ear,
And with monitions of mortality
Perturb the revelling year,
Thou goest forth and art anointed King.
Nature disdains not braveries: why should we
The sombre foil to all her splendours be?
Let London rustle with rich apparelling,
And all the ways, with festal faces lined,
Casement and coign and fluttering balcony,

Wave welcome on the wind.
Now the loud land flames with imperial gear,
And life itself, so late in hues austere
And the cold reign of iron custom bound,
Puts off its gray subjection, and is here
One moment throned and crowned.
Now the long glories prance and triumph by:
And now the pomps have passed, and we depart
Each to the peace or strife of his own heart:
And now the day whose bosom was so high
Sinks billowing down: and twilight sorceries change
Into remote and strange
What is most known and nigh:
And changelessly the river sends his sigh
Down leagues of hope and fear, and pride and shame,
And life and death; dim-journeying passionless
To where broad estuary and beaconing ness
Look towards the outlands whence our fathers came.
And high on Druid mountains hath the sun
Flamed valediction, as the last lights died
Beyond that fatal wave, that from our side
Sunders the lovely and the lonely Bride
Whom we have wedded but have never won.

IV

And night falls on an isle whose vassal seas
Remember not her prone regalities,
So withered from belief, so far and faint,
In such abjection before Time they lie,
Kingdoms and thrones forgotten of the sky.
Deira with her sea-face to the morn,
And Cumbria sunset-gazing; moist Dyvnaint,
A realm of coombs and tors; old greatnesses
From Dee to Severn, where the bards were born
Whose songs are in the wind by Idris' chair,
Whose lips won battles; and seats of puissance where,
With long grope of his desultory hand,
The ocean, prying deep into the land,

By Morven and the legends of wild Lorn,
Repents him, lost about Lochiel: all these
Have been and 'stablisht on their dust we stand;
Thy England; with the northern sister fair,
That hath the heath-bells in her blowing hair;
And the dark mountain maid
That dreams for ever in the wizard shade,
Hymning her heroes there.

V

O doom of overlordships! to decay
First at the heart, the eye scarce dimmed at all;
Or perish of much cumber and array,
The burdening robe of Empire, and its pall;
Or, of voluptuous hours the wanton prey,
Die of the poisons that most sweetly slay;
Or, from insensate height,
With prodigies, with light
Of trailing angers on the monstrous night,
Magnificently fall.
Far off from her that bore us be such fate,
And vain against her gate
Its knocking. But by chinks and crannies, Death,
Forbid the doorways, oft-times entereth.
Let her drink deep of discontent, and sow
Abroad the troubling knowledge. Let her show
Whence glories come, and wherefore glories go,
And what indeed are glories, unto these
'Twixt labour and the rest that is not ease
Made blank and darksome; who have hardly heard
Sound of her loftiest names, or any word
Of all that hath in gold been said and sung,
Since him of April heart and morning tongue,
Her ageless singing-bird.
For now the day is unto them that know,
And not henceforth she stumbles on the prize;
And yonder march the nations full of eyes.
Already is doom a-spinning, if unstirred

In leisure of ancient pathways she lose touch
Of the hour, and overmuch
Recline upon achievement, and be slow
To take the world arriving, and forget
How perilous are the stature and port that so
Invite the arrows, how unslumbering are
The hates that watch and crawl.
Nor must she, like the others, yield up yet
The generous dreams! But rather live to be
Saluted in the hearts of men as she
Of high and singular election, set
Benignant in the sea;
That greatly loving freedom loved to free,
And was herself the bridal and embrace
Of strength and conquering grace.

England

A kinsman's love beseech;
Coleridge, his locks aspersed with fairy foam,
Calm Spenser, Chaucer suave,
His equal friendship crave:
And godlike spirits hail him guest, in speech
Of Athens, Florence, Weimar, Stratford, Rome.

*   *   *

The seasons change, the winds they shift and veer;
The grace of yesteryear
Is dead; the birds depart, the groves decay:
Empires dissolve and peoples disappear:
Song passes not away.
Captains and conquerors leave a little dust,
And kings a dubious legend of their reign;
The swords of Caesars, they are less than rust:
The poet doth remain.
Dead is Augustus, Maro is alive;
And thou, the Mantuan of this age and soil,
With Virgil shalt survive,
Enriching Time with no less honeyed spoil,

The yielded sweet of every Muse's hive;
Heeding no more the sound of idle praise
In that great calm our tumults cannot reach,—
Master who crown'st our immelodious days
With flower of perfect speech.

Oscar Wilde

OSCAR WILDE (1854–1900) was born in Dublin. He attended
Trinity College before going to Magdalen College, Oxford, where
he graduated in 1878. Already as a student Wilde had attracted
attention both as a young scholar of promise and as an aesthete
of the more audacious kind, but after he came down from Oxford
he went to extravagant lengths to draw attention to himself,
dressing with overfine and over-extravagant taste, and holding
forth at society dinner tables with considerable charm and wit.
In 1882 he went on a lecture tour of the United States; in 1887
he edited *Woman's World;* but literary success came to him only
with the publication of his novel *The Picture of Dorian Gray*
(1891), which was quickly followed by his dramas, his most
successful being *The Importance of Being Earnest* (1895). Wilde
was a homosexual, and in 1895 was sent to prison for homosexual crimes. There he wrote *De Profundis,* a long confessional
epistle in which he acknowledged his sins and blamed his young
aristocratic friend, Lord Alfred Douglas, for leading him astray.
On his release two years later he withdrew to the Continent,
dying in Paris of cerebral meningitis three years later.

Wilde's poetry is the least substantial of his claims to literary
recognition, and though "The Ballad of Reading Gaol" ap-
proaches greatness and "The Harlot's House" deserves sympathetic consideration, the bulk of his poetry is heavily derivative
and full of false sentiment, drawing heavily on a number of
native poets as well as on the poetry of late nineteenth-century
France.

Theoretikos

This mighty empire hath but feet of clay:
   Of all its ancient chivalry and might
   Our little island is forsaken quite:
Some enemy hath stolen its crown of bay,
And from its hills that voice hath passed away
   Which spake of Freedom: O come out of it,
   Come out of it, my Soul, thou art not fit
For this vile traffic-house, where day by day
   Wisdom and reverence are sold at mart,
   And the rude people rage with ignorant cries
Against an heritage of centuries.
   It mars my calm: wherefore in dreams of Art
   And loftiest culture I would stand apart,
Neither for God, nor for his enemies.

Impression du Matin

The Thames nocturne of blue and gold
   Changed to a Harmony in grey:
   A barge with ochre-coloured hay
Dropt from the wharf: and chill and cold

The yellow fog came creeping down
   The bridges, till the houses' walls
   Seemed changed to shadows and St. Paul's
Loomed like a bubble o'er the town.

Then suddenly arose the clang
   Of waking life; the streets were stirred
   With country waggons: and a bird
Flew to the glistening roofs and sang.

But one pale woman all alone,
   The daylight kissing her wan hair,
   Loitered beneath the gas lamps' flare,
With lips of flame and heart of stone.

The Grave of Keats

Rid of the world's injustice, and his pain,
   He rests at last beneath God's veil of blue:
   Taken from life when life and love were new
The youngest of the martyrs here is lain,
Fair as Sebastian, and as early slain.
   No cypress shades his grave, no funeral yew,
   But gentle violets weeping with the dew
Weave on his bones an ever-blossoming chain.
O proudest heart that broke for misery!
   O sweetest lips since those of Mitylene!
   O poet-painter of our English Land!
Thy name was writ in water——it shall stand:
   And tears like mine will keep thy memory green,
   As Isabella did her Basil-tree.

In the Gold Room

A HARMONY

Her ivory hands on the ivory keys
   Strayed in a fitful fantasy,
Like the silver gleam when the poplar trees
   Rustle their pale leaves listlessly,
   Or the drifting foam of a restless sea
When the waves show their teeth in the flying breeze.

Her gold hair fell on the wall of gold
   Like the delicate gossamer tangles spun
On the burnished disk of the marigold,
   Or the sunflower turning to meet the sun
   When the gloom of the dark blue night is done,
And the spear of the lily is aureoled.

And her sweet red lips on these lips of mine
   Burned like the ruby fire set
In the swinging lamp of a crimson shrine,

Or the bleeding wounds of the pomegranate,
Or the heart of the lotus drenched and wet
With the spilt-out blood of the rose-red wine.

Taedium Vitae

To stab my youth with desperate knives, to wear
This paltry age's gaudy livery,
To let each base hand filch my treasury,
To mesh my soul within a woman's hair,
And be mere Fortune's lackeyed groom,—I swear
I love it not! these things are less to me
Than the thin foam that frets upon the sea,
Less than the thistledown of summer air
Which hath no seed: better to stand aloof
Far from these slanderous fools who mock my life
Knowing me not, better the lowliest roof
Fit for the meanest hind to sojourn in,
Than to go back to that hoarse cave of strife
Where my white soul first kissed the mouth of sin.

The Harlot's House

We caught the tread of dancing feet,
We loitered down the moonlit street,
And stopped beneath the harlot's house.

Inside, above the din and fray,
We heard the loud musicians play
The "Treues Liebes Herz" of Strauss.

Like strange mechanical grotesques,
Making fantastic arabesques,
The shadows raced across the blind.

We watched the ghostly dancers spin
To sound of horn and violin,
Like black leaves wheeling in the wind.

Like wire-pulled automatons,
Slim silhouetted skeletons
Went sidling through the slow quadrille,

Then took each other by the hand,
And danced a stately saraband;
Their laughter echoed thin and shrill.

Sometimes a clockwork puppet pressed
A phantom lover to her breast,
Sometimes they seemed to try to sing.

Sometimes a horrible marionette
Came out, and smoked its cigarette
Upon the steps like a live thing.

Then, turning to my love, I said,
"The dead are dancing with the dead,
The dust is whirling with the dust."

But she—she heard the violin,
And left my side, and entered in:
Love passed into the house of lust.

Then suddenly the tune went false,
The dancers wearied of the waltz,
The shadows ceased to wheel and whirl.

And down the long and silent street,
The dawn, with silver-sandalled feet,
Crept like a frightened girl.

Symphony in Yellow

An omnibus across the bridge
   Crawls like a yellow butterfly,
   And, here and there, a passer-by
Shows like a little restless midge.

Big barges full of yellow hay
  Are moored against the shadowy wharf,
  And, like a yellow silken scarf,
The thick fog hangs along the quay.

The yellow leaves begin to fade
  And flutter from the Temple elms,
  And at my feet the pale green Thames
Lies like a rod of rippled jade.

General Bibliography

PERHAPS the most useful survey of the poetry of the transitional period is Vivian de Sola Pinto's *Crisis in English Poetry, 1880–1940* (London, 1951) but R. L. Mégroz's *Modern English Poetry, 1882–1932* (London, 1932) is also well worth reading. Other surveys which may be recommended are David Daiches' *Poetry and the Modern World* (Chicago, 1940) and F. R. Leavis's *New Bearings in English Poetry* (London, 1932), but as both these writers tacitly assume that the poetry of the twenties and thirties is much superior to that which came immediately before, the transitional poets tend to be underrated or at best praised for the way in which they anticipated the achievements of more characteristically "modern" writers. B. Ifor Evans's *English Literature Between the Wars* (London, 1948), H. V. Routh's *English Literature and Ideas in the Twentieth Century* (New York, 1950), and R. A. Scott-James's *Fifty Years of English Literature, 1900–1950* (London, 1951) are all useful general surveys of the period, sharing, however, the usual limitations of concise literary histories, while William York Tindall's *Forces in Modern British Literature, 1885–1946* (New York, 1947) is an immensely readable but hardly impartial account which should be read with caution. Finally, Herbert Palmer's *Post Victorian Poetry* (London, 1938) may be recommended on account of its comprehensiveness, but when the author discusses poetry other than Georgian, his critical judgments tend to be either insensitive or idiosyncratic.

For the Nineties period Holbrook Jackson's *The 1890's* (New York, 1913) is still useful, and so is Granville Hicks's *Figures of Transition: A Study of British Literature at the End of the Nineteenth Century* (New York, 1939). On the Decadents, Osbert

Burdett's *The Beardsley Period* (New York, 1925) may be recommended, but the best brief account of these writers is the introduction to Karl Beckson's anthology, *Aesthetes and Decadents of the 1890's* (New York, 1966). There is no book-length account of the Counter-Decadent tradition, but the first chapter of Jerome H. Buckley's *William Ernest Henley* (Princeton, 1945) is a useful introduction.

The Georgians have been discussed in Frank Swinnerton's chatty survey, *The Georgian Literary Scene, 1910–1935* (London, 1950), but they received more scholarly treatment in Robert H. Ross's *The Georgian Revolt: Rise and Fall of a Poetic Ideal* (Carbondale and Edwardsville, Illinois, 1965). The 1914–1918 war poets have been discussed by Robert Graves in *The Common Asphodel* (London, 1949), but the most thorough and up-to-date study of these writers is undoubtedly John H. Johnston's *English Poetry of the First World War* (Princeton, 1964). There are at least two important books on the Imagists: Glenn Hughes's *Imagism and the Imagists* (Stanford, Calif., 1931) and Stanley K. Coffman, *Imagism: A Chapter for the History of Modern Poetry* (Norman, Okla., 1951).

Perhaps the two most stimulating books on the poetry of the 1880–1920 period are C. K. Stead's *The New Poetic* (London, 1964) and Frank Kermode's *Romantic Image* (London, 1957), which should be read in the light of John Bayley's *The Romantic Survival* (London, 1957). The first two of these books, especially, demonstrate with admirable clarity how much modern poetry owes to that which was written during the closing years of the nineteenth century and at the beginning of the twentieth, while the last serves as a reminder that we should be especially cautious in viewing the poetry of our day outside the context of the great nineteenth-century Romantic tradition.

Though not specifically concerned with the poetry of the 1880–1920 period, there are a number of important studies relevant to certain aspects of the poetry contained in this anthology. Enid Starkie's *From Gautier to Eliot* (London, 1960) and Ruth Z. Temple's *Critic's Alchemy* (New York, 1953) study the influence of nineteenth-century French literature on English literature, with special attention to the Symbolists, while James K. Robinson's "A Neglected Phase of the Aesthetic Movement, English Parnassianism" *(PMLA,* LXVIII, 1953, pp. 733–754) draws attention to the influence of the French Parnassians on late nineteenth-century English poetry and their importance in relation to the Imagist movement. Mario Praz's *Romantic Agony* (New York, 1956) considers the pathological aspect of nineteenth-century Decadence, and notes its appearance in late nineteenth-century English poetry. Hoxie Neale Fairchild's *Religious Trends in English Poetry,* Vol. IV (New York, 1957) and Raymond Tschumi's *Thought in Twentieth-Century English Poetry* (London, 1951) are relevant to the theological and philosophical preoccupations of many of the poets included in this anthology, while Joseph E. Duncan's *The Revival of Metaphysical Poetry* (Minneapolis, Minn., 1959) reminds us that far from being a twenties phenomenon, keen interest in the Metaphysicals was apparent throughout the nineteenth century.

There are also a number of book-length studies of the poetry of the Transition period which, though dated and of varying usefulness, are nevertheless interesting insofar as they reflect the attitude of contemporaries to the poetry of the time. Among the more significant are these: William Archer, *Poets of the Younger Generation* (New York, 1902); J. D. Beresford et. al., *Tradition and Experiment in Present Day Literature* (London, 1929); Arthur M. Clark, *The Realistic Revolt in Modern Poetry* (Oxford, 1922); H. P. Collins, *Modern Poetry* (London, 1925); Edward L. Davison, *Some Modern Poets and Other Essays* (New York, 1928); A. S. Hoyt, *The Spiritual Message of Modern English Poetry* (New York, 1924); Edwin Muir, *Transition: Essays on Contemporary Literature* (London, 1926); A. Noyes, *Some Aspects of Modern Poetry* (London, 1924); W. L. Phelps, *The Advance of English Poetry in the Twentieth Century* (New York, 1918); Harold Williams, *Modern English Writers* (London, 1918).

The Victorians and After by Edith Batho and Bonamy Dobrée (London, 1950) contains a useful survey of English literature from 1830 to 1914, but the most significant feature of the book is its bibliography, containing sections on the following poets included in this anthology: Austin Dobson; W. E. Henley; Henry Newbolt; Francis Thompson; Lionel Johnson; Alice Meynell; Robert Bridges; John Davidson; William Watson; A. E. Housman; Ernest Dowson; W. H. Davies; Walter de la Mare; John Masefield; Edward Thomas; Harold Monro; Lascelles Abercrombie;

James Elroy Flecker; J. C. Squire; Rupert Brooke; Oscar Wilde; Thomas Hardy; R. L. Stevenson; Rudyard Kipling; Arthur Symons; Edmund Gosse, Hilaire Belloc; G. K. Chesterton; and Owen Seaman. *The Present Age, From 1920* by David Daiches (London, 1958), in the same series as *The Victorians and After,* contains bibliographies on the following poets included in this anthology: W. H. Davies; Walter de la Mare; John Masefield; Harold Monro; Lascelles Abercrombie; J. C. Squire; Siegfried Sassoon; Edith Sitwell; Isaac Rosenberg; and Wilfred Owen. Useful as both these volumes are, they will probably be superseded shortly by a handbook to the Transition period compiled by Edward S. Lanterbach and W. Eugene Davis. This volume, which promises to be the most comprehensive guide to British Literature 1880–1920, will contain introductory essays on the background of the period, describe the development of major literary genres and movements, and also contain selective bibliographies of approximately 150 major and minor writers whose most important work was written between 1880 and 1920.

Finally, the journal *English Literature in Transition* publishes annotated bibliographies of the following poets included in this anthology: Robert Bridges; Rupert Brooke; G. K. Chesterton; John Davidson; Walter de la Mare; Ernest Dowson; James Elroy Flecker; Edmund Gosse; Thomas Hardy; W. E. Henley; A. E. Housman; Lionel Johnson; Rudyard Kipling; D. H. Lawrence; John Masefield; Wilfred Owen; Isaac Rosenberg; Siegfried Sassoon; R. L. Stevenson; Arthur Symons; Francis Thompson; Oscar Wilde. Some of these have already appeared; the others are in preparation.

Bibliographies of the Poets

Lascelles Abercrombie

Bibliography: Abercrombie's poems and some of his plays were published in *Collected Poems* (Oxford, 1930), which contained verse from his earlier volumes of poetry: *Interludes and Poems* (1908); *Mary and the Bramble* (1910); *Emblems of Love* (1911); *Twelve Idylls and Other Poems* (1928). His plays are as follows: *The Sale of St. Thomas* (1911); *Deborah* (1913); *Four Short Plays* (1928); *Phoenix* (1923); *The Sale of St. Thomas* (complete, revised version, 1930). Abercrombie's criticism is not especially memorable, but insofar as it throws light on his poetry, the following works may be recommended: "The Function of Poetry in Drama," *Poetry Review,* I (1912), pp. 107–108; *The Epic* (1914); *Poetry and Contemporary Speech* (1914); *Principles of English Prosody* (1923); *The Theory of Poetry* (1924); *The Idea of Great Poetry* (1925); *Romanticism* (1926); *Progress in Literature* (1929); *Colloquial Language in Literature* (1931); *Poetry, Its Music and Meaning* (1932). There is no single recent scholarly assessment of his work, but there are scattered references to him in such general surveys of early twentieth-century poetry as Robert H. Ross's *The Georgian Revolt,* mentioned in the general bibliography.

Hilaire Belloc

Bibliography: The most accessible collection of Belloc's writings is *An Anthology of Prose and Verse,* ed. W. N. Roughead (London, 1951). His individual volumes of verse are as follows: *Verses and Sonnets* (1896); *The Bad Child's Book of Beasts* (1896); *More Beasts— For Worse Children* (1897); *The Modern Traveller* (1898); *A Moral*

Alphabet (1899); *Cautionary Tales* (1907); *Verses* (1910); *More Peers* (1911); *New Cautionary Tales* (1930); and *An Heroic Poem in Praise of Wine* (1932). However, the recommended collection of Belloc's verse must be *Sonnets and Verse,* originally published in 1923, but newly edited with additional poems and an introduction by R. Jebb (London, 1954). There are two good "lives": J. B. Morton, *Hilaire Belloc: A Memoir* (London, 1955) and R. Speaight, *The Life of Hilaire Belloc* (London, 1956), which is the official biography. The best book-length study of his ideas and achievement as a writer is F. Wilhelmsen's *Hilaire Belloc: No Alienated Man* (London, 1954), but Sally Marguerite Furay's *The Poetry of Hilaire Belloc: A Critical Evaluation,* unpublished Ph.D. dissertation, Stanford, 1955, is a good assessment of Belloc's worth as a poet.

Robert Bridges

Bibliography: The standard, and also most accessible, volume of Bridges' poetry is his *Poetical Works* (2nd ed. rev.), published in the Oxford Standard Authors series in 1953. It includes the long *Testament of Beauty* as well as Bridges' shorter pieces, but excludes the eight poetical dramas. The *Poetical Dramas* (1885–1895) have not been reprinted in recent times, and the four-volume *Collected Essays, Papers, Etc.* (Oxford 1927–1929) is also out of print, but Bridges' *Poetry and Prose,* with an introduction and notes by John Sparrow (Oxford, 1955), the most compact and useful collection of Bridges' work, is still available. Essential to a proper understanding of Bridges' aims as a poet are: his anthology of poetry, *The Spirit of Man* (1916), which contains much incidental criticism; *Milton's Prosody* (1893); his study of *John Keats* (1895); and also his correspondence with G. M. Hopkins. In relation to the latter, see Hopkins' *Letters to Bridges,* ed. Claude C. Abbott (Oxford, 1955). The best book-length studies of Bridges are A. J. Guérard's, *Robert Bridges: A Study of Traditionalism in Poetry* (Cambridge, Mass., 1942) and E. J. Thompson's *Robert Bridges, 1844–1930* (London, 1944), which contains both biographical and critical material. Other important studies of Bridges' work are: T. Kelshall, *Robert Bridges* (London, 1924); E. de Selincourt, *Oxford Lectures on Poets* (Oxford, 1934), pp. 207–256; Oliver Elton, *Robert Bridges and the Testament of Beauty* (Oxford, 1932); E. C. Wright, *Metaphor, Sound and Meaning in Bridges' The Testa-*

ment of Beauty (Philadelphia, 1951); Jean-Georges Ritz, *Robert Bridges and Gerard Hopkins, 1863-1889, A Literary Friendship* (Oxford, 1960).

Rupert Brooke

Bibliography: Brooke's two volumes of poetry are *Poems* (1911) and *1914 and Other Poems* (1915), the contents of which have been reprinted in the *Complete Poems* (London, 1932); *Collected Poems,* with a Memoir by Edward Marsh, 3rd ed. rev. (London, 1942); and the *Poetical Works,* ed. Geoffrey Keynes (London, 1946), which is generally regarded as the most authoritative edition. Brooke's *Prose* has been edited and introduced by Christopher Hassal (London, 1956), and the standard bibliography is by Geoffrey Keynes, 2nd, ed. rev., *Soho Bibliographies* (London, 1954). Walter de la Mare's *Rupert Brooke and the Intellectual Imagination* (London, 1919) is an interesting study of the poet, which throws light on de la Mare's work as well, but the most significant study of Brooke is undoubtedly Christopher Hassal's critical biography, *Rupert Brooke* (London, 1964).

G. K. Chesterton

Bibliography: Chesterton's principal volumes of poetry are as follows: *The Wild Knight and Other Poems* (1900); *Greybeards at Play* (1900); *The Ballad of the White Horse* (1911); *The Flying Inn* (1914); *Poems* (1915); *The Ballad of St. Barbara and Other Verses* (1922); *The Queen of Seven Swords* (1926); *Gloria in Profundis* (1927); *Ubi Ecclegia* (1929); *The Turkey and the Turk: A Christmas Play* (1930); *The Grave at Athens* (1930). *The Collected Poems* were published in 1926, a new edition appearing in 1933. For Chesterton's life see his *Autobiography* (1936), which is perhaps to be preferred to Maisie Ward's *G. K. Chesterton* (London, 1944), which is generally regarded as the standard biography. Hilaire Belloc's *On the Place of G. K. Chesterton in English Letters* (London, 1940) is a sympathetic study by an admiring friend, while Maisie Ward's *Return to Chesterton* (London, 1952) is also recommended. For a brief comparative sketch of both Chesterton and Belloc, see Bernard Bergonzi, "Chesterton and/or Belloc," *Critical Quarterly,* I (1959), pp. 64-71. The standard bibliography is John Sullivan, *G. K. Chesterton: A Bibliography* (London, 1958).

John Davidson

Bibliography: Davidson's principal volumes of poetry are: *In a Music Hall and Other Poems* (1891); *Fleet Street Eclogues* (1893); *Ballads and Songs* (1894); *Fleet Street Eclogues: Second Series* (1896); *New Ballads* (1897); *The Last Ballad* (1899); *The Testament of a Vivisector* (1901); *The Testament of a Man Forbid* (1901); *The Testament of an Empire Builder* (1902); *The Testament of a Prime Minister* (1904); *Holiday and Other Poems* (1906); *The Triumph of Mammon* (1907); *Mammon and His Message* (1908); *The Testament of John Davidson* (1908); *Fleet Street and Other Poems* (1909). There is no collected volume of his poems, but there is a recent book, *John Davidson: A Selection of His Poems,* ed. Maurice Lindsay with a preface by T. S. Eliot, which contains a good representative sampling of his work. J. B. Townsend's *John Davidson: Poet of Armageddon* (New Haven, Conn., 1961) is the standard biography, which also contains a great deal of sound critical comment. Other recommended studies of his work are: John A. Lester Jr., "Friedrich Nietzsche and John Davidson: A Study in Influence," *Journal of the History of Ideas* (June, 1957), pp. 411–429, and the early study by A. S. Mories, "The Religious Significance of John Davidson," *Westminster Review,* CLXXX (1913), pp. 75–85.

W. H. Davies

Bibliography: Davies's individual volumes of poems are too numerous to list here, but there was a collected edition in 1916, another in 1923, a third in 1928, a fourth in 1943, while *The Complete Poems of W. H. Davies,* intro. by Osbert Sitwell, foreword by Daniel George, appeared in 1963. Of his prose works *A Poet's Pilgrimage* (London, 1918) and "Poets and Critics," *The New Statesman* XXI (September, 1923), 619, are relevant to his verse, but the spirit of his poetry is equally reflected in *The Autobiography of a Super-tramp* (London, 1907) and two late, rather slight volumes, *My Birds* (London, 1933) and *My Garden* (London, 1933). Thomas Moult's *W. H. Davies* (London, 1934) may be recommended both for its information concerning Davies's life and its critical estimate of his work, but Richard Stonesifer, *W. H. Davies: A Critical Biography* (London, 1963) is to be preferred.

Walter de la Mare

Bibliography: De la Mare's principal volumes of verse are as follows: *Songs of Childhood* (1902); *Poems* (1906); *The Listeners* (1912); *Peacock Pie* (1913); *The Sunken Garden* (1917); *Motley and Other Poems* (1920); *The Veil* (1921); *The Captive and Other Poems* (1928); *A Snowdrop* (1929); *Poems for Children* (1930); *Old Rhymes and New* (1932); *The Fleeting and Other Poems* (1933); *Memory and Other Poems* (1938); *Bells and Cross* (1941); *The Burning Glass* (1945); *Inward Companion* (1950); *Winged Chariot* (1951). Collected editions of his verse are as follows: *Poems, 1901–1918* (London, 1920); *Poems, 1919–1934* (London, 1935); *Collected Poems* (London, 1942); *Collected Rhymes and Verses* (1944). Because de la Mare's aesthetic and philosophical preoccupations are as apparent in his prose as in his poetry, his novels and short stories are relevant to his verse, and so are *Behold This Dreamer* (London, 1939), an anthology with intro. and commentary, and *Pleasures and Speculations* (London, 1940), a collection of critical essays. There is no official biography of de la Mare, but the following critical biographies may be recommended: R. L. Mégroz, *Walter de la Mare* (London, 1924); Forest Reid, *Walter de la Mare* (London, 1929); J. Atkins, *Walter de la Mare* (London, 1947); H. C. Duffin, *Walter de la Mare* (London, 1949). There is also *Tribute to Walter de la Mare on His 75th Birthday* (London, 1948), which includes essays on the poet by T. S. Eliot, Edmund Blunden, Lord David Cecil, et al., while H. Coombes, "Hardy, de la Mare and Edward Thomas" in *The Modern Age,* Pelican Guide to English Literature, Vol. VII (London, 1961), may also be recommended.

Austin Dobson

Bibliography: Dobson's principal poetic publications are: *Vignettes in Rhyme* (1873); *Proverbs in Porcelain* (1877); *Old World Idylls* (1883);

At the Sign of the Lyre (1885); *Poems on Several Occasions* (1895); and *Poems on the War* (1915). His *Selected Poems* were published in the World's Classics series in 1925, but the standard edition of his poetry is the *Complete Poetical Works,* ed. Alban Dobson (London, 1924). Dobson's uneventful life has not been an attraction for biographers, and the closest thing to an official "life" outside the *Dictionary of National Biography* is Alban Dobson's *Austin Dobson: Some Notes* (London, 1928). Recommended studies of his poetry are as follows: H. C. Lipscombe, "Horace and the Poetry of Austin Dobson," *American Journal of Philology,* L (1929), pp. 1–20; H. Monroe, "From Queen Anne to George the Fifth," *Poetry,* XIX (1921), pp. 90–94; Arthur Symons, "Austin Dobson," in *Studies in Prose and Verse* (London, 1904). The two most significant studies, however, are by James K. Robinson: "A Neglected Phase of the Aesthetic Movement: English Parnassianism," *PMLA,* LXVIII (1953), pp. 733–754; and "Austin Dobson and the Rondeliers," *Modern Language Quarterly,* XIV (1953), pp. 31–42.

Ernest Dowson

Bibliography: During his lifetime, Dowson's verse appeared in various periodicals and in his *Verses* (1896) and *Decorations* (1899). His verse playlet, *The Pierrot of the Minute,* was published in 1897, but no collected edition of his verse appeared until after his death. Desmond Flower's *The Poetical Works of Ernest Dowson* (London, 1934) is the standard collection of Dowson's verse, but *The Poems of Ernest Dowson* (London, 1905) is valuable for its memoir of the poet by Arthur Symons. The standard biography is Mark Longaker's *Ernest Dowson* (Philadelphia, 1944), but two other short biographical studies may be mentioned: John Gawsworth, "The Dowson Legend," *Royal Society of Literature Transactions,* XVII (1938), pp. 93–123, and Russell M. Goldfarb, "The Dowson Legend Today," *Studies in English Literature, 1500–1900,* IV (1964), pp. 653–662. The most recent study of Dowson's work is Thomas B. Swann's *Ernest Dowson* (New York, 1964).

James Elroy Flecker

Bibliography: Flecker's principal volumes of verse are as follows: *The Bridge of Fire* (1907); *Thirty-Six Poems* (1910); *Forty-Two Poems*

(1911); *The Golden Journey to Samarkand* (1913); *The Old Ships* (1915); *The Burial in England* (1915). *His Collected Poems,* with intro. by J. C. Squire, appeared in 1916. Flecker's two verse dramas were published posthumously: *Hassan* (1922) and *Don Juan* (1925). *The King of Alsander,* Flecker's only novel, was published in 1914, while his *Collected Prose* appeared first in 1920 and was republished in 1922. The standard biography of Flecker is Geraldine Hodgson, *The Life of James Elroy Flecker* (London, 1925), but there is other biographical material in the *Letters of James Elroy Flecker to Frank Savery* (London, 1926) and Flecker's *Some Letters from Abroad* (London, 1930). There is an intelligent but somewhat fulsome account of Flecker's achievement as a poet in J. C. Squire's introduction to the revised edition of the *Collected Poems* (London, 1946).

•

F. S. Flint

Bibliography: Flint's verse appeared in numerous anthologies and reviews of the day, but the three principal sources are *In the Net of the Stars* (1909); *Cadences* (1915); *Otherworld* (1915). Especially important to the study of Imagism is Flint's essay on the "History of Imagism," *Egoist,* II (1915), pp. 70–71. There is no standard biography of Flint, nor has his poetry been intensively studied. However, there are a number of references to him in *The Collected Letters* of D. H. Lawrence, ed. Harry T. Moore, 2 vols. (New York, 1962); Glenn Hughes, *Imagism and the Imagists* (Palo Alto, Calif., 1931); and J. G. Fletcher, *Life Is My Song* (New York, 1937). There is a sympathetic article by Richard Aldington on Flint's verse, "The Poetry of F. S. Flint," in the May 1, 1915, issue of the *Egoist.*

Edmond Gosse

Bibliography: Gosse's principal volumes of verse are as follows: *Madrigals, Songs and Sonnets,* with J. A. Blaikie (1870); *On Viol and Flute* (1873); *New Poems* (1879); *Firdausi in Exile and Other Poems* (1885); *In Russet and Silver* (1894); *The Autumn Garden* (1909). He also wrote a verse tragedy, *King Erik* (1876). *The Collected Poems* appeared in 1911, while *Selected Poems* was published in 1926. Gosse was a voluminous writer of criticism, and though not always a stickler for factual accuracy, he has many intelligent things to say. Many of his shorter pieces are relevant to the study of poets included in this anthology, and may be found in his *Collected Essays,* 12 vols. (London, 1912-1927). The standard biography is E. Charteris, *The Life and Letters of Edmund Gosse* (London, 1931). Other useful studies of his work are John Freeman, *English Portraits and Essays* (London, 1924) and P. Braybrooke, *Considerations: Edmund Gosse,* with an intro. by Gilbert Frankau (London, 1925).

Julian Grenfell

Bibliography: Grenfell's output was slight, and the only accessible collection of his verse is included in Viola Meynell's *Julian Grenfell* (London, 1917), a memoir which also contains some of his poems. Apart from scattered references to him in general studies of the poetry of the 1914-1918 war, such as those included in the General Bibliography, there is a brief account of him in T. Sturge Moore's, *Some Soldier Poets* (New York, 1920).

Thomas Hardy

Bibliography: Hardy's principal volumes of poetry are as follows: *Wessex Poems* (1898); *Poems of the Past and the Present* (1901); *The Dynasts* Pt. I (1903), Pt. II (1906), Pt. III (1908); *Times Laughing-Stocks* (1909); *Satires of Circumstance* (1911); *Moments of Vision* (1917); *Late Lyrics* (1922); *Human Shows* (1925). There are two main editions of Hardy's works, the Wessex (1912-1922) and the Mellstock (1920). The *Collected Poems* appeared in 1926. The most complete account of Hardy's life is Carl J. Weber's *Hardy of Wessex* (New York, 1940), but the following biographical studies should also be mentioned: E. Hardy, *Thomas Hardy* (New York, 1954); Florence E. Hardy, *The Early Life of Thomas Hardy, 1840-1891* (London, 1928); Florence E. Hardy, *The Later Years of Thomas Hardy, 1892-1928* (New York, 1930). There are numerous book-length studies of Hardy's work, but the following may be mentioned in relation to his poetry especially: S. C. Chew, *Thomas Hardy, Poet and Novelist* (New York, 1928); J. G. Southworth, *The Poetry of Thomas Hardy* (New York, 1947); H. C. Webster, *On a Darkling Plain: The Art and*

Thought of Thomas Hardy (Chicago, 1947); Samuel L. Hynes, *The Pattern of Hardy's Poetry* (Chapel Hill, N. C., 1961). The most up-to-date, lengthy appraisal of *The Dynasts* is Harold Orel's *Thomas Hardy's Epic-Drama: A Study of the Dynasts* (Lawrence, Kansas, 1963). Shorter studies of Hardy's poems which may be recommended are as follows: G. R. Elliott, "Hardy's Poetry and the Ghostly Moving-Picture," *South Atlantic Quarterly,* XXVII (1928), pp. 280–291; David Perkins, "Hardy and the Poetry of Isolation," *ELH,* XXVI (1959), pp. 253–270; Mark Van Doren, "The Poems of Thomas Hardy" in *Four Poets on Poetry,* ed. D. C. Allen (Baltimore, Maryland, 1959); John Crowe Ransom, "Thomas Hardy's Poems and the Religious Difficulties of a Naturalist," *Kenyon Review,* XXII, pp. 169–193.

W. E. Henley

Bibliography: The principal volumes of Henley's poetry are as follows: *A Book of Verses* (1888); *The Song of the Sword and Other Verses* (1892), 2nd ed. with additions published under the title of *London Voluntaries* (1893); *Poems* (1898); *For England's Sake* (1900); *Hawthorn and Lavender* (1901); *A Song of Speed* (1903). There are two collected editions of Henley's work: *The Works of W. E. Henley* (London, 1908) and *The Works of William Ernest Henley* (London, 1921). The best account of Henley's life is in Jerome H. Buckley's *William Ernest Henley* (Princeton, 1945), which also contains the most perceptive survey of his writings, but the following early studies of Henley's verse may be recommended: J. C. Bailey, "The Poetry of William Ernest Henley," *Monthly Review,* XII (1903), pp. 78–87; Gilbert Parker, "The New Poetry and Mr. W. E. Henley," *Lippincott's Magazine,* LII (1893), pp 109–116; Arthur Symons, "Mr. Henley's Poetry," *Fortnightly Review,* LVIII (1892), pp. 182–192.

A. E. Housman

Bibliography: Housman's poetry appeared in three separate volumes: *A Shropshire Lad* (1896); *Last Poems* (1922); and the posthumous *More Poems* (1936). *The Collected Poems* appeared in 1939, and were reprinted by Penguin in 1956, but the most authoritative edition is

The Complete Poems of A. E. Housman, ed. T. B. Haber (New York, 1959). Of his prose works, *The Name and Nature of Poetry* (1933), is the most relevant to his achievement as a poet, but his editions of Manilius (1903–1930), Juvenal (1905), and Lucan (1926) all reflect his appreciation of discipline and form, which are perhaps the most notable features of his poetry. A. F. S. Gow's *A. E. Housman, A Sketch* (New York, 1936); Percy Withers' *A Buried Life: Personal Recollections of A. E. Housman* (London, 1940); George L. Watson's *A Divided Life* (London, 1957); and Norman Marlow's *A. E. Housman: Scholar and Poet* (London, 1958) are all recommended studies of Housman's life and work. See also John W. Stevenson, "The Pastoral Setting in the Poetry of A. E. Housman," *South Atlantic Quarterly,* LV (1955), pp. 487–500.

T. E. Hulme

Bibliography: Hulme's five poems were printed as an appendix to *Speculations,* ed. Herbert Read (London, 1924), a collection of essays and fragments culled from his notebooks and MSS after his death. The principal study of Hulme is Alun R. Jones, *The Life and Opinions of T. E. Hulme* (Boston, 1960), though Michael Roberts, *T. E. Hulme* (London, 1938) is also recommended. Hulme's relationship with the Imagist movement is discussed in Frank Kermode's *Romantic Image* (London, 1957) and in A. R. Jones, "Notes Towards a History of Imagism: An Examination of Literary Sources," *South Atlantic Quarterly,* LXV (1961), pp. 262–285, while the same writer's "T. E. Hulme, Wilhelm Worringer, and the Urge to Abstraction," *British Journal of Aesthetics,* I (1960), pp. 1–7, is especially relevant to Hulme's aesthetic and the poetry of the Imagist movement.

Lionel Johnson

Bibliography: Johnson's principal volumes of poetry are *Poems* (1895) and *Ireland, with Other Poems* (1897). The standard edition of his verse is the *Complete Poems of Lionel Johnson,* ed. Iain Fletcher (London, 1953), which is especially valuable for the editor's biographical and critical introduction. There is no standard biography, but the following studies of his work may be recommended: A. B.

Feldman, "The Art of Lionel Johnson," *Poet Lore* LVII (1953), pp. 140–160; Arthur Patrick, *Lionel Johnson, Poète et Critique* (Paris, 1939); and Ezra Pound's introduction to *The Poetical Works of Lionel Johnson,* reprinted in *Literary Essays,* ed. T. S. Eliot (London, 1954). The best brief survey of Johnson's work is included in Barbara Charlesworth's *Dark Passages: The Decadent Consciousness in Victorian Literature* (Madison, Wis., 1965).

Rudyard Kipling

Bibliography: Kipling's principal volumes of verse are as follows: *Departmental Ditties* (1886); *Barrack-Room Ballads* (1892); *The Seven Seas* (1896); *The Five Nations* (1903); *Songs from Books* (1913); *The Years Between* (1918). The best collected edition of Kipling's writings as a whole is the Sussex Edition of the *Complete Works in Prose and Verse* (London, 1937–1939), while the volume *Rudyard Kipling's Verse* (London, 1940) is the definitive edition of his poetry. The standard biography is Charles Carrington's *Rudyard Kipling* (London, 1955); a good brief introduction to his verse is the preface to *A Choice of Kipling's Verse* (London, 1941) by T. S. Eliot, but a more extended study is François Leaux, *La Poétique de Rudyard Kipling* (Paris, 1958). Critical studies of Kipling are, as one would expect, especially numerous, but E. B. Shanks, *Rudyard Kipling: A Study in Literature and Political Ideas* (London, 1940) should be mentioned for its objective assessment of an aspect of Kipling which is frequently given biased or distorted treatment—namely, his conservative, imperialistic political philosophy. The standard bibliography is F. V. Livingstone's *A Bibliography of the Works of Rudyard Kipling* (Cambridge, Mass., 1938).

D. H. Lawrence

Bibliography: Lawrence's principal volumes of poems are as follows: *Look, We Have Come Through* (1917); *New Poems* (1918); *Buy: Book of Poems* (1919); *Tortoises* (1921); *Birds, Beasts and Flowers* (1923); *Pansies* (1929); *Nettles* (1930); *The Triumph of the Machines* (1930); *Last Poems* (1932). *The Collected Poems* appeared in 1932, and *The Complete Poems* of D. H. Lawrence, ed. with intro. and notes by V. de Sola Pinto and W. Roberts, 2 vols., was published in 1964. Of his prose writings the following are relevant to his verse: "Review of Georgian Poetry 1911-1912"; "Introduction" to *New Poems;* "Chaos in Poetry"; "Review of a Second Contemporary Verse Anthology," all of which are included in D. H. Lawrence, *Selected Literary Criticism* (London, 1956). There is also much valuable criticism of poetry in *The Collected Letters of D. H. Lawrence,* ed. Harry T. Moore, 2 vols, (New York, 1962). Two other essays relevant to Lawrence's poetry are: "The Georgian Renaissance," *Rhythm,* II (1913), pp. xvii-xx; and "Verse Free and Unfree," *Voices,* IV (1919), pp. 129-134. *The Life and Works of D. H. Lawrence,* ed. H. T. Moore, (London, 1951) is an excellent critical biography, while the following studies may be recommended as being especially relevant to Lawrence's verse: J. Arrow, *J. C. Squire v. D. H. Lawrence* (London, 1930); R. L. Mégroz, *Five Novelist Poets of Today* (London, 1933); *The Achievement of D. H. Lawrence,* ed. Harry T. Moore and F. J. Hoffman (Norman, Okla., 1953). There is a brief but sane chapter on Lawrence's verse in Graham Hough's *The Dark Sun* (London, 1958).

John Masefield

Bibliography: Masefield's poetry has been published in a steady flow of volumes, beginning with *Salt Water Ballads* (1902). Among the more significant of his early verse publications the following may be mentioned: *Ballads* (1903); *Ballads and Poems* (1910); *The Everlasting Mercy* (1911); *The Widow in the Bye Street* (1912); *Dauber: A Poem* (1913); *The Daffodil Fields* (1913); *Good Friday and Other Poems* (1916); *Lollingdon Downs and Other Poems* (1917); *Reynard the Fox* (1919); and *Enslaved and Other Poems* (1920). *The Collected Poems* was first published in 1923, but this volume has been newly edited and enlarged in 1932 and again in 1938; his *Collected Works,* Wanderer Edn., 10 vols. (London, 1935-1938), contain the bulk of his voluminous writings. There is as yet no definitive biography of Masefield, but the following studies of his work may be mentioned: W. M. Hamilton, *John Masefield: A Critical Study* (London, 1922); C. Biggane, *John Masefield* (Cambridge, 1924); G. O. Thomas, *John Masefield* (London, 1932); Muriel Spark, *John Masefield* (London, 1953); and M. Fisher, *John Masefield* (London, 1963). G. Handley-Taylor's *John Masefield, O.M., the Queen's Poet Laureate:*

A Bibliography and Eighty-First Birthday Tribute (London, 1960) is also recommended.

Alice Meynell

Bibliography: Meynell's principal volumes of poetry are: *Preludes* (1875); *Poems* (1893); *Collected Poems* (1913); and *Last Poems* (1923), but the most accessible collection is *The Poems*, ed. Frederick Page (London, 1940) in the Oxford Standard Authors series. Other important collections are as follows: *Prose and Poetry*, ed. F. Page et al., with a biography and critical intro. by V. Sackville-West (London, 1947); *Poems*, ed. Sir Francis Meynell (London, 1948); *Poems* (London, 1926). There are two biographies of Meynell which are worth reading: Viola Meynell, *Alice Meynell: A Memoir* (London, 1947) and Anne K. Tuell, *Mrs. Meynell and Her Literary Generation* (New York, 1925). Meynell's poetry has received comparatively little critical attention, and what has been written is not especially noteworthy. *Alice Meynell Centenary Tribute, 1847–1947*, ed. T. L. Connolly (Boston, 1948) is worth looking at, however, and so is T. B. Reilly's "A Study of Alice Meynell's Poems," *Catholic World*, LXXIII (1901), pp. 521–530.

Harold Monro

Bibliography: Monro's principal poetry volumes are as follows: *Poems* (1906); *Judas* (1908); *Before Dawn* (1911); *Children of Love* (1914); *Trees* (1915); *Strange Meeting* (1917); *Real Property* (1922); *The Earth for Sale* (1928); *The Winter Solstice* (1928); and *Elm Angel* (1930). *The Collected Poems*, ed. Alida Monro (London, 1933) is, however, the most accessible volume of his verse, and is especially recommended on account of its biographical sketch by F. S. Flint and its critical note by T. S. Eliot. Monro's three major prose works, *The Evolution of the Soul* (1907), *The Chronicle of a Pilgrimage* (1910), and *Some Contemporary Poets* (1920) especially, all throw light on his verse, and so do his editorial comments in *Poetry Review* (1911–1912), which later became *Poetry and Drama* (1912–1913). The best brief account of Monro's achievement as a poet and also his influence on the contemporary poetry scene is the chapter devoted to him in Robert H. Ross's, *The Georgian Revolt: The Rise and Fall of a Poetic Ideal* (Carbondale and Edwardsville, Ill., 1965).

Henry Newbolt

Bibliography: Newbolt's principal volumes of verse are as follows: *Mordred: A Tragedy* (1895); *Admirals All and Other Verses* (1897); *The Island Race* (1898); *The Sailing of the Long-Ships* (1902); *Clifton Chapel and Other School Poems* (1908); *Songs of Mercy and Hope* (1909); *Poems New and Old* (1912); *Drake's Drum and Other Songs of the Sea* (1914); *St. George's Day and Other Poems* (1918); *The Linnet's Nest* (1927); *A Child Is Born* (1931). His *Collected Poems, 1897–1907,* appeared in 1910, while *Prose and Poetry,* selected by the author, was published in 1920. Of his prose writings, "Poetry and Time," the Warton Lecture he delivered in 1919, is relevant to his own verse, while *Studies in Gray and Green* (1926) contains criticism of some of the poets of his day. Coulson Kernahan's *Six Famous Living Poets* (London, 1922) includes a brief but sympathetic study of Newbolt's achievement, and also some biographical material. Other information about his life may be found in Newbolt's *My World as in My Time* (1932) and *The Later Life and Letters of Sir Henry Newbolt* (London, 1942). A short appreciation of his verse is included in Herbert Palmer's *Post Victorian Poetry* (London, 1938).

Wilfred Owen

Bibliography: The standard edition of Owen's verse is *The Collected Poems of Wilfred Owen,* ed. with an intro. and notes by C. Day Lewis (London, 1964); the other major collection of his verse is *Poems,* ed. Edmund Blunden (New York, 1931). The standard biography is by his brother, Harold Owen, *Journey From Obscurity: Wilfred Owen, 1893–1918,* 3 vols. (London, 1963–1965). The best book-length critical study of Owen's verse is D. S. R. Welland, *Wilfred Owen* (London, 1960), but Joseph Cohen has published two important articles: "Wilfred Owen's Greater Love," *Tulane Studies in English,* VII (1957), pp. 105–117, and "Owen Agonistes," *English Literature in Transition,* VIII (1965), pp. 253–268. Cohen has also published an account of the various editions of Owen's poetry: "Fresher Fields Than Flanders," *English Literature in Transition,* VII (1964), pp. 1–7.

Isaac Rosenberg

Bibliography: Rosenberg's poetry appeared in various literary journals during his lifetime, and in two privately printed pamphlets, *Night and Day* (1912) and *Youth* (1915). Collected editions of his writings are *Poems,* ed. Gordon Bottomley (London, 1922) and *Collected Works,* ed. Gordon Bottomley and Denys Harding (London, 1937). The *Collected Poems,* extracted from the 1937 edition of the *Collected Works,* was published in 1949 and reprinted in 1962. There are several good short studies of Rosenberg's life and poetry, the two most notable being Horace Gregory, "The Isolation of Isaac Rosenberg," *Poetry,* LXVIII (1949), pp. 30–39, and Joseph Cohen, "Isaac Rosenberg: From Romantic to Classic," *Tulane Studies in English,* X (1960), pp. 129–142.

Siegfried Sassoon

Bibliography: Sassoon's principal volumes of verse are as follows: *Poems* (1906); *Orpheus in Dilocrym* (1908); *Sonnets* (1909); *The Redeemer* (1910); *Hyacinth* (1912); *Discoveries* (1915); *The Old Huntsman and Other Poems* (1917); *Counter-Attack and Other Poems* (1918); *The War Poems of Siegfried Sassoon* (1919); *Selected Poems* (1925); *Satirical Poems* (1926); *The Heart's Journey* (1927); *Poems of Pinchbeck Lyre* (1931); *Vigils* (1934); *Rhymed Ruminations* (1941); *Sequences* (1950). *The Collected Poems* was first published in 1947. For his life readers are referred to his various memoirs, *Memoirs of a Fox-Hunting Man* (1928); *Memoirs of an Infantry Officer* (1931); *Sherston's Progress* (1936); *Sherston's Journey, 1916–1920* (1945), and especially *Siegfried's Journey* (1947). Though somewhat lacking in factual accuracy, these semi-autobiographical, fictional narratives provide a clear and sympathetic picture of the man, and at the same time illuminate certain aspects of the last half-century which appeal to Sassoon most, notably the life of a cultivated, rural squire. Among critical studies of his poetry, the following may be mentioned: Joseph Cohen, "The Three Roles of Siegfried Sassoon," *Tulane Studies in English,* VI (1957), pp. 169–185, and C. E. Maguire, "Harmony Unheard: The Poetry of Siegfried Sassoon," *Renascence,* XI (1959), pp. 115–124. The only book-length study of Sassoon is Michael

Thorpe's recent *Siegfried Sassoon: A Critical Study* (London, 1967), but this should be supplemented by Geoffrey Keynes's *A Bibliography of Siegfried Sassoon* (London, 1962).

Owen Seaman

Bibliography: Seaman's best verse parodies and satires are included in *The Battle of the Bays* (1896), though there are others included in the volume called *In Cap and Bells* (1899) and *Borrowed Plumes* (1902). *Tillers of the Sand* (1895) contains political verse satires on the Rosebery administration, while *War Time* (1915) is a mixture of satiric verse and patriotic doggerel.

Edith Sitwell

Bibliography: There are four major volumes of Edith Sitwell's verse: *Collected Poems* (London, 1930); *Selected Poems* (London, 1936); *The Canticle of the Rose* (London, 1949); and *Facade and Other Poems 1920–1947* (London, 1950). Among her prose writings *Poetry and Criticism* (London, 1925), *Aspects of Modern Poetry* (London, 1934), and *A Poet's Notebook* (London, 1943) throw some light on her verse, while her anthologies, *The Pleasures of Poetry* (London, 1930–1932) and *Edith Sitwell's Anthology* (London, 1940) give a clear indication of her poetical preferences. R. L. Mégroz's *The Three Sitwells* (London, 1927), Osbert Sitwell's *Left Hand! Right Hand!* (London, 1945), C. M. Bowra's *Edith Sitwell* (Monaco, 1947), and *Celebrations for Edith Sitwell,* ed. J. B. Villa, (New York, 1948) may all be recommended for the light they throw on the poet's life as well as her work. *Sitwelliana, 1915–1927,* ed. T. Balston (London, 1928) is a useful hand-list of the early writings of all three Sitwells. The most detailed account of Edith Sitwell's achievement as a poet is *Development of the Poetry of Edith Sitwell,* unpub. Ph.D. diss., Wisconsin, 1956.

Charles Sorley

Bibliography: Sorley's verse was published in *Marlborough and Other Poems* (Cambridge, 1916), the fourth edition, enlarged and rearranged, appearing in 1919. There is no standard biography of Sorley, but we can learn a great deal about him from his *Letters* (Cambridge, 1919). Apart from discussions of his writing published in general surveys of the poetry of the 1914–1918 war, the best study of his poetry is John Press, "Charles Sorley," *A Review of English Literature,* VII (1966), pp. 43–60.

J. C. Squire

Bibliography: Squire's principal poetry volumes are as follows: *The Three Hills and Other Poems* (1913); *The Survival of the Fittest and Other Poems* (1916); *The Lily of Malud and Other Poems* (1917); *Poems, First Series* (1918); *The Birds and Other Poems* (1919); *Poems, Second Series* (1921); *Poems in One Volume* (1926); *A Face in Candlelight and Other Poems* (1932). For his parodies see *Tricks of the Trade* (1917) and *Collected Parodies* (1921). *The Collected Poems of Sir John Squire,* with a preface by John Betjeman, was published in 1959. Of his criticism, *Essays on Poetry* (1923) may be recommended for its relevance to Squire's own verse and to that of some of his contemporaries, but the volume as a whole is hardly distinguished. *Selections from the Modern Poets* (London, 1921), an anthology, gives some indication of Squire's poetical preferences, but more pertinent are his contributions to *The New Statesman,* "Books in General," written under the pseudonym of "Solomon Eagle": II ·(1913), 341, 439; III (1914); VII (1916); IX (1917), *passim.* Squire's *Reflections and Memories* (1935) contains interesting biographical material, and there is a sympathetic discussion of Squire's achievement as a poet in Herbert Palmer's *Post Victorian Poetry* (London, 1938).

Robert Louis Stevenson

Bibliography: Stevenson's principal volumes of verse are as follows: *A Child's Garden of Verses* (1885); *Underwoods* (1887); *Ballads* (1890); and *Songs of Travel* (1896). The definitive collection, however, is the *Collected Poems,* ed. with intro. and notes by Janet Adam Smith (London, 1950). There have been numerous biographical studies of varying authority, but the two best are J. A. Stewart, *Robert Louis Stevenson: Man and Writer* (London, 1924) and J. C. Furnas, *Voyage to Wind-*

ward: The Life of Robert Louis Stevenson (London, 1952). Of the many book-length studies of his writings, the following are recommended: Frank Swinnerton, *R. L. Stevenson: A Critical Study* (London, 1924); H. D. MacPherson, *R. L. Stevenson: A Study in French Influence* (New York, 1930); J. Adam Smith, *Robert Louis Stevenson* (London, 1937); and David Daiches, *Robert Louis Stevenson* (Glasgow, 1947).

Arthur Symons

Bibliography: The most accessible collection of Symons' poetry is probably the first three volumes of the *Collected Works of Arthur Symons* (London, 1924), which includes the contents of his major verse collections: *Days and Nights* (1889); *Silhouettes* (1892); *London Nights* (1895); *Images of Good Evil* (1900); *The Fool of the World* (1906); *The Knave of Hearts 1894–1900* (1913); the privately printed *Loom of Dreams* (1901); and the poems published later under the title *Jezebel Mort and Other Poems* (1931). Of his many critical works "The Decadent Movement in Literature," *Harper's New Monthly Magazine,* LXXXVII (1893), pp. 858–867 and *The Symbolist Movement in Literature* (London, 1899) throw most light on his poetry, and indeed are also important in relation to other poets' work of the time. The standard biography is Roger Lhombreaud's *Arthur Symons* (London, 1963), and the two most useful studies of his poetry are John M. Munro's "Arthur Symons as Poet: Theory and Practice," *English Literature in Transition,* VI (1963), pp. 212–222 and Edward Baugh's "Arthur Symons, Poet: A Centenary Tribute," *Review of English Literature,* VI (1966), pp. 70–80. Also recommended are the chapter on Symons in Frank Kermode's *Romantic Image* (London, 1957) and the section on the poet in Barbara Charlesworth's *Dark Passages: The Decadent Consciousness in Victorian Literature* (Madison, Wis., 1965).

Edward Thomas

Bibliography: The bulk of Thomas's verse appeared in *Poems* (1917) and *Last Poems* (1918), followed by the first collected edition in 1920. *The Collected Poems* were newly edited in 1928 and again in 1936, the 1928 edition containing an appreciation by Walter de la Mare. Thomas's life has been described by his widow, Helen Thomas, in

As It Was (London, 1926) and *World Without End* (London, 1931), which were republished in one volume in 1956, but her account should be supplemented by R. P. Eckert's *Edward Thomas: A Biography and a Bibliography* (London, 1937), while J. Moore's *The Life and Letters of Edward Thomas* (London, 1939) is preferable to both. The best book-length study of the poet is H. Coombes, *Edward Thomas* (London, 1956), but some other shorter studies may be mentioned, notably C. Day Lewis, "The Poetry of Edward Thomas" in *Essays by Divers Hands,* Transactions of the Royal Soc. of Lit., XXVIII (Oxford, 1956) and H. Coombes, "Hardy, de la Mare and Edward Thomas," in *The Modern Age,* Pelican Guide to English Literature, Vol. VII (London, 1961).

Francis Thompson

Bibliography: Thompson's best verse was published in *Poems* (1893); *Sister Songs* (1895); and *New Poems* (1897). After his death appeared *Selected Poems,* with a biographical note by Wilfrid Meynell (London, 1908) and later still the bulk of his poetry was reprinted in the first two volumes of *Works,* ed. W. Meynell (London, 1913), the third volume containing a selection of his prose. Two modern editions are *Poems,* ed. T. L. Connolly (New York, 1932, rev. ed. 1941), and *Poems* (London, 1937) in the Oxford Standard Authors series. There have been several biographical studies of Thompson, as for example E. Meynell's *The Life of Francis Thompson* (London, 1913) and Viola Meynell's *Francis Thompson and Wilfrid Meynell: A Memoir* (London, 1952), both of which were written by people who knew the poet personally. However, the most scholarly and objective account of Thompson's life and work is P. Danchin's *Francis Thompson: la vie et l'oeuvre d'un poète* (Paris, 1959). J. C. Reid's *Francis Thompson: Man and Poet* (London, 1959) is also recommended.

William Watson

Bibliography: The standard editions of Watson's poetry are as follows: *Collected Poems* (London, 1899); *Poems,* with an introduction by J. A. Spender (New York, 1905); and *Poems 1878–1935* (London, 1936), the latter being the most complete. The most useful collection, however, is *Selected Poems,* selected with notes by the author (London, 1928). Watson's criticism was published in *Excursions in Criticism* (London, 1893), and though uninspired is worth looking at insofar as it throws light on his criteria for literary excellence and reflects his own poetical intentions. There is no standard biography of Watson, but there is something of his life in Coulson Kernahan's *Six More Famous Living Poets* (London, 1928). Similarly there is no standard critical study of his work, but the following articles, though dated, may be recommended: G. White, "An Agnostic Poet," *Sewanee Review,* VIII (1900), pp. 305–377; G. E. Woodberry, "William Watson," *Century Magazine,* LXIV (1902), pp. 801–805; J. Griffith Fairfax, "William Watson: The Poet of Public Affairs," *Poetry Review,* I (1912), pp. 160–163; Arthur Symons, "William Watson," in *Dramatis Personae* (Indianapolis, 1923). Three recent articles provide some basic bibliographical information: Cecil Woolf, "Some Uncollected Authors: William Watson," *The Book Collector,* V (1957), pp. 375–380; Norman Colbeck, "Some Uncollected Authors: William Watson, Additions and Corrections," *The Book Collector,* VI (1958), pp. 66–67; Walter E. Swayze, "Some Uncollected Authors: William Watson," *The Book Collector,* VI (1958), pp. 285–286, 402.

Oscar Wilde

Bibliography: Wilde's writings have been reprinted many times, but probably the most authoritative edition is *The Works of Oscar Wilde,* ed. Robert Ross (London, 1909). His three principal publications, with regard to his verse, are: *Poems* (1881); *The Sphinx* (1894); and *The Ballad of Reading Gaol* (1898). The standard biography is Hesketh Pearson, *Oscar Wilde: His Life and Wit* (New York, 1946), but *The Letters of Oscar Wilde,* ed. Rupert Hart-Davis (London, 1962) is an indispensable supplement. Of the numerous studies of Wilde few have paid more than passing attention to his poetry. Among the best, however, are: B. Brasol, *Oscar Wilde* (New York, 1938); Edward Roditi, *Oscar Wilde* (Norfolk, Conn., 1947); and Robert Merle, *Oscar Wilde* (Paris, 1948). In relation to Wilde's poetry specifically, see J. D. Thomas, "Wilde's The Harlot's House," *Modern Language Notes,* LXV (1950), pp. 485–488. There is also a *Bibliography of Wilde's Poems* by Stuart Mason [C. S. Millard] (London, 1907).